COOKING WIZARDRY for KIDS

Margaret Kenda and Phyllis S. Williams

BARRON'S

New York London Toronto Sydney

For Our Children
(Rowena, Bethany, Jeremy, and Wesley Williams; Mary, Ann, and John Kenda)
Who Taught Us All We Know

All inquiries should be addressed to:
Barron's Educational Series, Inc.
250 Wireless Boulevard
Hauppauge, New York 11788

International Standard Book No. 0-8120-4409-6

Library of Congress Catalog Card No. 90-33280

Library of Congress Cataloging-in-Publication Data

Kenda, Margaret.
    Cooking wizardry for kids / by Margaret Kenda and
Phyllis S. Williams.
        p.   cm.
    Summary: Instructions for nearly 200 creative kitchen
projects, including a copper plating experiment, invisible
ink, experiments with liquids, and recipes for astronaut
cookies, fried worms, and various kinds of cakes, puddings, and salads.
    ISBN 0-8120-4409-6
    1. Cookery—Juvenile literature. 2. Science—
Experiments—Juvenile literature. [1. Science—
Experiments. 2. Experiments. 3. Cookery.] I. Williams,
Phyllis S. II. Title.
TX652.5.K36   1990
641.5'123—dc20   90-33280
                                            CIP
                                              AC

Book & cover design by Milton Glaser, Inc.
Illustrations by Tim Robinson

PRINTED IN THE UNITED STATES OF AMERICA

0123 8800 987654321

CONTENTS

INTRODUCTION

This is your chance to become the Wizard of the Kitchen.

This is an opportunity to create your own secret recipes and your own special projects.

Think up what you'd like to do. We'll show you how. Here are almost 200 projects for just about anything you want to create, cook, bake, microwave, mix, test, design, twist, punch, or grow.

If you like having fun in the kitchen . . .

Try twisting up your own pretzels. Create cheese eyeballs. Roll up a popcorn ball. Decorate a snowbaby cake. Slice cucumber wheelies.

If you like science experiments . . .

Try "growing" sugar crystals for your own rock candy. Collect an invisible gas that can inflate a balloon for you. Try the eerie "blood red experiment." Find out if plants have feelings.

If you want to send secret messages . . .

Write with your own invisible ink. Or bake cupcakes full of good-luck messages. Create applesauce that says "I love you."

If you're curious . . .

Try astronaut's cookies (suitable for eating on a spaceship). Or how about brain food, a sports-power pita pocket, pioneer delicacies?

If you like art . . .

    You'll love making dough ornaments, bird's nests, and elephant's ears. Try your hand at a tomato rose, turkey in the straw, or fancy butter.

If you like eating in restaurants . . .

    You can operate your own restaurant at home. Design your own pizza. Create a Chinese dinner, stuff your own baked potato, or bake your own giant chocolate chunk cookies.

If you like to work with the microwave oven . . .

    Learn how to tell if a dish is safe for the microwave. Use the microwave to dry flowers that cannot wilt. Zip up mini-pizzas and pure chocolate designs.

If you like animals . . .

    Stir up a birthday cake for your cat, biscuits for your dog, or wild bird feed.

If you like to get outside . . .

    Create outdoor treats such as trail mix and s'mores.

If you're in a mood to celebrate . . .

    Try green milkshakes for St. Patrick's Day or (very careful) flaming cherries for Presidents' Day. Learn the stories behind Haman's hats, racing pancakes, and carrot coins. Construct your own Christmas gingerbread house.

If you're feeling a little weird . . .

    Go for a cheese puffs pig-out project. Or get up your nerve to try a fried-worms gross-out project. (Don't worry. They taste delicious.)

You're the Wizard of the Kitchen. You're in charge.

How Parents Can Use COOKING WIZARDRY FOR KIDS

Cooking is the favorite quality-time activity between parents and children.

It's fun. It's necessary. It's part of the daily routine. Food preparation is a good time to chat, to be together, to be happy—and to learn.

Outside of school—and sometimes in school—cooking is the main source of a child's knowledge of any number of fascinating subjects.

Best of all, cooking with a loved adult brings a child closer to a lifetime of good eating, good for the body and good for the soul.

COOKING WIZARDRY FOR KIDS is a creative projects book to enhance that delightful time between parents and children.

How Teachers Can Use COOKING WIZARDRY FOR KIDS

COOKING WIZARDRY FOR KIDS is the first book to take the approach of the new children's cooking schools, and we intend the book partly as a support manual for these popular courses.

The cooking school approach appeals to both boys and girls, and is most often an activity of choice, not an imposition. It is devoted to serious creative projects.

We hope COOKING WIZARDRY FOR KIDS will help you to teach "why" as well as "what" to do in the kitchen—and to teach with love and a sense of fun.

Margaret Kenda
Phyllis S. Williams

SAFETY AND CLEANUP RULES

The basic, basic rules:

1 Have fun while you cook. Take your time.
Accidents happen when you get frustrated or when you're in too much of a hurry.

2 Don't worry about failures.
You can learn from failure. Start out easy, but don't be afraid to try something different, too.

3 Keep things clean and organized.
If you get to do the cooking, then it's only fair to do the cleaning up, too.
Besides, cleaner is safer.

4 Pay attention to your cooking from start to finish.
Don't assume that someone else will remind you when it's time to take the cookies out of the oven or stop the vegetables from boiling over.

Before you start:

1 Read before you cook.
Read the recipe all the way through, and make sure that you understand what to do and that you have all the ingredients on hand.
2 Wash your hands before you cook.
Pull back your hair. Wear a smock or an apron. Roll up your sleeves.
3 Get organized before you cook. Assemble equipment, utensils, and ingredients. Have a system so you won't forget anything.
4 Make sure you have permission before you invade the kitchen. You need to have permission to work in the kitchen and to use knives and machines. Teamwork is more fun, anyway.
5 Before you use machines, get someone to show you how. Read the instruction book and try out the microwave oven, mixer, blender, or food processor. Start with something easy first. Boil a cup of water in the microwave oven. Or make a simple milkshake in the blender.
6 Check that your ingredients are fresh.
Don't be in so much of a hurry that you don't notice color, looks, smell—especially if you're noticing something wrong.

While you are working:

1 Work slowly and carefully. Take your time.
2 As you add each ingredient, put it back in its right place. Then you won't forget whether you've already added that ingredient or not.
3 Especially remember to put meats and frozen foods back into the refrigerator or freezer—right away.
4 Wipe up spills immediately.

While you are cutting:

1 Treat knives with respect.
2 Use a good solid cutting board that won't move. Don't ever cut or chop directly on the counter or table.
3 Always work so that the cutting blade of the knife is directed away from your hand. Pare or cut away from your hand.
4 If you drop a knife, don't try to catch it.

While you are measuring:

1 Use a transparent cup to measure liquids. Stoop down, so that you see the measure at eye level.
2 To get the measure for dry ingredients just right, fill the cup or spoon and then level off with a spatula or knife.
3 As you measure dry ingredients, press them down. You don't want to be measuring air space. But don't pack down flour. Sift the flour (if the recipe calls for sifting), and then spoon it gently so that you *don't* pack it down.

While you are preparing ingredients:

1 Wash, chop and otherwise prepare all ingredients *before* you begin cooking.
2 Wash most fruits and vegetables in cool, clear water. Then drain.
3 Crack an egg by tapping it firmly but gently. Hold the egg over a bowl, and use the fingers of both hands to break it in half. If you see pieces of shell in the bowl, scoop them out with another part of the broken eggshell. Eggshell pieces stick together naturally.

While you are using a blender or food processor:

Put the lid on before you turn on the machine. (Some machines will not turn on until the lid is tight.)

To prevent food spoiling:

1 Put food back in the refrigerator as soon as you are finished using it. Wrap refrigerator and freezer food tightly, and close milk cartons. If wrapping is torn, get new wrapping.
2 Wash your cutting board each time you use it.
3 Never cut meat on a cutting board and then cut vegetables. Wash the board first.
4 Wash your can opener after you use it. Otherwise, bits of food on it can turn rotten—and drop into the next can you open.
5 Wash can lids before you open the can. You don't need dust or dirt dropping into the open can.
6 Don't let meat defrost out on the counter.

Here are three safe ways to defrost food:

1 Move it from the freezer to the refrigerator, and let it thaw slowly.
2 Thaw it in a bowl of cold water. (Make sure the food is very well wrapped so that the water doesn't soak through.)
3 Or if you're in a hurry, thaw frozen food in the microwave oven. Take off the wrappings. Put the frozen food into a covered dish, or put it on a plate and cover loosely with waxed paper or plastic wrap. Then process at low (or half) power for just a few minutes. Keep an eye on the food so that it thaws but does not overheat.

While you are using a mixer:

1 Unplug the mixer while you are putting the beaters in and out.
2 Most often, it's best to turn off the mixer before you add new ingredients.
3 Be sure to use a large enough mixing bowl. Allow room for whipping.
4 Start the mixer up slowly so that ingredients don't come splashing out. Then you can turn up the speed gradually.
5 Don't put your fingers near a moving mixer, and keep your hair out of the way.
6 Break eggs into a separate bowl before you put them in the mixer bowl. Then if one egg is spoiled, you don't contaminate the rest of your ingredients.

3

While you are using the stove:

1 Cook at low heat and check often.

2 Know for sure whether things are cool enough to touch before you touch them.

3 Always have pot holders, oven mitts, and tongs within easy reach.

4 Make sure pot holders are dry. Wet ones let the heat through.

5 Do not leave a spoon in a hot pan. Before you know it, a metal spoon gets too hot to touch. And some plastic spoons could melt if you left them in a hot pan long enough.

6 Have a safe place to set a hot pan *before* you pick it up. Never set a hot pan directly onto the kitchen counter or directly onto a table. Put it on a cutting board, on a cooling rack, or on a hot plate.

7 Turn pan handles toward the middle of the stove. (A small child could reach up and pull them over the edge of the stove. An older person could bump into them.) Keep the handles turned from you and away from other hot burners.

8 Whenever you are around a stove, remember about steam. Steam is dangerous. Steam is very hot and can be completely invisible. Open pan lids away from you. And when you stir or pour from a pan, remember that steam can surge up at you when you're not expecting it.

9 Turn off the stove when you are finished.

When you are finished with cooking:

1 Clean up.

2 Put away foods. Cover and wrap foods tightly. Close boxes tightly (with tape, if necessary) and roll up the inner plastic.

3 Return equipment and ingredients to their proper places.

SUPERMARKET SECRETS

The grocery store is full of mysteries. How can you figure out the real costs? Can you tell the difference between the real and the fake? How do the grocery store managers convince people to buy particular foods?

You can find solutions to the secrets of the supermarket.

AN OBSERVATION EXPERIMENT ON HUMAN BEHAVIOR IN THE GROCERY STORE

Supermarket researchers study what people buy and why they buy—and what makes people change their minds about what they buy.

These supermarket researchers are especially interested in studying impulse buying.

When shoppers buy something they did not plan on buying, that's called impulse buying. Impulse buying is a good way for grocery stores to take in extra money.

The supermarket researchers have found out that shoppers mainly do impulse buying of two types of food:

1 The fruits and vegetables in the produce department

2 The baked goods in the bakery section

Of course, some impulse buying is purely practical. If strawberries are in, if the tomatoes look good, if the fresh vegetables are really cheap today, then that's what we buy.

And the supermarkets are practical when they try to sell food fast. Fruits and vegetables spoil quickly, and baked goods go stale.

But much of our buying has to do with emotions. We buy what we feel good about—and grocery store managers try to arrange their products so that we feel good about them.

Tour your grocery store and observe ways the store encourages people to buy.

Observe your own reactions. What looks attractive to you in the grocery store? What gives you the impulse to buy?

Consider the big displays, the bright colors, the highly visible locations for certain foods.

But also remember to notice the small ways that grocery stores make food look good and stay fresh.

· · · · · · · · · · ·

AN OBSERVATION EXPERIMENT ON IMPULSE BUYING IN THE GROCERY STORE

· ·

If you ran a grocery store, you might be thinking about how to capture the attention of small children. You might be considering what attracts small children—and what they might ask their parents to buy.

In a supermarket, small children might especially notice:

Large displays with bright colors

Pictures of children on packages or pictures of toys and cartoon characters that children like

Displays at a child's eye level or where a child riding in a grocery cart would look first

Displays at the checkout line, where children wait and are liable to get restless and bored

Write down the names of grocery store items that you see displayed in ways that appeal to small children.

Then note how each display falls into one of these categories:

1 *Nutritious foods* such as milk, vegetables, fruits, eggs, meats, fish, poultry

2 *Sometimes nutritious* foods such as cereals, breads, crackers, cookies, fruit juices, frozen desserts

3 *Never nutritious* foods such as snack foods, soft drinks, candy, and chewing gum

4 *Non-food items* such as toys and magazines

(We'd be surprised if you find any items from the nutritious food category in child-attractive displays. You will probably find most child appeals are never-nutritious foods and non-food items.)

Note: *A few grocery stores feature a no-candy checkout station. You can see the advantage to parents who don't want to cope with children who are crying for candy. What is the advantage to the grocery store managers in an arrangement like this?*

AN OBSERVATION EXPERIMENT ON THE MAP OF THE SUPERMARKET

Try making a map of the grocery store, and you will see clever planning. Good locations help keep food from spoiling. Good locations make the job of transporting food easier. Good locations help sell food.

Notice the delivery areas where delivery trucks come into the grocery store. What grocery store departments are nearest the delivery area? Where do you find the large refrigerated areas?

Why do you expect to find freezer and refrigerator foods at the backs and sides of the store rather than in the middle aisles?

Why are meats at the back of the store?

Look at what goes next to what in the grocery store. Sometimes you find odd arrangements of items that don't seem to have much in common. Consider why you might find these groups in the same locations:

1 Crates of soft drinks, along with fireplace logs, large bags of charcoal, and kitty litter

2 Cuts of meat wrapped together with a few potatoes, carrots, turnips, and maybe a packet of herbs and spices

3 Magazines, newspapers, candy, chewing gum, and first-aid kits

4 Baby food and pet food

The more people see in a grocery store, the more people buy. What areas do you see first as you enter the store? List several items you see displayed in those highly visible locations.

Milk is the item that people purchase most frequently. Where is milk in your supermarket? What other displays might tempt you if you walked directly to the milk section and then to the checkout counter?

The end of each aisle is a special location for grocery stores. Displays show up well there. And the grocery store employees can easily change the end-of-the-aisle displays. List several items you see displayed at the ends of the aisles in your grocery store, and consider the reasons for special display of those items.

. . . .
AN OBSERVATION EXPERIMENT ON THE GROCERY STORE OF THE FUTURE
. . . .

Here are some changes you will probably see in your local grocery store, either now or in the future:

Bigger and bigger stores with a greater variety of non-food merchandise for sale

(Some day you may buy a television set or new clothes at the "hyper-market.")

More and more non-food services

(You may already see a bank machine or a video rental counter at your local supermarket.)

More high-quality prepared food

(You will probably find a salad bar, ready-made sandwiches, hot soup, fresh and frozen gourmet dinners.)

More food made especially for the microwave oven

More use of computer technology, with fewer employees to help you check out and bag your groceries

(In some supermarkets, shoppers order and pay for groceries by pushing computer buttons.)

More use of biodegradable plastic wrap and recycled paper

(We need food packaging that does not damage the environment.)

More and more information about the ingredients, nutritional values, and calories of packaged foods

Which changes do you think are good ideas?

What changes would you like to see in the grocery store? And what new products?

FRUIT JUICE LABEL-READING PROJECT

You might think that a fruit juice and a fruit drink are pretty much the same. But that's not necessarily so.

Take notes, and fill in a chart for as many brands and types as you can find:

COMPARISON OF CANNED FRUIT JUICES

Brand of Drink	Price of the Can
Type of Fruit or Fruit Flavor	Number of Ounces in Can
Labeled as "Juice" or "Juice Drink"	Price of the Drink per Ounce
Percentage of Juice	

Hint: To find the price of the drink per ounce, divide the price of the can by the number of ounces in the can.

Puzzler: Find a drink in the canned drink section that contains no juice at all. Even though they are in the juice section, drinks like these are manufactured drinks with no natural ingredients.
Answer: Gatorade—and others

Puzzler: Which flavor of canned juice drink is never labeled "100% juice"?
Answer: Cranberry juice cocktail

. . . .
FRUIT JUICE LABEL-READING
continued

Now fill in a chart for bottled fruit drinks in as many brands and types as you can find. You'll find some bottled fruit drinks in the refrigerator cases, some in the soft drink section, and some with the canned fruit drinks.

. . . .

COMPARISON OF BOTTLED FRUIT JUICES

Brand of Drink	*Percentage of Juice*
Type of Fruit or Fruit Flavor	*Price of the Bottle*
Labeled as "Juice," "Juice Drink," or "Soda"	*Number of Ounces in Bottle*
Refrigerated or Not Refrigerated	*Price of the Drink per Ounce*

. . . .

Now fill in a chart for frozen fruit juices in as many brands and types as you can find:

. . . .

COMPARISON OF FROZEN FRUIT JUICE CONCENTRATE

Brand of Drink	*Price of the Can*
Type of Fruit or Fruit Flavor	*Number of Ounces of Concentrate in Can*
Pure or with Sugar Added	*Price of the Concentrate per Ounce*

. . . .

Now compare overall. Which juices cost the most per ounce, and which cost the least per ounce?

Which tends to cost most: a canned drink, a bottled drink, or a bottled drink from the refrigerator case?

A PINT'S A POUND

If you have one cup juice, how much does the juice weigh? If you have 12 ounces of juice, how many cups is that?

Your great-grandparents had a way to remember automatically. The old-fashioned saying is:

A pint's a pound
The world around.

Now all you have to do is remember that a pint equals 2 cups (or half a quart), and you can always know what liquid weighs:

1 cup = 8 ounces (or ½ pound)
2 cups (or 1 pint) = 16 ounces (or 1 pound)
3 cups = 24 ounces
4 cups (or 1 quart) = 32 ounces (or 2 pounds)

An easy way to remember (by a verse or a saying or a funny sentence) is called a *mnemonic*. The first m is silent.

A COMPARING-SIZES-AND-PRICES PROJECT

Comparing sizes and prices at the supermarket is not always easy.

Most supermarkets display the price of the product in large numerals on the shelf under the product. That seems simple enough.

Then next to the product price, many stores list the unit price.

The unit price is how much a product costs per quart, per liter, per pound, per ounce—or by whatever size the store uses for comparison.

Carry a small calculator with you in the grocery store, and figure unit prices on three similar food items.

For instance, compare three cereals, three brands of flour, three types of pancake syrups, three kinds of cooking oil, three cheeses.

Decide which costs most—and which costs least—per pound, ounce, quart, liter.

Here is the formula:

- Divide the total price by the number of ounces (or pounds, quarts, liters). That gives the unit price.

Hint: Even if the store displays a unit price, figure the cost yourself. Store clerks can make mistakes.

Another Hint: Always check to be sure you are comparing the same unit of measure. You don't want to confuse quarts with liters, or ounces with pounds.

Unit prices are a good way to figure out the best values. For an example, look at your favorite brand of popcorn. Calculate the unit cost (cost per ounce) for a large bag of popcorn. Then calculate the unit cost (cost per ounce) for a medium-sized bag of popcorn.

Next figure the unit cost for the smallest bags (the kind you might pack in your lunch box).

Which size offers you the lowest cost per ounce of popcorn? Which size offers you the highest cost per ounce of popcorn?

If you want to buy 16 ounces of popcorn, what is the best size bag to buy?

Mystery Tour: Usually the largest packages offer the best values. The bigger the box or bag or can or bottle, the smaller the unit cost. But that's not always so. Can you find a grocery store item that costs less per unit in small packages?

YOUR OWN FOOD FACTORY

Start a fabulous food factory today right in your own kitchen.

Commercial food factories make all sorts of food these days. But you can make your own. You can discover the top-secret formula for your own cola. You can create your own juice drinks and make them taste better than food factory drinks.

And you can make your own "instant" mixes and convenience foods any time you want.

Your own food-factory recipes cost less, too.

The food factories can't keep secrets from you.

··········
A MAKE-YOUR-OWN FRUIT DRINK PROJECT
································

Here's how to make a fruit drink similar to the food-factory flavors.

Here's what you do to make a simple syrup:

1 Measure one cup sugar in a one-pint or one-quart glass measuring cup.

2 Pour boiling water into the measure while stirring until you have about 1½ cups.

   : *Caution: You need adult help*
   : *with boiling water.*

3 Continue stirring until the sugar dissolves.

4 Pour the simple syrup into a jar with a tight-fitting cover, and save for sweetening your drinks.

Here's what you need to make your fruit drinks:

A 1-quart container

4 to 6 tablespoons simple syrup

*1 teaspoon orange or lemon extract (**or** 1 tablespoon frozen orange or lemon juice concentrate)*

6 tablespoons plus 1 teaspoon of your favorite juice (100%, of course)

4 to 6 ice cubes

Water to fill the quart container

Here's what you do:

Measure the simple syrup, orange or lemon flavoring, juice, and ice cubes into the one-quart container. Then fill the rest of the way with water.

You decide what color you want your drink to be.

Stir in food coloring, ONE DROP AT A TIME, until the color is just right.

: **NOW YOU HAVE ONE QUART**
: **OF YOUR OWN FRUIT DRINK.**

AN ADD-UP-THE-COSTS-OF-YOUR-OWN-FRUIT-DRINK PROJECT

Here's how to figure the cost of your fruit drink:

$\frac{1}{10}$ of the price of the fruit juice

+

$\frac{1}{160}$ of the price of 5 pounds of sugar

+

$\frac{1}{6}$ of the price
of orange or lemon extract

=

The final cost of your quart of fruit drink

Puzzler: *How does your cost compare with a food-factory brand of 10% juice drink?*

Suggestion: *Pure juice tastes better than mixtures of sugar, flavorings, and colorings. Just dilute juice with an equal amount of water—and you will have a better tasting drink than the 10% juice drinks.*

Another Suggestion: *If you'd like to try something more creative, try the Make-Your-Own Fruit Juice project in MAKE UP YOUR OWN SECRET RECIPES.*

A MAKE-YOUR-OWN NATURAL FRUIT SODA PROJECT

You'll love the real fruit flavor with bubbles. And this sort of "soft drink" is better than any you'll find in the supermarket.

You decide your favorite juice (or two juices blended).

Hint: We recommend seltzer water rather than soda water. Seltzer water contains no sodium, and besides seltzer water has fine carbon dioxide bubbling through it.

You can buy a bottle of seltzer water for this project. Or you can make your own if you have a seltzer maker. A seltzer maker works by bubbling pure carbon dioxide through water.

Here's what to do:
Mix one part juice with one part seltzer water.

Caution: You can use a seltzer maker only with water, not with juice. Add the juice to the seltzer water later.

NOW YOU HAVE YOUR OWN NATURAL FRUIT SODA. DRINK IMMEDIATELY.

A MAKE-YOUR-OWN FAKE COLA EXPERIMENT

The secret recipe for Coca-Cola is supposedly locked in a safe. Only a few top company officials know the secret recipe, and they are sworn not to tell.

But you can probably make up something similar.

Here's what you need to begin the experiment:

- ½ cup sparkling mineral water or seltzer
- 1½ tablespoons simple syrup (See the Make-Your-Own Fruit Drink project for the recipe for simple syrup.)
- 1 teaspoon vanilla extract
- 1 teaspoon lemon juice
- ⅛ teaspoon cinnamon

Here's what you do:

1 Mix the mineral water with the simple syrup, vanilla extract, lemon juice, and cinnamon.

2 You will need to experiment with the flavorings. Try a bit more here, a bit less there until the drink tastes like cola.

3 If you are still not entirely satisfied with the flavor, try adding ¼ teaspoon decaffeinated coffee for even more cola flavor.

4 To create the right brown color, mix in droplets of red, yellow, and either green or blue food coloring. Or use brown coloring available at baking supply stores.

5 If the taste is still not just right, try putting in ice cubes. Any soft drink tastes better with plenty of ice.

> **YOU'RE ON YOUR WAY TO CRACKING THE SECRET FORMULA.**

An Almost-Instant Oatmeal Project

You can make your own breakfast convenience oatmeal mix.

Here's what you need for your mix:

4 cups quick oatmeal

¼ cup sugar, brown or white

1 to 2 teaspoons spice
(**You Decide:** allspice, cinnamon, cloves, nutmeg—or ½ teaspoon nutmeg mixed with allspice, cinnamon, or cloves)

1 cup whole raisins or 1 cup other dried fruit, chopped
(**You Decide:** dried apples, apricots, dates, peaches, pears.)

Hint: The generic brand of oatmeal in the plain white box is the least expensive. And you'll like it just as well.

Here's what you do:

1 Mix thoroughly.

2 If you wish, store your mix in plastic bags in ⅓-cup serving sizes. Tie the bags tightly. Your mix will keep up to six months in a cool place, and even longer in the freezer. But you'll want to eat oatmeal long before then.

: **Now You Have About Five**
: **Cups Of Your Own**
: **Almost-Instant Oatmeal.**

Here's how to prepare your oatmeal:

1 Pour ⅓ cup mix into a bowl.

2 Pour in ½ cup warm water. Then heat in the microwave oven for two minutes, until hot.

3 OR add ½ cup boiling water.

: *Caution: You need adult help*
: *with boiling water.*

4 Let stand two or three minutes, covered, while the oatmeal mix absorbs the water.

5 Serve with milk.

: **Now You Have A Bowl Of**
: **Your Own Instant**
: **Oatmeal.**

GENERIC TIDBITS

Generic brands come in plain white boxes with plain black names like "OATMEAL," "RICE," or "FLOUR."

With generic brands you get no company name, no advertising, no pictures, no promises—and no high costs. Nothing is special about generics except the price.

Generic brands are often food-factory leftovers, and often they are not as good as the big-name brands.

But you can sometimes save money with generic brands. And with a few products you can't really tell the difference in quality. Generic oatmeal and generic rice, for instance, taste as good and are just as good for you as most of the expensive brands.

Try a comparison test to see if you can tell the differences between the generics and the big names.

A MAKE-YOUR-OWN ALL-PURPOSE MIX PROJECT

There's no mystery to mixes. You can mix up your own mix—and then use it to make brownies, pancakes, and all sorts of cookies.

Here's what you need:

9 cups all purpose or unbleached flour

3 cups nonfat dry milk

1/3 cup baking powder

1/4 cup sugar

1 tablespoon salt

2 cups shortening

Here's what you do to mix up the mix:

1 In a large mixing bowl, mix the flour, nonfat dry milk, baking powder, sugar, and salt. Stir thoroughly.

2 Cut in the shortening with a pastry blender or with two forks until the shortening is well blended with the dry ingredients.

3 Store in an airtight container in a cool place. You can store the mix up to six months—or even longer if you keep it in the freezer.

: **NOW YOU HAVE ABOUT 15**
: **CUPS OF YOUR OWN**
: **ALL-PURPOSE MIX,**

enough to make:

*About 15 batches of brownies, or
*About 7 batches of chocolate chip cookies, or
*About 15 batches of oatmeal cookies, or
*About 10 batches of peanut butter cookies, or
*About 10 batches of pancakes

USE YOUR MIX TO MAKE BROWNIES

Here's what you need:

1 cup mix
½ cup unsweetened cocoa powder
½ cup sugar
1 egg
¼ cup water
¼ cup (½ stick) butter or margarine

Here's what you do:

1 Preheat the oven to 350°F (180°C).

2 In a large bowl, combine mix, cocoa, and sugar. Do not use an electric mixer.

3 Crack the egg into a small bowl, and beat the egg lightly with a fork. Then pour in the water, and stir to combine the egg and water.

4 Melt the butter or margarine. (To melt, put into a heatproof dish, and heat in the microwave for about 30 seconds.)

5 Stir the egg mixture into the dry ingredients.

6 Stir in the melted butter.

7 Butter an 8 × 8-inch square baking pan. Spread the batter in the pan.

8 Bake for 20 minutes.

> **NOW YOU HAVE 16 BROWNIES FROM YOUR OWN MIX. COOL IN PAN BEFORE CUTTING.**

Suggestion: For ways to top off your brownies, see the make-your-own blondies project in *MAKE UP YOUR OWN SECRET RECIPES.*

USE YOUR MIX TO MAKE CHOCOLATE CHIP COOKIES

Here's what you need:

½ cup (1 stick) butter or margarine, softened

1 cup brown sugar, well packed

1 egg

2 cups mix

1 cup (6 ounces) semisweet chocolate chips

½ cup chopped nuts, if you want

Here's what you do:

1 Preheat oven to 375°F (190°C).

2 Use a good strong spoon, and beat together the butter, brown sugar, and egg in a large bowl.

3 Stir in the mix.

4 Stir in chocolate chips and nuts.

5 Drop by teaspoonfuls onto ungreased baking sheet, about two inches apart.

6 Bake for 10 to 12 minutes until light brown. Let cool on the baking sheet for a couple of minutes. Then use a spatula to transfer the cookies to a wire rack to finish cooling.

> **NOW YOU HAVE ABOUT 48 CHOCOLATE CHIP COOKIES FROM YOUR OWN MIX.**

USE YOUR MIX TO MAKE CHOCOLATE CHIP SQUARES

1 Be especially careful to wash your hands before you begin making chocolate chip squares.

2 Preheat the oven to 375°F (190°C).

3 Look back at the recipe for chocolate chip cookies. Make this recipe just the same way, mixing together the butter or margarine, brown sugar, egg, and mix. BUT DON'T PUT IN THE CHOCOLATE CHIPS OR NUTS JUST YET.

4 Grease a 9 × 13-inch baking pan. Spread the batter in the pan. Use a rubber spatula—and smooth the batter with your clean hands.

5 Now sprinkle the batter with chocolate chips and nuts. Gently pat the chips and nuts partway into the dough.

6 Bake for 20 minutes or until lightly browned.

> **NOW YOU HAVE ABOUT 36 CHOCOLATE CHIP SQUARES FROM YOUR OWN MIX. COOL IN THE PAN BEFORE CUTTING.**

USE YOUR MIX TO MAKE OATMEAL COOKIES

Here's what you need:

1 cup mix

1 cup rolled oats

⅔ cup brown sugar, well packed

¼ teaspoon cinnamon

1 egg

2 tablespoons water

1 teaspoon vanilla extract

Here's what you do:

1 Preheat oven to 375°F (190°C).

2 Use a large spoon to beat together the mix, rolled oats, brown sugar, and cinnamon.

3 Crack the egg into a small bowl, and beat lightly with a fork. Stir in water and vanilla extract.

4 Add the egg mixture to the dry ingredients. Stir until well blended.

5 Butter or grease a baking sheet. Drop batter by teaspoonfuls onto the baking sheet, about 1½ to 2 inches apart.

6 Bake for 10 to 12 minutes.

7 Let the cookies cool on the baking sheet for two minutes. Then use a spatula to transfer the cookies to a wire rack to finish cooling.

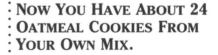

NOW YOU HAVE ABOUT 24 OATMEAL COOKIES FROM YOUR OWN MIX.

USE YOUR MIX TO MAKE PEANUT BUTTER COOKIES

Here's what you need:

1½ cups mix
⅔ cup brown sugar, well packed
1 egg
⅓ cup peanut butter
1 tablespoon water
1 teaspoon vanilla extract

Here's what you do:

1 Be especially careful to wash your hands before you begin making peanut butter cookies.

2 Preheat oven to 375°F (190°C).

3 In a large bowl, stir together the mix and the brown sugar.

4 In a small bowl, beat the egg lightly with a fork, and combine it with the peanut butter. Then stir in the water and vanilla extract.

5 Add the egg–peanut butter mixture to the dry ingredients, and blend thoroughly with the back of a large spoon.

6 Form your peanut butter batter into one-inch balls.

7 Place two inches apart on an ungreased cookie sheet. Flatten with the tines of a fork to form a cross-hatch design.

8 Bake for 8 to 10 minutes.

9 Cool on a wire rack.

: **NOW YOU HAVE ABOUT 36
: PEANUT-BUTTER COOKIES
: FROM YOUR OWN MIX.**

USE YOUR MIX TO MAKE SHAKE-AND-POUR PANCAKES

Here's what you need:

1½ cups mix
1 egg
¾ cup water
2 tablespoons vegetable oil

Here's what you do:

1 Put 1½ cups mix into a pint or quart jar with a tight cover.

2 In a small bowl, beat egg lightly with a fork.

3 Add egg and water to the jar.

4 Cover the jar tightly, and shake vigorously. Shake until all the ingredients are well combined.

5 Heat a griddle. You can tell the griddle is hot enough when drops of water dance on the surface when tossed from your fingertips.

6 Pour two tablespoons oil on the griddle. Tip the griddle very slightly so that the oil coats the griddle evenly.

7 Pour or spoon pancake batter onto the griddle, the equivalent of about one large spoonful at a time.

8 Cook until the bubbles that form on the surface of the pancakes break and the surface dries slightly.

9 Then slide the spatula under each pancake, and flip to the other slide. FLIP ONLY ONCE. Cook the second side until golden.

10 Transfer your first batch of pancakes to a heated platter. Then cover the platter to keep those pancakes hot while you are cooking the rest.
You decide how to serve your pancakes: Serve pancakes with butter, syrup, or fruit preserves. Or sprinkle your pancakes with cinnamon and brown sugar.

NOW YOU HAVE ABOUT TEN PANCAKES FROM YOUR OWN MIX.

A MAKE-YOUR-OWN CAKE MIX PROJECT

Here's what you need:

3⅓ cups shortening, at room temperature

7⅔ cups sugar

11 cups sifted all purpose flour

5 tablespoons baking powder

3 tablespoons salt

Taste Comparison: *Get your family and friends to compare tastes. We hope they like your cakes better than food-factory cakes.*

Here's what you do:

1 Measure shortening into a large mixer bowl. Use the electric mixer to beat for about 30 seconds at medium speed. Stop the mixer, and scrape the sides and bottom of the bowl with a rubber spatula. Then beat again for another 30 seconds.

2 Add one cup sugar, and beat into the shortening for one minute.

3 Repeat this step three more times until you have added a total of four cups sugar and beaten them into the shortening. (This is called creaming.)

4 In another large bowl, mix together the rest of the sugar (3⅔ cups), the flour, the baking powder, and the salt.

5 Add two cups of this flour-sugar mixture to creamed shortening and sugar. Beat at medium speed until thoroughly mixed. Once in a while, stop the mixer and scrape the sides of the bowl.

6 Add the creamed mixture to the remaining sugar-flour mixture. Blend together thoroughly with the back of a spoon. When you are finished, the mixture ought to look somewhat like cornmeal.

7 Store in an airtight container in a cool place. You can store this mix as long as six months.

NOW YOU HAVE 21 CUPS OF YOUR OWN MIX, ENOUGH FOR SIX LARGE CAKES.

25

USE YOUR CAKE MIX TO BAKE A YELLOW CAKE

Here's what you need:

3½ cups cake mix

2 large eggs

¾ cup milk

1 teaspoon vanilla extract

Here are types of pans you can choose:

(1) Two 8-inch or 9-inch round cake pans
(2) One 8-inch round pan and one 8 × 8-inch square pan
(3) One 9 × 13-inch oblong pan
(4) Two 8 × 8-inch square pans
(5) Two dozen-muffin pans

Hint: For ideas on shapes, look at the cake-for-every-occasion project in FOODS TO PUNCH, TWIST, SHAPE, AND DESIGN. For another interesting idea, look at the cupcake cones project in FOODS THAT LOOK LIKE SOMETHING (OR SOMEONE).

Hint: Look for interesting frosting recipes and creative cake decorating ideas in the FOODS TO PUNCH, TWIST, SHAPE, AND DESIGN section, in the HOLIDAY SURPRISES, and in FUN FOOD WITH SECRET MESSAGES.

Here's what you do:

1 Preheat oven to 350°F (180°C).

2 In a large mixer bowl, combine the mix, eggs, milk, and vanilla extract. Use the electric mixer to beat for one minute at low speed. Stop the mixer, and scrape the sides of the bowl with a rubber spatula.

3 Beat at medium speed for two more minutes until the batter is smooth and free of lumps.

4 Grease and lightly flour pans.

5 *You decide the shape of cake you want.*

6 Spread the batter in evenly.

7 Bake. If you are using round or square pans, bake your cake for 20 to 25 minutes. If you are using a 9 × 13-inch oblong pan, bake your cake for 35 to 40 minutes. If you are using muffin pans, fill each cup about ⅔ full, and bake for 20 to 25 minutes.

8 Your cake is done when a toothpick poked into the center comes out clean.

9 Cool for ten minutes before you remove the cake layers from the pans. Then cool on wire racks.

10 When the cake layers are completely cool, put them together and frost.

NOW YOU HAVE A TWO-LAYER YELLOW CAKE FROM YOUR OWN CAKE MIX (OR AN OBLONG CAKE OR TWO DOZEN MUFFINS).

USE YOUR CAKE MIX TO BAKE A CHOCOLATE CAKE

1 Look back at the recipe for yellow cake. Make this recipe *just* the same way. ***But Add These Ingredients.***

> *2 more tablespoons milk (in addition to the ¾ cup milk)*
>
> *2 squares (2 ounces) unsweetened chocolate, melted*

Here are two ways to melt the chocolate:

(1) Put the chocolate squares in a small, heatproof dish. Cover and microwave at low power for two minutes. Stir gently.

(2) Or melt in the top of a double boiler over simmering water. Stir gently.

2 Bake the chocolate cake just the same as the yellow cake.

> **NOW YOU HAVE A TWO-LAYER CHOCOLATE CAKE FROM YOUR OWN CAKE MIX.**

USE YOUR CAKE MIX TO BAKE A WHITE CAKE

1 Look back at the recipe for yellow cake. Make this recipe *just* the same way. ***But instead of two eggs, use three egg whites.***

Here's how to separate an egg white from the yellow egg yolk:

Have two small bowls ready. Over one bowl, crack the egg by tapping it firmly but gently. Use the fingers of both hands to break the egg in half (slowly).

Keep the egg upright, and hold the yolk in the eggshell while you let the egg white drop into the bowl. Then pour the egg yolk into the other bowl.

2 Bake the white cake just the same as the yellow cake.

> **NOW YOU HAVE A TWO-LAYER WHITE CAKE FROM YOUR OWN CAKE MIX.**

A MAKE-YOUR-OWN PUDDING MIX

Here's what you need:

4 cups nonfat dry milk
2 cups sugar
1½ cups cornstarch
1½ teaspoons salt

Here's what you do:

Mix the dry milk, sugar, cornstarch, and salt together in a jar with a tight-fitting lid. Store in a cool place. You can store the mix for as long as six months—or longer if you keep it in the freezer.

NOW YOU HAVE 7½ CUPS OF YOUR OWN PUDDING MIX, ENOUGH FOR ABOUT 30 SERVINGS OF PUDDING.

USE YOUR PUDDING MIX TO MAKE VANILLA PUDDING

Here's what you need:

1 cup plus 2 tablespoons pudding mix
2 cups water
2 tablespoons butter or margarine
1 teaspoon vanilla extract

Here's what you do:

1 Measure the pudding mix into a one-quart saucepan. Add the water slowly as you stir. Stir until the water is completely blended in.

2 Bring the mixture to a boil over medium heat. **Stir constantly. The pudding will burn if you don't keep stirring.**

3 Then turn the heat to low. Boil gently, while stirring, for two to three minutes. Remove from heat.

4 Stir in the butter or margarine along with the vanilla extract. (The butter will melt.)

5 Let stand 15 minutes. Stir once more. If you wish, pour the warm pudding into pudding or custard cups.

Caution: You may need adult help with pouring.

6 Refrigerate until set and ready to eat.

NOW YOU HAVE FOUR ½-CUP SERVINGS OF VANILLA PUDDING FROM YOUR OWN PUDDING MIX.

A MAKE-YOUR-OWN COCOA MIX PROJECT

Here's what you need:

 3 cups nonfat dry milk
⅔ cup sugar
⅔ cup unsweetened cocoa powder
½ teaspoon salt

Here's what you do:

1 Mix dry milk, sugar, cocoa, and salt thoroughly.

2 Store in an airtight container in a cool place. You can store this mix practically forever—but you won't want to. You'll want to drink hot cocoa too often for that.

> NOW YOU HAVE 4⅓ CUPS OF YOUR OWN COCOA MIX, ENOUGH FOR ABOUT 17 CUPS OF COCOA.

USE YOUR COCOA MIX TO MAKE HOT COCOA

Here's what you do:

1 Measure ¼ cup mix into a heatproof cup. Then fill the cup with warm water. Stir well. Heat in the microwave oven for about one minute, and stir again.

2 Or measure ¼ cup mix into a cup. Then fill the cup with boiling water and stir well.

> *Caution: You need adult help with boiling water.*

> NOW YOU HAVE ONE CUP OF HOT COCOA FROM YOUR OWN COCOA MIX.

A SUPER-INSTANT MUFFIN MIX PROJECT

This is a total mix. You can keep the mix in the refrigerator for as long as a month. Then when you want muffins, just pour the mix into muffin pans and bake.

Here's what you need:

- 1 15-ounce box of raisin bran cereal
- 5 cups flour (if you wish, use a combination of whole wheat flour, white flour, and wheat germ.)
- 2 teaspoons baking soda
- 2 teaspoons salt
- 1 quart buttermilk
- 4 large eggs
- 1 cup vegetable oil
- ¾ cup honey or molasses (Or use a combination of honey and molasses.)

Here's how to make the mix:

1 In a large bowl, combine the raisin bran cereal, flour, baking soda, and salt.

2 In a second large bowl, stir together the buttermilk, eggs, oil, and honey or molasses.

3 Add the buttermilk mixture to the raisin bran mixture. Stir until combined.

4 Refrigerate in a covered plastic or glass container.

Here's how to use the mix:

1 When you're ready to bake muffins, preheat the oven to 400°F (200°C).

2 Then pour or spoon the muffin mix into greased muffin tins. Fill each tin about ⅔ full, or use paper muffin cups.

3 Bake for 20 to 25 minutes. Muffins are done when they are light brown and the tops pop back when you touch them.

> NOW YOU HAVE A REALLY INSTANT READY-TO-BAKE MUFFIN MIX—ENOUGH FOR THREE BATCHES (A DOZEN MUFFINS EACH) WHENEVER YOU WANT.

Hint: Instead of fresh buttermilk, you can use dry buttermilk powder. Add ¾ cup dry buttermilk powder to the cereal-flour mixture, and then add a quart of water with the wet ingredients.

QUICK KITCHEN SCIENCE EXPERIMENTS

Do you know why cakes rise, how yeast works,why you cook potatoes? Would you like to write secret messages and bounce blueberries?

Here are kitchen science experiments. You can learn about food and cooking from all of them, and you can eat a few of them.

Rule: An adult ought to help you with these experiments.

CHEMICALS

Everything on earth is composed of chemicals. Our own bodies, animals and plants, rocks and air, are all basically chemical.

Basic chemical elements are of two types. There are metallic elements like gold, copper, and iron. And then there are non-metallic elements like the oxygen we breathe and the carbon that is a part of living things. You see carbon in the black ash left over when wood or food is burned.

When elements combine, they form compounds. And chemical compounds look and behave much differently from the basic elements.

For example, sugar is a compound of carbon, hydrogen, and oxygen. Yet obviously sugar does not look or act like carbon, hydrogen, or oxygen by themselves. If you burn sugar, the oxygen and hydrogen are released in the form of water, and the carbon is left behind.

Table salt, our most common seasoning for food, is composed of two poisonous chemicals. The two are sodium, a metallic element, and chlorine gas, a non-metallic element. By themselves, each of these chemicals is poison. Chemically combined, they are nothing more than ordinary salt.

CHEMICAL REACTIONS IN COOKING

Cooking depends on chemical reactions like these. A chemical reaction makes biscuits rise and puts the carbonation into soft drinks.

Chemical reactions can even take place between the pans you use and the food you cook in them. In some cases, that can be good for you.

For instance, if you cook an acid food like spaghetti sauce in a cast iron pot, the acid and the iron react chemically and the sauce actually takes in a small amount of valuable iron. Since your body needs iron, that is good for you nutritionally.

Here is an experiment to show you how copper pennies react with acid.

. . . .

A COPPER PLATING EXPERIMENT

. . . .

Cooking an acid food in an iron pot might produce chemical reactions that are good for you nutritionally. Cooking an acid food in an aluminum or copper pot might not be so good. Your body does need tiny amounts of aluminum and copper, but not as much as you might get from the cooking chemistry of an acid food in a copper or aluminum pot.

This experiment shows how copper reacts with acid. You can actually take the copper from copper pennies and use it to coat an iron nail.

Here is what you need:

Vinegar

Salt

A few dull copper pennies

A glass container

An iron nail

Steel wool or cleanser

Here's what you do:

1 In the glass container, mix vinegar with ½ teaspoon salt.

2 Drop the dull pennies in the solution and leave them until they become clean. Your solution now contains a copper salt from the pennies.

3 Clean an iron nail with steel wool and soap or cleanser. Rinse it thoroughly.

4 Drop the nail into the vinegar solution.

> **AFTER FIVE OR TEN MINUTES, YOU WILL FIND THAT THE NAIL IS COVERED WITH A BRIGHT COATING OF COPPER.**

. . . .

EXPERIMENTS WITH LIQUIDS

Molecules of liquids stick together. Molecules stick together on the surface of a liquid, and molecules also adhere (or stick) to the walls of the container. You can see how molecules stick together in this next experiment.

· · · · · · · · · ·
A FLOATING NEEDLE EXPERIMENT
· ·

Here is what you need:

Water
A bowl
A small piece of newspaper
A sewing needle
Some liquid detergent

Here's what you do:

1 Fill a bowl with water.

2 Cut out a piece of newspaper about 1½ inches square.

3 Float the newspaper on the surface of the water.

4 Place the needle in the middle of the newspaper.

5 Carefully push the edges of the newspaper down into the water. As the newspaper gets wet, it will sink and leave the needle floating.

6 Now add a drop of liquid detergent to the water at the edge of the bowl. Notice how quickly the needle sinks to the bottom.

The detergent causes the molecules to disassociate or to stop adhering to one another. One result is that anything dropping into the water (like the needle) gets wet much faster than it ordinarily would. Clothes washed in water with detergent in it get soaked through more quickly—and that is one way that detergent helps get clothes clean. Because the detergent seems to be making the water (and things in the water) "wetter," the detergent is known as a wetting agent.

Surface tension makes it possible to float the needle on water. That is because the molecules on the surface stick together. Look closely, and you will see how the needle is supported by the water.

A MEASURING EXPERIMENT

Liquid molecules don't only stick to one another. They also are attracted to the molecules of the wall of their container. In this experiment, you can see evidence of how the molecules do that. You will need a one-cup glass measuring cup and a small pitcher of water.

1 Set the cup on a flat surface.

2 With your eyes even at the level of the cup, carefully pour water into the cup. You can see the water curve downward because the water molecules adhere to the sides of the measuring cup.

3 To measure ½ cup of water, pour the water into the cup until the bottom of the curve is on the ½-cup line. This is the most closely accurate way to measure liquids.

EXPERIMENTS WITH SOLUTIONS, MIXTURES, SUSPENSIONS, AND EMULSIONS

Here are experiments on how liquids and solids mix—or cannot mix— together.

Solutions
The first experiment dissolves a solid into a liquid. The next dissolves two liquids.

A SOLUTIONS EXPERIMENT WITH SALT

Salt water is an example of dissolving a solid into a liquid.

1 Stir ½ teaspoon of salt into warm water until the salt disappears.

2 You can no longer see the salt, but you can taste it. The salt has not changed its taste. And the same salt has not changed chemically.

　　The salt molecules have disappeared in the water, but without a chemical reaction.

3 Boil the water to make it evaporate, and the salt will appear again.

A SOLUTIONS EXPERIMENT WITH VINEGAR

Here is an experiment that dissolves two liquids.

1 Pour a small amount of wine vinegar into a glass. Or use cider vinegar if you wish. Smell and taste it.

2 Now add water. The color will become paler, but you ought still to be able to smell and taste the vinegar.

3 Boil the solution. Some of the water will evaporate, and the vinegar will again become concentrated—and you will see the natural color of the vinegar again.

MIXTURES

Mixtures are not the same as solutions, partly because they don't last.

Mixtures separate like the dirt and water you mixed together to make mud pies when you were little. You stir them together, and either slowly or quickly, they separate out.

Mixtures that separate very slowly are called suspensions. Suspensions are very important in cooking because you often create suspensions when you mix ingredients together for cakes, cookies, and other baked goods.

The flour and water in dough form a suspension as you beat them. The more you beat the dough, the more stable and long-lasting the suspension becomes.

Heating flour and water together causes the flour particles to absorb water and become suspended. That is how flour thickens puddings and sauces.

As the dough cooks, the blended ingredients become solid as water is both absorbed and evaporates.

Here are experiments on mixtures and suspensions.

A MIXTURES EXPERIMENT WITH FLOUR

1 Sprinkle a tablespoon of flour into a cup of water. Stir rapidly.

2 Now let the mixture stand for a few minutes.

    You can mix the flour into water, but you cannot dissolve it. No matter how hard you stir, the flour will eventually separate from the water.

A MIXTURES EXPERIMENT WITH OIL

Pour a tablespoon of cooking oil into a cup of water.

    Again, you can mix oil into the water, but the oil will immediately separate and float on top of the water.

A solid can be suspended in a liquid, and a liquid can be suspended in another liquid.

A SUSPENSIONS EXPERIMENTS WITH FLOUR

Pour one cup of water and one tablespoon of flour into a blender jar. (You can use the same flour and water you used for the mixtures experiment.) Blend at high speed for one minute. Then pour the flour-and-water suspension back into the glass.

    The flour is now suspended in the water. The flour will still separate from the water eventually, but it will take much longer than with a simple mixture.

. . . .

AN EMULSION EXPERIMENT WITH OIL

. . . .

An emulsion is the suspension of a liquid within another liquid. Oil and water naturally separate. (You can often see motor oil floating in a puddle of rain.) But you can create a suspension and make oil and water stay together.

Pour one cup of water and one tablespoon oil into the blender jar. (Again, you can use the same oil and water you used for the mixtures experiment.) Cover the blender, and blend on high speed for one minute. Pour the oil and water back into the glass.

Now you have an emulsion. Notice that now the oil is distributed throughout the water. The oil takes much longer to separate from the water than it does with a plain mixture of oil and water.

1 Put your finger into the oil-and-water emulsion. Your finger feels oily when you take it out.

2 Add a few drops of liquid detergent to the oil and water. Pour into the blender and blend for one minute. You will find that the oil is evenly distributed throughout.

3 Put your finger into the emulsion again. Does your finger feel oily now when you take it out?

The detergent acts as an emulsifier that helps the oil stay in suspension.

Examples of emulsions:

1 Homogenized milk is an example of an emulsion in which milk fat is suspended within the liquid milk.

2 Lecithin is a substance found in egg yolk that holds oils in suspension. Mayonnaise is an emulsion in which egg yolk is the emulsifier.

. . . .

EXPERIMENTS WITH SUPERSATURATED SOLUTIONS

When you heat a liquid, you usually increase its ability to dissolve a solid substance. When you heat water to boiling, you can dissolve much more salt than you can in cold water.

When you cool the boiled water, the salt will still remain in solution. This is a supersaturated solution.

This is how it works. A super-saturated solution contains more salt or sugar than it normally would at room temperature. It is not a stable solution.

Hard shaking, adding more crystals, or letting the solvent (in this case, the water) evaporate into the air will cause the extra crystals to settle out of the solution.

If you add a foreign substance to the container, the crystals will grow on that substance. That's how to grow large crystals from a supersaturated solution.

These next experiments show how to grow crystals from both sugar and salt solutions.

A Rock Candy Experiment

Here's what you need:

A clean one-quart large-mouth canning jar

A piece of clean white string

A metal weight, such as a paper clip or a metal washer

A pencil

A knife or fork

Sugar

Boiling water

> **Caution: An adult needs to handle the boiling water for this experiment.**

1 Fill the jar with sugar.

2 Slowly pour boiling water into the jar. Push a kitchen knife down into the water so that the sugar gets wet all the way down to the bottom of the jar. Add more water slowly and then stir to make sure that all of the sugar dissolves.

3 Tie the paper clip weight to one end of the string.

4 Tie the other end of the string to the pencil.

5 Place the pencil across the mouth of the jar.

6 Roll the string around the pencil until the weight is almost touching the bottom of the jar.

7 Set the uncovered jar aside undisturbed in a warm place for several days.
   Crystals will grow on the string, on the jar, and on the surface of the sugar solution.

8 Break up the crust from time to time so that the water can evaporate. As the water evaporates, more crystals grow.

> **NOW YOU HAVE ROCK CANDY YOU CAN EAT.**

A SALT CRYSTAL EXPERIMENT

You can perform exactly the same experiment with table salt. Of course, you will not want to eat the salt crystals. But if you have a salt mill, you can put the crystals in the mill and grind them over salads.

You'll find that the large salt crystals don't wilt salad greens as ordinary salt crystals might.

Here's why.

Large salt crystals have less surface area than the same amount of salt formed into small crystals. Less of the large salt crystal is in contact with the greens. Since salt absorbs water from greens and can cause them to wilt, the large crystals will withdraw less water and therefore cause less wilting.

EXPERIMENTS WITH ACIDS AND BASES

Acids are useful for cooking and useful for flavoring and preserving food.

Vinegar is an example. So is lemon juice. Acids are sour to the taste. Some nutrients, like vitamin C (ascorbic acid), are acids.

Bases or alkalies are the opposite of acids. In fact, acids and bases neutralize each other to form salts. Bases are soapy or bitter to the taste.

Don't taste strong acids or bases, though, since they can be dangerous.

A Very Edible Red Cabbage Experiment to Test for Acids and Bases

Over the years, chemists have learned that certain substances change color when exposed to an acid or to a base.

You can use extracts from many vegetables, flowers, and spices to test for acids and bases. Here is an indicator test with red cabbage water.

Here is what you need:

A red cabbage

Substances to test, such as:
　White vinegar,
　Baking soda,
　Orange or lemon juice,
　A vitamin C tablet, etc.

4 or more small jars

A white paper towel

Here's how to prepare the test strips:

1 Grate about three cups of the cabbage into a stainless steel pan. You will probably want some adult help with this.

2 Pour in water until you can just see the water through the cabbage. Boil the cabbage until tender.

3 The water will turn a shade between blue and red. Carefully strain the colored water into a jar. Let the cabbage water cool slightly.

4 Now make indicator strips from the cabbage water. Cut a white paper towel into strips. Dip the strips into the cabbage water and allow to dry. You can dip these strips into liquids to test for acids and bases.

Here's how to test:

1 Pour some of the cabbage water into three or four small jars.

2 Into one jar add a tablespoon of white vinegar. Add lemon juice to the second jar, and baking soda to the third. Crush the vitamin C tablet with a spoon and add to the fourth jar.

3 Bases cause the cabbage water to turn a deep blue. Acids make the water a bright red.

4 Record how the water changes color when you add vinegar, juice, baking soda, vitamin C, and other substances.

5 Add the solution of baking soda to the jar containing the white vinegar. How does the color change?

Here are other substances you can test:

Save some cabbage water to test other substances. (If you wish, refrigerate some cabbage water for later tests.)
　Baking powder
　Cream of tartar
　Detergent
　Eggshell (crushed and wet)
　Household ammonia
　Milk of magnesia (magnesium hydroxide)
　Salt
　Sugar
　Toothpaste or tooth powder
　Washing soda

AFTER THE EXPERIMENT, FIX THE CABBAGE FOR DINNER

Here's what you need:

The cooked red cabbage
Vinegar
Butter
Salt
Sugar
An apple (if you want)
Raisins (if you want)

Here's what to do:

1 The cooked cabbage is a bluish color, not very appetizing. To make the cabbage look more edible, mix in a small amount of vinegar. The cabbage will turn bright red.

2 Add a little butter and salt. A little sugar will offset the acid taste of the vinegar.

3 If you wish, add chopped apple and a few raisins. Some cooks like to add caraway seeds, but they need to be cooked with the cabbage in order to add their flavor to it.

Taste-test the cabbage as you add each ingredient. Cabbage is a good source of vitamin C, because the acid (vinegar) helps preserve the vitamin C of the cabbage, even after you cook the cabbage.

NOW YOU HAVE SWEET AND SOUR RED CABBAGE.

MORE MYSTIFYING RED CABBAGE EXPERIMENTS

1 You can mystify your friends by pouring a little white vinegar, which looks just like water, into a glass of the bluish cabbage water. Watch the water turn ruby red.

2 To confuse your friends even more, make a clear solution of baking soda and water. Add your solution to the cabbage water containing the vinegar. The solution will foam and then turn back to a bluish color.

YET MORE COLOR CHANGING EXPERIMENTS TO TEST FOR ACIDS AND BASES

You can use other vegetables and fruits as indicators, as long as the vegetables and fruits are highly colored. Try beet juice and blueberry juice. Or try deeply colored blossoms from flowers such as dark red geranium or rose petals. You can test with elderberry juice, and turn the juice from purple to green.

A BLOOD RED EXPERIMENT

Turmeric is an especially good indicator. In India, turmeric is a spice to flavor food. In the United States, turmeric is mainly used to add color to mustard.

Here's what you need for a turmeric indicator test:

Turmeric

Rubbing alcohol

Small jars

Baking soda and other substances you wish to test

Here's how to go about the experiment:

1 Mix one teaspoon turmeric with ⅓ cup rubbing alcohol.

2 Label the container: "TURMERIC IN ALCOHOL—POISON."

3 Let the mixture sit until the mixture becomes bright yellow.

> *Caution: Keep this mixture separate from food and out of the reach of small children. The alcohol is poisonous.*

4 Next make a solution of baking soda and water in a small jar. (You may find extra undissolved baking soda in the bottom of the jar. That is all right.)

5 Carefully pour a little of the colored alcohol into the baking soda solution.

The yellow alcohol becomes blood red and floats on top of the baking soda solution.

The color is the indicator for a base. In this experiment, the baking soda is the base. The colored alcohol floats on top because it is lighter than the baking soda solution.

Notice how clearly the two liquids separate. If you shake or stir the solution, the alcohol dissolves in the soda solution, and the color is diluted. If you add acid, the solution foams, and the color turns to a pale yellow.

FOAMS, FIZZES, AND BUBBLES

Sparkling, bubbling, fizzing water holds a special charm. Everyone likes to pop open a soft drink bottle and watch the fizz.

The bubbles are carbon dioxide.

Carbon dioxide bubbles out of water naturally in many places of the world, often where people have vacationed over many generations, enjoying the hot bubbly water and letting the water relax them and cure their ills. The ancient Romans used to call those mysterious bubbles the "spirit" *of the waters. The ancient Mohawk peoples called their natural springs the* "medicine waters of the Great Spirit."

Then in 1772, a British scientist, Joseph Priestley, discovered how to collect carbon dioxide gas from fermenting beer. He was the first to figure out how to bubble carbon dioxide gas—"fixed air," as he called it—through water artificially.

And so he invented the first bubbly, fizzy, carbonated drink.

A DANCING BLUEBERRIES EXPERIMENT

Here's how you can see the carbon dioxide bubbles act in a fizzy drink:

1 Pour a glass of fresh mineral water, ginger ale, or other light-colored soft drink.

2 Immediately pop in a few blueberries.

You'll see the carbon dioxide bubbles cling to the blueberries and make them dance.

AN EXPERIMENT ON WHAT MAKES BREADS AND CAKES RISE

Chemical reactions that release carbon dioxide are what make breads and cakes rise in the oven as you bake them.

When you mix baking soda (sodium bicarbonate) with an acid like vinegar, sour cream, buttermilk, or molasses, a chemical reaction makes the mixture foam right away. And that chemical reaction produces carbon dioxide bubbles.

Cream of tartar is an acid that also causes a reaction with baking soda. Cream of tartar is useful in cooking because sometimes you want the chemical reaction of baking soda and an acid but without adding extra flavor.

Here's how to see baking soda work:

1 Mix ¼ teaspoon cream of tartar and ½ teaspoon baking soda.
2 Add ½ cup warm water.
   The mixture will foam immediately. You can use a mixture like this to make cookies rise.

Or you can use baking powder.

Baking powder is a mixture of two salt powders: one acid and one base. When the mixture heats, it foams. And when it heats while baking in something like biscuits, baking powder makes the biscuits rise.

Look at the ingredients listed on a can of baking powder. One ingredient is bicarbonate of soda. Bicarbonate of soda is the chemical name for baking soda, and it is a base salt.

Another ingredient may be acid phosphate of calcium. That's an acid salt.

When they mix, the mixture is called double-acting baking powder.

Here's how to see baking powder work:

1 Mix ¾ teaspoon double-acting baking powder into ½ cup warm water in a one-quart glass measuring cup.
2 Put the cup into the microwave, and heat for one minute.
   Take the cup out of the oven, and notice how the mixture continues to bubble.
   Baking powder reacts twice, once when you mix it and once when you heat it. That's why it's called double-acting.

A YEAST EXPERIMENT WITH A BALLOON

Yeast makes bread rise. This experiment will help explain how.

Here's what you need:

1 teaspoon dry yeast
$\frac{1}{4}$ cup sugar
Water
A measuring cup
Measuring spoons
A clean one-quart soda bottle
A balloon
A piece of string
A two-quart cooking pot

Here's what to do:

1 Add the dry yeast and sugar to one cup of very warm tap water. Stir to dissolve.

2 Pour the mixture into the one-quart soda bottle.

3 Blow up the balloon once or twice and let the air out to soften it.

4 Put the balloon over the lip of the bottle and tie it in place with the string.

5 Fill the cooking pot half full of very warm tap water.

6 Stand the soda bottle in the water. Yeast likes warmth.

Within an hour, you will see frothy bubbles fill the bottle. The empty balloon is no longer empty. The yeast has slowly begun to blow up the balloon.

The gas in the balloon is carbon dioxide.

Baking soda and baking powder produce carbon dioxide bubbles, too, but the yeast does it in a different way. Yeast is a living organism, a type of plant. It feeds on the sugar in the water and produces carbon dioxide gas.

When yeast is mixed with flour and water (and, of course, other ingredients) to make bread, it digests some of the flour. The yeast grows and multiplies and forms the carbon dioxide gas that makes the bread rise.

When you knead or punch bread dough, you help break up gas bubbles. As you make the gas bubbles smaller, you give the bread a fine, even texture. Perhaps an angry cook makes good bread. And after punching and kneading the bread, the cook should be less angry.

A BALLOON AND CANDLE EXPERIMENT WITH CARBON DIOXIDE

Carbon dioxide puts out fires. Fire extinguishers use carbon dioxide foam. So a good test for carbon dioxide is to see if it puts out fire.

After your yeast experiment, you have a balloon full of carbon dioxide.

Here's how to tell for sure:

1 Remove the balloon from the bottle. Slowly release the "air" from the balloon into a small jar. Quickly cover the jar.

2 Now light a candle in a secure candle holder. *You must have adult help with this part of the experiment.* For extra safety, set the candle in the kitchen sink.

3 Remove the cover from the jar, and pour the gas from the jar over the flame. Carbon dioxide is heavier than air. That's why you can pour it down over the flame.

You should be able to put out the candle immediately. Your fire extinguisher is the carbon dioxide gas in the jar.

Try a repeat of this experiment using the gas from the vinegar and baking powder experiment.

. . . .

A YEAST STARTER EXPERIMENT

. . . .

In the time before grocery stores, people needed to keep yeast growing from one bread batch to the next. When they made bread, they saved a cup of the batter to become the starter for the next batch.

If their starter yeast died or dried up, they borrowed more from a neighbor. If they didn't have a neighbor, they made new starter from potatoes or from fresh milk.

In those days, if people left an uncovered pint of milk in the kitchen all night, the milk would collect some of the yeast plants floating in the air. Picture the air full of tiny, invisible yeast plants waiting to settle into a nice warm pint of milk.

You can't try this experiment with ordinary milk from the grocery store. Most milk from the grocery store is pasteurized and would spoil before the yeast could grow.

But in your great-grandmother's day, milk fresh from the cow provided a perfect place for yeast to grow.

Of course, fresh milk also turns sour quickly. The bread your great-grandmother made might have been called sourdough bread because the sour milk gave it a sour flavor.

Sometimes today, you can buy sourdough bread and see how it tasted to your great-grandfamily. Or make some modern sourdough starter.

Here's how to make sourdough starter for yourself:

1 Buy active-cultured buttermilk. (Buttermilk does not spoil like ordinary milk. Acid-making bacteria make it turn sour in the natural, old-fashioned way.)

2 Leave one cup of the buttermilk out, uncovered, for 24 hours.

3 After 24 hours, add one cup flour and let the mixture stand, uncovered, for two to five days. It should be in a warm place, ideally about 80°F (25°C). You might put it in an oven that has a pilot light or near a heater. And wait for a good sour aroma and for the bubbly yeast to grow.

4 Use right away, or cover and store in the refrigerator for no more than a week.

Hint: If you leave your starter in the refrigerator for longer than a week, you can still save it. Mix one cup starter with one cup milk and one cup flour. Leave at room temperature, uncovered, for several hours or overnight. Soon your starter will be bubbly again.

AFTER THE EXPERIMENT, MAKE SOURDOUGH BREAD

Sourdough bread takes 24 hours from start to finish. Plan ahead! Begin one afternoon. Let it rise all night. Work on it the next morning. Let it rise again. Bake it in the afternoon.

Here's what you need:

1½ cups very warm water

1 cup sourdough starter

4 cups unsifted all-purpose or unbleached flour

2 teaspoons sugar

2 teaspoons salt

2 more cups unsifted flour

½ teaspoon baking soda

Here's what to do on the first afternoon:

1 In a large bowl, stir together warm water, sourdough starter, four cups flour, sugar, and salt.

2 Place in a crockery bowl at room temperature for 18 hours. Cover the bowl with a clean dish towel.

Hint: If you start at 4 o'clock in the afternoon, you can be ready to work on your dough at 10 o'clock the next morning.

Here's what to do the next morning:

1 Remove one cup of the risen dough, and add it to your old sourdough starter. Then you'll have more starter the next time you want to make bread. The old-fashioned name for your risen dough is the "sponge."

2 Mix one cup flour with baking soda, and stir into the sponge. At this point, the dough will be very stiff.

3 Find a large wooden or plastic board, and flour it with one cup flour. Turn the dough onto the board, and knead it with the palms of your hands. Knead gently, pushing the dough again and again. Be patient! Knead for about eight minutes until the dough is smooth and cannot absorb any more flour.

. . . .

SOURDOUGH BREAD
continued

4 ***You decide how to shape your bread.*** Shape the dough into two oblong loaves or one large round loaf.

5 Lightly butter a baking sheet, and gently slide your bread dough onto the sheet. Cover with a clean dish towel.

6 Let sit in a warm place for three or four hours. An oven with a pilot light will be warm but not too hot. Or put the baking sheet on a rack over a pan of warm water.

Here's what to do that afternoon:

1 Preheat the oven to 400°F (200°C).

2 Just before you bake your dough, use a sharp knife (carefully!) to make diagonal slashes in the top.

3 ***You decide if you want the bread crust to be crispy or tender.***

If you want a crispy crust, brush your loaves with water, and put a pan of hot water in the bottom of the oven as the loaves bake.

If you want a tender crust, brush your loaves with melted butter or oil.

4 If you made two oblong loaves, bake them for 45 minutes. If you made one large round loaf, bake it for 50 minutes. The crust ought to be a medium dark brown.

5 Cool the loaves. Keep them in plastic bags.

: **NOW YOU HAVE ONE OR**
: **TWO LOAVES OF YOUR OWN**
: **SPECIAL OLD-FASHIONED**
: **SOURDOUGH BREAD.**

· · · · · · · · · ·

KNEADING BREAD THE REALLY OLD-FASHIONED WAY

· ·

A popular 19th-century cookbook called *Practical Housekeeping* directed American cooks to knead bread for 45 minutes to one hour. The author further pointed out that any interruption in the process would injure the bread. For our great-grandparents who followed this advice, bread-making was a very time-consuming process indeed.

· ·

EXPERIMENTS WITH STARCHES

You could divide all food, essentially, into three components: protein, fat, and carbohydrate.

Starch is one major type of carbohydrate. Here's how to test for starch in a food—and, while you're at it, here's how to make up secret messages with invisible ink.

> : *Caution: These experiments use*
> : *iodine. Iodine is a poison. You*
> · *must have an adult help you*
> : *with these experiments.*
> : *Carefully dispose of everything*
> · *you use in the experiments that*
> : *might contain iodine. Keep*
> : *small children away.*

· ·

IODINE TESTS FOR STARCH

Here's what you need:

Water

A small bottle or other container

Iodine
(Note: Any antiseptic iodine will do, such as tincture of iodine or Betadine R.)

A white salad plate

Bread

Flour

Uncooked white rice

Dry instant rice

Cooked white rice

Uncooked macaroni

Cooked macaroni

Cornstarch

Raw potato

Cooked potato

Sheets of different types of paper, such as newsprint, a white paper towel, white lined paper, bond stationery paper

A drinking straw

Note: To cook cornstarch, put ½ teaspoon in a glass measuring cup. Slowly stir in ¼ to ½ cup water. Place the cup in the microwave oven and heat on high for one minute. Stir after 30 seconds. The heated mixture should be thick and clear in color. Remove a sample and save the rest. You will want it for your invisible ink experiments.

Here's how to do the experiment:

1 Put about ⅓ cup water into a small bottle or other container.

2 Add enough iodine to color the water a deep tan. Label the container with a gummed sticker: "IODINE— POISON."

3 On the white plate, arrange tiny samples, each about ¼ or ½ teaspoon: bread, flour, uncooked white rice, dry instant rice, cooked white rice, uncooked macaroni, cooked macaroni, cornstarch, cooked cornstarch, raw potato, cooked potato. Label each sample on the plate. Line up sample pieces of the papers also.

4 Chew a small piece of bread until it is completely mixed with saliva. Put the chewed bread on the plate along with the rest of your samples.

5 Put the drinking straw into the bottle of iodine water, and put your finger over the other end of the straw. Lift the straw from the iodine, and hold it over the samples on the plate. Lift your finger slightly and quickly as you drop tiny bits of iodine onto each of your samples.

6 Now keep careful record of what happens to each of your samples when they come in contact with the iodine. Note differences in color change between cooked and uncooked food samples.

Here is what we think you will see:

1 Most of the food samples turn deep blue or pale lavender.
2 The uncooked white rice does not change color in the same way the cooked rice does. The instant rice changes slightly.
3 The cooked cornstarch changes to a deeper blue than the light blue change of the raw cornstarch.
4 The white flour and the unchewed bread turn lavender. The chewed bread hardly changes color at all.
5 The cooked potato turns a deeper color than the raw potato.

Why did these food samples change color?

The starch in your food samples reacts to the drops of iodine and causes the color changes.

The cooked food samples turn a deeper color than do the uncooked food samples. Cooked food reacts strongly to the iodine because cooking has helped to break down cell walls and release the starch.

Starch reacts most intensely when it is in a purified or refined form or when it is very finely ground. The starch is pure and finely ground in the cornstarch and the flour samples. You should see color changes in those samples.

Grind a small amount of rice in a blender or grinder and see how fine ground rice reacts to the iodine.

Notice the differences in color between the unchewed bread and the chewed bread. When you chewed the bread, your saliva caused a chemical reaction. The starch in the bread broke down into sugar. So the chewed sample could not change color in the way other bread does.

. . . .

IODINE TESTS ON PAPER

. . . .

Now test the paper samples in the same way you tested the foods. Probably you will find that the newsprint, paper towels, and other rough papers do not react to the iodine. They do not change color. But the fine stationery papers may turn a deep lavender.

Of course, most modern paper comes from the wood of trees, and that wood contains cellulose. (Cellulose is a carbohydrate. It gives structure to plant walls, and we actually eat cellulose when we eat vegetable foods. And cellulose is good for us since it provides fiber in our diets.) When rough papers are manufactured, the cellulose stays. It does not become starch. When the more expensive fine papers are manufactured, however, the cellulose is chemically changed, and starch is released. So the fine papers usually change color when you test them with iodine.

Save the papers that did *not* react to the iodine, and use them for your secret message experiments. Save the cooked cornstarch solution for your invisible ink.

AN IODINE TEST FOR VITAMIN C

Here's what you need:

Cornstarch

Measuring cups and spoons

Water

Jars with lids and jar labels

Iodine

A vitamin C tablet (250-milligram, nonchewable)

A medicine dropper or drinking straws

Lemon juice

White vinegar

Here's how to test for vitamin C:

1 Measure ½ teaspoon cornstarch into a one-quart glass measuring cup.

2 Stir in one cup water.

3 Heat in the microwave on high setting for one minute. Stir after 30 seconds. If the cornstarch has not dissolved by then, stir and heat 20 more seconds.

4 In a clean test jar, stir one teaspoon of the cornstarch solution into one cup water. This will be your test solution.

5 Add four drops of iodine. Of course, your test solution contains cornstarch, so you can expect the starch to turn blue.

6 Dissolve the vitamin C tablet in one cup water.

7 Put two tablespoons of the test solution into a small glass container. Using the medicine dropper or straw, add a drop of the vitamin C solution. Stir, and watch the blue color disappear. If the blue doesn't vanish right away, add another drop of the vitamin C solution.

8 Repeat the experiment using lemon juice and the white vinegar. The vinegar is a control so that you can be sure it is the vitamin C and not the acid which causes the change.

   Now you can test other liquids to see if they contain vitamin C. If the blue in the iodine solution disappears, you know your sample contains vitamin C. Try fruit juice, vegetable juice, and water used to cook potatoes. This test will detect even very small amounts of vitamin C.

· · · · · · · · · ·
INVISIBLE INK EXPERIMENTS
· ·

Here are ways to write secret messages with invisible ink.

· · · · · · · · · ·
A WAY TO WRITE SECRET MESSAGES WITH IODINE
· ·

Here's how to write the secret message:

1 Choose a paper you saved from your iodine tests. Choose a paper that did *not* react to the iodine.

2 This is the time to use the cooked cornstarch solution from that experiment.

3 Find a calligraphy or other straight pen. This ought to be a pen without ink inside it. You need only your own invisible ink.

4 Dip the pen into the cooked cornstarch solution. Now write your secret message. Put the paper aside to dry.

Here's how to read the secret message:

When the paper is dry, lightly sponge the iodine solution over it. Your message will show up in lavender or blue.

. . . .
MORE WAYS TO WRITE SECRET MESSAGES WITH LEMON JUICE, MILK, ONION, AND ALUM
. . . .

Here's what you need:

Lemon juice

Milk

Alum or a styptic pencil

Note: *Alum is a chemical used in pickling and an ingredient in antiperspirant. You can find alum for sale in the spice department at the grocery store. (A styptic pencil is made from alum.)*

Water

A calligraphy or straight pen or toothpick

An onion or a small amount of onion juice

A candle

4 small glass containers

A teaspoon

4 pieces of paper

Here's how to write the secret messages:

1 Put some lemon juice in one container, milk in a second. In a third container, dissolve ½ teaspoon alum in some water.

2 Using a calligraphy pen or toothpick, write messages on the three pieces of paper. For your three types of ink, use the lemon juice, the milk, and the alum. Note which you used on each piece of paper.

3 Cut an onion or use onion juice. Stick the pen into the onion to wet it or dip it directly into onion juice. Now write on the fourth piece of paper.

4 Allow the paper to dry. You will find that your secret messages have become invisible.

Here's how to read the secret messages:

: Caution: You need an adult to
: help with this part of the
· experiment.

1 Light the candle in a secure candle holder. For extra safety, set the candle in the sink.

2 Hold each paper about two or three inches above the flame, and move the paper back and forth until the writing appears.

Compare the colors in which your secret messages reappear.

. . . .

A BIG COOKING STORY

. . . .

Paul Bunyan was a big, big man who liked a breakfast of old-fashioned sour-dough pancakes.

How big was Paul Bunyan?

He was so big that when he was a baby, his cradle was a boat—and it took the waves of the entire Atlantic Ocean to rock the cradle.

And when Paul Bunyan grew up, he really grew UP.

As soon as Paul Bunyan was big enough, he left his birthplace in Eastport, Maine, to go west to cut the tall (really tall) lumber. Paul Bunyan could cover hundreds of miles with each giant step, so traveling west didn't take long.

Of course, like all lumberjacks, Paul Bunyan had a big (big) appetite. Paul Bunyan's cook was Hot Biscuit Sam, and Paul Bunyan's cookhouse was as big as Mammoth Caves.

Hot Biscuit Sam worked with assistant cooks who had names to show how low-down and inferior they were. The poor cooks, like real cooks in lumber-jack camps back then, were called "boilers" or "sizzlers." Of course, cooking Paul Bunyan's food was a great deal of work, so even the assistant cooks had helpers, more inferior and low-down than the assistant cooks themselves, and these helpers were called "flunkies."

As you can imagine, Paul Bunyan could really pack in the sourdough pancakes.

In fact, the griddles for Paul Bunyan's pancakes were so big that there was only one way to grease them. Flunkies skated around the griddles with whole sides of bacon strapped to their feet, greasing as they skated.

If you ever travel to Bangor, Maine, you can see a giant statue of Paul Bunyan. The statue looks as if Paul Bunyan had swallowed his morning pancakes and has picked up his tools to go to work for the day.

QUICK TASTEBUD EXPERIMENTS

Y ou have more tastebuds than your parents do.

Your baby sister or brother has more tastebuds than you do.

Because people lose tastebuds as they grow older, you can taste food better than your parents can, and a small child can taste food better than you can.

When you look at your tongue, you see tiny bumps. Those are not tastebuds. The tiny bumps are the papillae, and there are hundreds of them.

The actual tastebuds are on the papillae, but they are so small that you cannot see them. And there are thousands of them.

The tastebuds themselves are made of even tinier little cells.

The cells change over every ten days or so, so that you have a constant supply of fresh taste cells. (You'll be glad of the constant turnover if you ever burn your tongue on hot food.)

Tastebuds are specialized. Each tastebud can taste only one type of basic flavor: sweet, salt, sour, and bitter. Some scientists add two more basic tastes: alkaline (or soapy taste) and metallic taste.

Tastebuds do not exist just to make our food taste good. Tastebuds also exist to help us to recognize poison and to get rid of spoiled foods.

Taste is not all. Our sense of smell is really part of our sense of taste. When you have a cold and cannot catch the aroma of your foods, your foods taste dull and boring.

Taste and smell are not all either. In many ways, people also taste food by looks, by temperature, and by texture.

A MAKE-THE-MAP-OF-YOUR-TONGUE EXPERIMENT

Some areas of your tongue taste only one flavor. You can make a map of your tongue to show the areas for each of the four basic flavors: sweet, salt, sour, or bitter.

(We'll forget about soapy and metal taste for now. If your tastebuds recognize soapy and metal tastes specifically, it is only to warn you to get those things out of your mouth.)

Here's what you'll need:

For the sweet taste, two tablespoons sugar dissolved in one cup room-temperature water

For the salty taste, two tablespoons salt dissolved in one cup room-temperature water

For the sour taste, two tablespoons lemon juice mixed into one cup room-temperature water.

(You can also use two tablespoons cream of tartar.)

For the bitter taste, 2 tablespoons instant coffee dissolved in one cup room-temperature water. (You can also use one cup room-temperature strong coffee.)

For a neutral taste, one cup room-temperature water

Five flat toothpicks, cotton swabs, or small paintbrushes

1 Label each glass. Draw a diagram of your tongue so that you can keep notes on specific areas for each taste sensation.

2 Use a separate toothpick, cotton swab, or paintbrush for each one of your solutions.

3 Dip the toothpick or brush into one of your glasses and dot the solution on one part of your tongue. Decide whether you can distinguish the basic flavor, and note what part of your tongue was able to distinguish that flavor. You will probably also find some overlap, especially between sweet and salty flavors on the tip of your tongue.

4 Rinse your mouth out with water from time to time. You don't want to get confused by an "aftertaste."

5 Draw a diagram of your tongue, and mark the divisions for sweet, salty, sour, and bitter.

59

A Color and Taste Experiment on Scrambled Eggs

Dr. Seuss says, "I do not like green eggs and ham." What if a food is really, really the wrong color?

Fix some scrambled eggs and see.

Here's what you need:

1 egg, beaten

A few drops red and blue food coloring

1 Beat food coloring into the egg until the egg looks dark and purple.

2 Now cook the beaten egg in a heated, buttered skillet. Stir the egg as you cook until it looks good enough to eat.

But is it good enough to eat?

The purple scrambled egg tastes the same as regular egg as far as your tastebuds are concerned—but perhaps not as far as the rest of you is concerned.

A Sweet and Sour Experiment on Grapefruit

Salt does not always make food taste salty. Salt can make food taste sweet. People often sprinkle salt on grapefruit, melons, and cantaloupes in order to make them sweeter. Try some for yourself.

Here's what you need:

1 grapefruit, cut in half

Some salt and some sugar

1 Sprinkle salt on one half of the grapefruit. Sprinkle sugar on the other. Sprinkle both very lightly.

2 Now decide which side tastes sweeter.

A TEMPERATURE AND TASTE EXPERIMENT

Our tastebuds react most strongly when the food they taste is not too hot and not too cold. The tastebuds react most sensitively when the food is between 72 and 105 degrees Fahrenheit (22 to 41 degrees Centigrade).

To test this, try a variation on the making-a-map-of-your-tongue experiment.

Keep your sweet, salty, sour, and bitter solutions just as you had them. But before you taste them, rub an ice cube on your tongue.

See if your tastebuds still work as well as they did.

A TEMPERATURE AND TASTE EXPERIMENT ON MILK

This is an experiment not on how well your tastebuds work but on what sort of temperature you prefer. Do you still like good food when the food is the "wrong" temperature?

Taste test milk at different temperatures.

1 Try milk at room temperature. (To bring milk to room temperature quickly, heat in a microwave oven for about ten seconds.)

2 Try very warm milk. (Heat in a microwave for 30 seconds. Or heat milk at low heat in a pan for just a couple of minutes. Do not let it boil.)

3 Try very cold milk. (To chill milk quickly, blend with two small ice cubes until smooth.)

You may find you have definite preferences on the temperature of milk. Imagine how strongly you might feel about eating a cold scrambled egg or a hot hard-cooked egg.

Hint: *Many people do not like to drink milk during the heat of the summer. But milk will taste good again if you get it cold enough. Blend in an ice cube or a scoop of ice cream.*

61

FOOD PUZZLERS

$\mathbf{C}$an you figure out food mysteries? Here are some experiments to help.

You can eat most of these experiments—and they're delicious.

MICROWAVE MYSTERIES

$\mathbf{C}$an you imagine using radio waves to cook food?

A microwave oven is like a small broadcasting station sending out short waves similar to radio waves. Microwaves are invisible. Yet they can cook food.

Here is how they work.

All matter is composed of molecules. At normal temperatures, some are close together, like the molecules of steel. Others, like the molecules of carbon dioxide gas, tend to spread apart. But all molecules contain space and are surrounded by space. And molecules are constantly in motion within that space. As molecules move, they produce heat.

The molecules collide and transfer heat from one molecule to another. Each molecule is not necessarily hot itself. The molecules just have a strong tendency to transfer heat to cooler bodies.

· · · · · · · · · · ·
MICROWAVE MYSTERIES
continued

Microwaves work by increasing the movement of molecules.

As the waves hit the surface of food, they rub against the food molecules, and then the molecules move more rapidly. In turn, these molecules transfer energy to other inner molecules, and food continues to heat and cook.

Remember a few limitations to microwave cooking:

1 *You cannot use a metal pan to cook in a microwave.*

Microwaves bounce off metals without going through them. You cannot even use dishes with small amounts of metal, such as plates with gold metal edges.

Microwaves do pass through glass, paper, plastic, china, porcelain, pottery, and most ordinary kinds of dishes.

2 *Sometimes a microwave oven heats one part of a food and leaves other parts cold.*

Fats and sugars especially tend to attract microwave energy and to heat up more rapidly than other foods. If you heat a jelly roll in a microwave oven, for instance, the jelly inside becomes much hotter than the roll.

Some microwave ovens rotate the dish automatically or turn the microwaves themselves around so that food cooks evenly.

But to make sure the food heats all the way through in your microwave oven, you often need to stir food or turn the dish.

3 *Because the air inside the microwave oven is not hot and dry as in a regular oven, foods do not turn brown as they cook.*

Since most people agree that brown is the only right color for meats, cooks usually finish browning meat in a regular oven.

4 *You can't use just any paper towel in a microwave oven.*

The paper towels you use in the microwave need to be able to absorb moisture and prevent your food from getting soggy. Use paper towels that do not contain bleaches, dyes, or recycled paper.

Put several folds of paper towels under and over bread or rolls that you want to heat in the microwave oven. Let the towels get wet, not the bread.

A MICROWAVE MELTING EXPERIMENT

1 Mix some water with drops of food coloring, any color you like. Pour the colored water into an ice cube tray, and freeze until solid.

2 Remove six colored ice cubes. Arrange them in a glass pie plate, with one ice cube in the center and the five others surrounding it.

3 Melt the ice cubes in the microwave oven on high for three minutes.

4 Notice how the ice melts, and compare the size of the cubes to see which have melted most. Observe how the melted water tunnels through the ice. You will probably find that the center cube has melted least.

5 Repeat the experiment with six more ice cubes. This time, melt them for three minutes at the low-power or "defrost" setting of the microwave. Notice that the ice cubes melt more slowly and also more evenly than they do on the full-power setting.

A HOW-TO-TELL-IF-A-DISH-IS-SAFE-FOR-MICROWAVING EXPERIMENT

Here's how to find out if a particular dish is safe to use in your microwave oven.

1 Place the dish in the center of the microwave oven. In one corner, place one cup of water in a glass measuring cup.

2 Heat on high power for one minute.

3 At the end of one minute, the water ought to be warm, and the dish ought to be cold.

If the dish is warm, that means the dish contains some metal or else the dish has absorbed moisture because it was not made properly in the first place.

What happens if you put aluminum foil in the microwave? You'll get a crackling sound and maybe even some sparks.

A Microwave Potato Experiment

1 Select three potatoes, and make sure they are the same size. Scrub them, pierce each of them several times with a fork, and arrange them in the microwave oven on a paper towel or paper plate. Put one potato directly in the middle, and one on each side.

2 Bake on full power for ten minutes.

3 Remove each potato with a pot holder. Cut the center potato and one of the side potatoes in half. Wrap the third potato in foil. Let them stand for five minutes.

4 Now cut the other potato in half, and observe all three. Pierce each with a fork to see which is softest. Which is fully cooked and still hot?

5 Notice the difference oven position makes. Observe whether potatoes cook faster in the center or on the edge of the oven.

6 When you cut open two of the potatoes, you stopped the cooking time. But essentially, the foil-wrapped potato was still cooking. The standing time for that potato allowed the rapidly moving potato molecules to pass the energy or heat to the molecules in the center of the potato.

Which potato looks best to eat?

Hint: *If you'd like to get creative with your potatoes, look at the stuff-your-own baked potatoes project in MAKE YOUR OWN FAVORITE RESTAURANT FOODS.*

A WHAT-MAKES-POPCORN-POP EXPERIMENT

Your popcorn has water in it, just a tiny bit but powerful enough to make the corn pop.

If you cut a popcorn kernel in half, you see a soft, moist material sealed tightly inside. Moisture keeps the seed alive and ready to sprout when the time is right.

Moisture also makes the corn pop.

When you heat a kernel of popcorn quickly enough, the water inside vaporizes into steam. Steam expands rapidly and blows the kernel open.

Here's how you can tell:

Measure popcorn kernels into three batches of ¼ cup each.

1 Use the same brand of popcorn, so you are sure the popcorn all begins the same.

2 Let ¼ cup popcorn kernels (Batch #1) just sit for 90 minutes.

3 Soak ¼ cup popcorn kernels (Batch #2) in a bowl of cool water for 90 minutes.

4 Spread ¼ cup popcorn kernels (Batch #3) on a baking sheet. Put them in the oven at 200°F (93°C) for 90 minutes. Let them cool.

When Batch #3 is cool, pop each batch of kernels separately. Now compare your results. Keep careful notes.

5 Line up ten popped kernels from each batch. Measure the line, and divide by ten. Now you have the average size of each popped kernel.

6 Count the kernels from each batch that did not pop. Write down the count.

7 Taste popped kernels from each batch, and write down your opinion.

	Average Size of Popped Kernels	*Number of Unpopped Kernels*	*Taste Test Comparison*
Batch #1			
Batch #2			
Batch #3			

You dried most of the moisture out of Batch #3. What were the results? _____

You put extra moisture into Batch #2. What were the results? _____

You left Batch #1 with its natural amount of moisture. What were the results? _____

WHY ONIONS MAKE YOUR EYES WATER

Onions add such delicious flavors to our food that devoted cooks often find themselves slicing and dicing, peeling and chopping onions.

But there is one problem. Onion chopping stings the cook's eyes.

The onion is defending itself. The sting is the onion's defense mechanism. That's a built-in attempt to convince you not to chop it up and eat it.

To attack, the onion uses a special amino acid that contains a few molecules of sulfur. As soon as you cut the onion, the sulfur molecules explode. If those molecules reach your eyes, they mix with the natural fluids of your eyes and actually create sulfuric acid.

Fortunately, this type of sulfuric acid is weak and does not last long.

But maybe for a moment, you feel like the co-star in a horror movie featuring evil onions who lurk on kitchen counters and plot to toss acid in your face.

People who like to cook also like to think of ways to stop onions from stinging their eyes.

Here are some of the most common ways to relieve onion sting:

Consider what effect each method might have on the ability of the acid molecules to reach your eyes.

Clue: Some of these common methods do not work at all. Some work just fine.

1 Put the onion in the refrigerator so it's cold when you slice it.

2 Hold the onion in a bowl of water as you slice it.

3 Hold a piece of bread between your teeth as you slice the onion.

4 Drop the onion into a pan of boiling water for one minute, and then use tongs to drop it into a pan of cold water.

5 Use a very sharp knife to slice the onion.

6 Wear safety goggles.
(Hold bread between your teeth and wear safety goggles at the same time, and you might take more trouble from your friends than you do from the onion.)

. . . .
A HOW-TO-CORN-BEEF PROJECT
. . . .

How did people keep meat and fish before they had refrigerators and freezers? Preserving food was difficult for them. But one way that worked was to preserve meat with salt, or to "corn" the food.

Why does salt keep meat from spoiling?

Salt molecules have the power of drawing water out of the cells of bacteria or mold that might spoil the meat. Without water, the bacteria die—or stop growing so that they can't take over the meat.

And what does "corn" mean? Of course, this meaning for the word "corn" does not refer to the vegetable. This kind of "corn" was the name for the whole grains of salt that people in England used to preserve their meat.

Salting dries out the meat as well as the bacteria—and that creates a distinctive taste.

Here's what you need:

3- to 4-pound boneless beef roast
(round, brisket, or chuck)

Salt

Water

1 egg

Preserve the beef with salt.

1 Half-fill a large stainless steel or crockery bowl with water (just enough to cover the beef).

2 Place the unbroken raw egg into the water.

3 Add salt and stir to dissolve. You have enough when the egg floats in the water. Then spoon out the egg.

4 Place the beef into the salted water. Find a plate slightly smaller than the bowl, and put it on the beef. Fill a jar or plastic container with water and place it on top of the plate. The idea is to keep the beef under the salt water.

5 Cover lightly, and set in a cool place for three or four days.

Cook the beef.

1 At the end of three or four days, remove the meat from the bowl, and put it into a large pot. Fill the pot with cold water, just enough to cover the beef. Bring to a boil at medium-high heat. Then lower the heat so that the surface of the water barely moves. This is simmering.

2 Simmer the beef for three to four hours, until it is tender (easily pierced with a fork).

HERE'S HOW TO FIX THE BEEF FOR AN OLD FASHIONED NEW ENGLAND BOILED DINNER

Here's what else you need:

6 carrots, peeled

6 potatoes, scrubbed with a brush
(Be sure to cut out eyes and bad spots.)

1 yellow turnip, pared and cut into 6 pieces

1 small head cabbage, cut into 6 pieces
(Be sure to remove bruised or wilted cabbage leaves.)

Here's what else you do:

1 Let the beef cook until it is tender and you can easily pierce it with a fork. Then add the carrots, potatoes, and turnip pieces to the pot with the beef and simmering water.

2 Turn heat up again until the water boils. Then turn heat down and let your dinner simmer for another 20 minutes.

3 Add cabbage pieces. Turn heat up once again until the water boils. Then turn heat down and let your dinner simmer another 15 minutes.

4 Carefully remove the beef, and put it on a large platter. You may need some help.

5 Spoon out the vegetables, and arrange them around the beef. Spoon some broth over the beef and vegetables.

6 Serve immediately for a full New England dinner.

A HOW-TO-FIGURE-OUT-AN-EGG EXPERIMENT

. . . .

To tell the difference between a hard-cooked egg and a raw egg, give them each a spin.

The hard-cooked egg is all of one piece, so it spins rapidly and smoothly and takes longer to stop than does the raw egg.

The raw egg, on the other hand, has a semi-liquid yolk (the yellow center of the egg) and a liquid albumin (the white of the egg). The raw egg wobbles as the yolk shifts its weight during the spin. Since the insides are sloshing around in different directions, the raw egg spins slowly and comes to a stop first.

To tell if an egg is fresh, put it in a bowl of water.

If the egg sinks to the bottom, you have a fresh egg.

If the egg floats, you have a rotten egg. The rotten egg weighs less than the fresh egg. Its yolk and albumin are disintegrating, and the air pocket is getting larger.

. . . .

A HOW-TO-TELL-A-FRUIT-FROM-A-VEGETABLE PUZZLER

. . . .

Ordinarily, we think of fruit as tasting much sweeter than vegetables. And we usually eat vegetables as a main course, while we think of fruit as dessert or as a snack.

But that's not technically true. A student of plants would give a different definition:

A fruit contains seeds. A vegetable does not. (The seeds for a vegetable plant are in another part of the plant that we don't eat.)

Most fruits grow above ground (like apples on a tree), and many vegetables grow under ground (like carrots) or on the ground (like lettuce).

Which of these foods are fruits (with seeds) and which are vegetables (without seeds)? • Cucumbers •Eggplants •Pumpkins • Tomatoes

If you really want to get technical, you'd even have to add one more unusual "fruit": nuts.

A HOW-TO-TELL-WHEN-FOOD-IS-SPOILED PUZZLER

Lucky for us, we can almost always tell when food is spoiled because the food looks strange, smells rotten, or tastes so bad that we don't eat more than one bite.

But you can't be too careful.

Never eat food or drink milk too hastily. You need to savor the taste—and notice any problems.

And get rid of food that seems wrong. Beware of bread with green spots, fruit turning mushy, vegetables growing white fuzz, raw meat that has turned dark, bitter green blemishes on potatoes, rubbery gelatin, watery pudding.

Beware of swollen-looking cans. A tiny, invisible hole can let in bacteria—and the bacteria can grow until the can is bursting with poison.

The most prevalent cause of food poisoning is salmonella bacteria. And unfortunately, if you accidentally eat salmonella bacteria with your food, you can get very sick without ever being aware of a bad taste or rotten smell.

Salmonella bacteria don't show themselves.

Yet they can proliferate in eggs (or in foods with eggs in them like custards or egg salad), in chicken and turkey (and in the stuffings that go with chicken and turkey), and in other meats and dairy products.

One good way to avoid food poisoning is to keep things very clean—your hands, your dishes, your cutting board, even your can opener.

Another good way to avoid food poisoning is to cook meats slowly and completely. Barbecued meats sometimes look seared (or even burned) on the outside but actually remain dangerously uncooked inside.

And remember to keep hot foods hot and cold foods cold. Food-poisoning bacteria cannot live in either very hot or very cold food. It's the in-between temperatures you need to avoid. Your food could be just sitting around on the kitchen table or in a well-packed picnic basket—breeding trouble.

You don't want the puzzler of food poisoning, ever.

A HOW-DID-THEY-EVER-INVENT-BUTTER PUZZLER

Legend has it that the Arabs discovered butter by accident. They loaded skins full of milk on their camels, and as the camels moved slowly across the desert, their rolling gait churned the milk into delicious butter.

For many generations, churning butter was a job for children.

The children had to push and push at cream in a churning machine—until they were surely very tired of the job.

As a churner works, the cream very, very slowly takes in air. Bubbles form, and drops of fat from the cream stick to the walls of the bubbles. The drops of fat get knocked around, and eventually they begin to stick together.

Slowly, they stick in larger and larger masses of a semi-solid butter. (The leftover liquid is buttermilk.)

And then the person churning could run off to play at last—and the camel could find an oasis and a rest.

GROW YOUR OWN

You don't need to have a farm to grow some of your own food. You can grow sprouts under the sink or herbs on a windowsill. Try lettuce in a planter or an avocado in a pot. You can even try an experiment to see if plants have feelings.

· · · · · · · · · ·
AN UNDER-THE-SINK SPROUTING PROJECT
· ·

First, you decide what you want to grow:

1 Buy untreated alfalfa, radish, or dill seeds.

2 Or you can use dried whole peas, lentils, mung beans, or wheat berries.

Here's what else you need:

A quart jar, washed and rinsed with hot water

A small piece of clean cotton cheesecloth

A large rubber band

Here's how to start:

1 Into the quart jar, measure one tablespoon of seeds or ⅓ cup beans, peas, or wheat berries.

2 Fill the jar with warm water and let the seeds sit overnight.

3 The next day, pour off the soaking water. Cover the top of the jar with a piece of cheesecloth. Hold the cheesecloth in place with the rubber band.

4 Rinse the seeds through the cheesecloth, and then pour off all the water.

5 Now put your jar of seeds under the sink or in any dark cupboard. For best results, lay the jar on its side.

Here's how to continue:

1 Twice a day, rinse the sprouts through the cheesecloth. Pour off all the water each time.

2 Expect the seeds to sprout and be ready to eat in two to four days. Do not wait until they become plants with roots.

Here's how to continue:

1 Twice a day, rinse the sprouts through the cheesecloth. Pour off all the water each time.

2 Expect the seeds to sprout and be ready to eat in two to four days. Do not wait until they become plants with roots.

Here's how to finish:

1 Wash the sprouts in cold water, and get rid of unsprouted seeds. Drain.

2 For better color, let your sprouts sit in the sun for an hour.

3 Pack in a clean container. Cover tightly and refrigerate.

> **NOW YOU HAVE YOUR OWN HOME-GROWN SPROUTS.**

Eat them in salads or sandwiches. Or add your bean sprouts to Oriental foods.

A WINDOWSILL HERB GARDEN PROJECT

First, you decide what herbs you want to grow. Here are some suggestions: basil, oregano, parsley, rosemary, sage, tarragon, or thyme.

Here's what you need:

Seeds for your favorite herbs

4-inch plant pots with underdishes (Clay pots are best, but you can also use plastic.)

Potting soil

Pebbles

Old newspapers

Here's how to start:

1 Spread old newspapers over your work space, or else take this job outside.

2 Cover the bottom of each pot with pebbles.

3 Fill each pot with potting soil, to within one inch of the top.

4 Water the soil with lukewarm water.

5 Sprinkle about ten seeds on the top of the soil in each pot.

6 Cover the seeds with a sprinkling of soil.

7 Lay a piece of old newspaper over the top of each pot. (Some gardeners use plastic over their seeds, but sometimes plastic lets the seedings get moldy—or "damp off"—and die.)

8 Keep the pots in a warm (but not hot) place. A windowsill with indirect sunlight would be perfect.

A WINDOWSILL HERB GARDEN
continued

Then watch your plants grow:

1 Check your seeds every couple of days. You can expect to see sprouts in two weeks—or some seedlings may come up much sooner.

2 Touch the surface of the soil with your finger. If the soil is dry, water your plant gently. Add just enough water to make the soil feel damp, not soggy.

3 After you see tiny seedlings appear, wait until each one grows its second leaf. Then, in each pot, select the three most vigorous seedlings. Remove all the rest from each pot. At this point, you no longer need to cover the seedlings with newspaper.

4 As the plants grow, water them gently every couple of days. After the third set of leaves has developed, pinch back the growing tip of each plant. Pinching back the tip helps the plants grow thick and bushy.

Here's how to continue:

1 When the plants are strong and thick, you can begin to harvest leaves.

2 Be sure to continue to pinch the growing tips to keep the plants from flowering.

3 Some herb plants, like rosemary, grow quite large. Transplant them to bigger pots as they outgrow the little pots, and let them keep growing on your windowsill.

Here's how to make the transfer:

1 Spread old newspapers over your work space, or else take this job outside.

2 Cover the bottom of the bigger pot with pebbles, and then with just an inch or so of potting soil.

3 Thoroughly wet each plant just before the transplant.

4 Tip the pot so that the plant and soil come out as a whole. If the roots have become potbound (growing tightly around and around instead of growing outward), gently pull out the roots a little, and rough up the soil around them. You will be helping the potbound roots grow outward into the bigger pot.

5 Set plant and soil in the center of the new pot, and fill the space around with new potting soil. Gently pack the soil all around the plant.

NOW YOU HAVE YOUR OWN
WINDOWSILL HERB GARDEN.

And you can harvest leaves year round. Use fresh herb leaves for cooking, or dry your herbs for an unusual and special holiday gift.

A MICROWAVE HERB-DRYING PROJECT

Anyone who likes to cook will love the gift of a special package of herbs.

Here's how to dry herbs in a microwave oven:

1 Select one of your home-grown herbs to dry. (One kind at a time, please.) Pick and wash the leaves.

2 Neatly fold two layers of paper towels in the center of your microwave oven. Spread 1½ to two cups of fresh herb leaves on the paper towels.

3 Microwave on high power for four to six minutes. Gently stir the herb leaves every 90 seconds. As the herbs dry, they will become crisp. They'll rattle when you shake them.

NOW YOU HAVE ABOUT ¾ TO ONE CUP OF YOUR OWN DRIED HERBS.

Store your herb leaves in an airtight jar.

....

A Lettuce Project

....

Here's what you need:

A package of seeds for dwarf lettuce

4-inch plant pots (or larger) with underdishes OR you may want to grow several lettuce plants in a 2-foot box

Pebbles

Potting soil

Old newspapers

Here's how to start:

1 Spread old newspapers over your work surface, or else take this job outside.

2 Cover the bottom of the pots or box with pebbles.

3 Then fill each with potting soil to within one inch of the top.

4 Water the soil with lukewarm water.

5 Sprinkle about six seeds on the top of the soil in each pot. In the box, sprinkle six seeds in groups four or five inches apart.

6 Cover the seeds with a sprinkling of soil.

7 Lay a piece of old newspaper over the top of each group of seeds.

8 Keep your pots or box in a warm (but not hot) place.

Then watch your lettuce grow:

1 Check your seeds every day. You can expect to see tiny lettuce plants in just a few days.

2 Touch the surface of the soil with your finger. If the soil is dry, water your plants gently. Add just enough water to make the soil feel damp, not soggy.

Here's how to continue:

1 When your lettuce plants are strong, you can begin to harvest leaves.

2 Keep watering every couple of days.

Now You Have Your Own Lettuce Garden.

You can pick lettuce, leaf by leaf, as it continues to grow. Use your lettuce in salads and sandwiches.

AN AVOCADO PROJECT

The next time you eat an avocado from the grocery store, save the pit and grow a lovely house plant.

Here's what you need:

A large avocado seed
(Take it from the center of a ripe avocado.)
A 6-inch to 8-inch plant pot with underdish
Pebbles
Potting soil
Old newspapers
A glass

Here's how to start:

1 Cover your work surface with old newspapers, or else take this job outside.

2 Carefully cut a very thin sliver from both the top and the bottom of the avocado seed. Use a very sharp knife, and cut no more than ⅛ inch.

　　Caution: You need an adult to help with this step.

3 Cover the bottom of the pot with pebbles, and then fill about halfway with potting soil.

4 Plant your seed with the large end down. Stick the seed only about ⅔ of the way into the soil. Leave the top third of the seed above the soil line.

5 Water well, and put a glass over the top of the seed. That will trap the water with the seed and help keep the seed moist.

6 Keep your plant on a windowsill or in another warm place.

7 Within a few days, the seed will split. At that time, remove the glass and cover the rest of the seed with soil.

8 When your avocado plant is about six inches tall, cut off the top two inches. Cutting back the plant helps it to grow thick and bushy.

9 Gently water your plant every couple of days, and pinch back the growing tip whenever your plant threatens to grow too tall and scraggly.

NOW YOU HAVE YOUR OWN AVOCADO PLANT.

As your plant grows, you may need to transplant it to larger containers. Don't expect to get an avocado to eat. But do expect to get a very pretty house plant.

A SWEET POTATO PROJECT

You can grow a sweet potato from the grocery store into a lovely vine with delicate little flowers.

Here's what you need:

A sweet potato
A quart jar with a wide mouth
Four to six toothpicks

Later you will need:

6-inch pot with underdish or a hanging pot
Pebbles
Potting soil
Old newspapers

Here's how to start:

1 Stick toothpicks into each side of the sweet potato. Fill the jar with lukewarm water, and use the toothpicks to balance the sweet potato halfway in and halfway out of the water. Keep your sweet potato jar away from direct light.

2 Your sweet potato ought to sprout leaves and roots in less than a week. Some grocery stores treat sweet potatoes so that they won't sprout, so if yours has not sprouted after ten days, try another sweet potato.

Hint: *If you get discouraged, buy a sweet potato seedling from a garden center, and plant it directly into a pot of soil.*

When your sweet potato sprouts to about six inches high, transplant it.

Here's how to make the transfer:

1 Spread old newspapers over your work area, or else take this job outside.

2 Cover the bottom of the pot with pebbles, and then fill with potting soil to within one inch of the top.

3 Plant your sweet potato seedling in the center of the pot, and gently pack the soil all around it.

4 Water the soil with lukewarm water.

5 Keep your plant in a windowsill or in another sunny spot, and gently water every couple of days.

NOW YOU HAVE YOUR OWN SWEET POTATO PLANT.

A HOW-TO-TELL-IF-PLANTS-HAVE-FEELINGS EXPERIMENT

Do your house plants care if you love them? Do they thrive on love and affection? Here's how to tell.

1 You need three identical plants. And you need to provide identical physical conditions for each plant. Give each the same kind of pot, same soil, same sunlight, exactly the same amount of watering.

2 Label each plant.

3 One plant is the "control" plant. You give it physical attention, but you never speak to it one way or the other.

4 Select one as your "hated" plant. Every day tell it in loud angry tones that you hate it, and that you plan for it to shrivel up and die. Play loud raucous music. Keep up the noise at least fifteen minutes each day. (Remove the other two plants during this time.)

5 Select one as your "loved" plant. Every day praise it and tell it how strong and beautiful it is. Play soft classical music. Without touching it, gently move your hands on each side of the plant. Pay attention to your plant and play the music for at least fifteen minutes each day. (Remove the other two plants during this time.)

: *Caution: This is a science experiment. Do not let yourself actually "hate" or "love" the plants. Continue to give each plant exactly the same physical care, or the experiment will not be valid.*

6 Observe your plants carefully, and take notes over a month. Decide if you see differences in the growth and vigor of each plant. Or maybe one of them will start talking back.

MAKE UP YOUR OWN SECRET RECIPES

Begin with the basic recipe. Then LOOK FOR WAYS TO MAKE YOUR OWN SPECIAL CHANGES. You'll finish with a delicious secret recipe all your own!

A MAKE-YOUR-OWN FRUIT JUICE PROJECT

Choose your favorite fruit juice (maybe orange, apple, cranberry, grape, or pineapple). Then add your own secret ingredients to make it specially delicious.

Here's how to start:

1 Pour ½ cup pure fruit juice into a blender. Choose ONE of your favorite juices.

You decide what to blend in next:

2 Blend in ONE of these options:
   ½ cup of another fruit juice
   or 2 tablespoons pure lemon or lime juice
   or 1 cut-up banana
   or 2 small carrots, pared and cut into pieces
   or 2 small ice cubes

3 Blend well until all is smooth.

You decide how to finish.

Consider ONE or TWO of these final touches:

1 Scoop in some sherbet or ice cream.

2 Add a few strawberries, grapes, cherries, or pineapple chunks.

3 Decorate the edge of your glass with a sprig of mint.

4 Decorate the edge of your glass with a slice of lemon, lime, or orange.

: **NOW YOU HAVE ONE TALL**
: **FROST GLASS OF YOUR OWN**
: **SPECIAL FRUIT DRINK.**

Drink immediately.

A HEAT-YOUR-OWN HOT CHOCOLATE PROJECT

Hot chocolate is great even before you add secret ingredients. It will be double great when you invent your own special flavorings.

Here's what you need:

2 tablespoons unsweetened cocoa powder

2 tablespoons sugar

1 pinch salt

2 cups milk

Here's how to start:

1 In a small saucepan, stir the cocoa, sugar, and salt with ½ cup of the milk. Stir well.

2 Stir in the rest of the milk. Some cooks like to use an egg beater to make sure the cocoa is completely blended in.

3 Simmer over low heat.

Or if you use a microwave oven:

1 In a heatproof glass pitcher, stir cocoa, sugar, and salt with ½ cup of the milk. Heat on high power for one minute.

2 Stir in the rest of the milk. Heat on high power for another 1½ minutes.

You decide how to flavor your hot chocolate:

Here are some options:

After the hot chocolate is heated,

Add ½ teaspoon vanilla.

or Add ⅛ teaspoon mint or peppermint extract. Then decorate with a couple of mint leaves on top.

or Put in a dash of cloves, and then add a cinnamon stick.

or Top with a spoonful of whipped cream.

or Top with a scoop of ice cream.

NOW YOU HAVE TWO CUPS OF YOUR OWN SPECIAL HOT CHOCOLATE BEVERAGE.

Drink immediately.

AN INVENT-YOUR-OWN SANDWICHES SMORGASBORD PROJECT

A smörgåsbord is a Swedish invention. You display a wide variety of foods and let people choose as much or as little as they want, in all possible combinations. Maybe you can come up with a never-before-seen, one-of-a-kind sandwich.

Here's how to start:

1 Select a *different* bread, perhaps a kind of bread you've never tried before. Or try *two* kinds of bread, one on top and one on bottom.

Then mix and match what goes inside:

2 Select a *different* meat or cheese perhaps a kind you've never tried before.

3 Or try a salad sandwich: chicken, egg, ham, tuna, or turkey salad.

4 Or try a spread for your sandwich: cream cheese, peanut butter, or another kind of nut butter.

You decide how high to pile on the extras.

5 What will you put on next?
   Consider different choices:
   Apple slices with raisins
   or Cranberry sauce slices
   or Cucumber slices
   or Hard-cooked egg slices
   or Lettuce with olive bits
   or Onion slices with pickle relish
   or Pickle slices
   or Sauerkraut
   or Sprouts
   or Tomato slices

You decide how to shape your sandwich.

Here are some options:
   Pile your sandwiches high, and secure them with toothpicks.
   Cut off the bread crusts, and cut your sandwiches into shapes.

NOW YOU CAN HAVE YOUR OWN SPECIAL SANDWICH INVENTION.

A TOAST-YOUR-OWN SANDWICHES PROJECT

Here's how to start:

1 Make a sandwich with sliced bread and cheese.

2 Put on just a few extras, maybe some thin-sliced ham, onions, tomatoes, a little mayonnaise. Don't pile on the extras, or your sandwich will come apart while you're grilling it.

3 Butter each slice of bread *on the outside.* Then your sandwich won't stick to the griddle.

Here's how to grill your sandwich:

1 Heat a griddle or a frying pan on the stove.

2 Using a large spatula, carefully slide each sandwich onto the griddle.

3 Grill for two or three minutes until your sandwich is light brown on one side.

4 Then carefully turn it over and grill your sandwich on the other side.

5 Your sandwich is done when both sides are brown and the cheese is melted.

Here's another way to toast your sandwich:

1 Put your sandwich in a toaster oven. Toast the sandwich for three or four minutes on each side.

2 Or toast your sandwich on a baking sheet in an oven heated to 350°F (180°C) for about four minutes on each side.

> NOW YOU HAVE YOUR OWN SPECIAL GRILLED SANDWICH INVENTION.

SANDWICH FAVORITES

What is your favorite sandwich?

In August 1989, Archie Comic Publications asked kids at four camps across the U.S.

The first-place favorite sandwich is ham and cheese.

Two sandwiches tied for second place: Turkey sandwiches and peanut butter with jelly.

A MAKE-YOUR-OWN PEANUT BUTTER PROJECT

Here's what you need:

1½ cups (8 ounces) unsalted roasted peanuts

1 tablespoon peanut or vegetable oil

You decide how chunky you want your peanut butter.

1 Set aside a few peanuts (¼ cup or less) for the chunky part of your peanut butter.

Process the rest of your peanuts.

2 Mix them with the peanut oil, and put them into a food processor. Process until smooth.

3 Then just stir in the peanuts that you set aside until your peanut butter is as chunky as you like it.

Store your peanut butter in the refrigerator.

4 Your peanut butter will keep up to two weeks in a sealed container.

NOW YOU HAVE ONE CUP OF YOUR OWN SPECIAL PEANUT BUTTER.

A MIX-YOUR-OWN FRUIT SALAD PROJECT

Here's how to start:

1 Select a variety of good fresh fruits.

2 Wash and cut the fruits you select into large, colorful chunks, and gently mix them in a bowl.

Here's what not to do:

Don't use canned fruit when you can find fresh fruit. If you decide to buy canned pineapple chunks, buy the kind that sits in its own juice, not the kind packed in sugar syrup.

Do not peel the apples or pears.

Don't cut up the berries or grapes. Fruit looks good in large, colorful chunks, and besides the peels are good for you.

You decide how to dress up your salad.

Here are some options:

1 Squeeze on a little juice from the orange or grapefruit. Or put in a little lemon, lime, or pineapple juice. Citrus juice keeps the fruit from turning brown.

2 Pour in one or two tablespoons of sparkling ginger ale.

3 Sprinkle on some chopped walnuts or dried coconut.

4 Mix in raisins.

5 Stir in a few chopped celery pieces or chopped carrots.

6 Mix in a small amount of mayonnaise.

7 Scoop on yogurt, frozen yogurt, or sherbet.

8 Fluff on some whipped cream or sour cream.

9 Serve on a bed of lettuce.

10 String chunks of fruit on toothpicks, and call them fruit kabobs.

NOW YOU HAVE YOUR OWN UNIQUE FRUIT SALAD.

Serve your fruit salad right away, or else cover and refrigerate for no more than a day.

A Dip-Your-Own Fruit Project

Dip chunks of fruit in delicious chocolate sauce, and see if your friends will let you keep any for yourself.

Here's what you need:

6 ounces semisweet baking chocolate or chocolate chips

1 teaspoon vegetable oil or shortening

Here are two ways to melt the chocolate and oil:

1 Melt the chocolate chips with oil or shortening in the top of a double boiler over simmering water. Stir gently.

2 Or melt your chocolate in the microwave. Put the chocolate in a small, heatproof glass dish. Cover and microwave at low power for two minutes. Stir gently.

You decide what fruits to dip in delicious chocolate.

1 Strawberries with the leaves left on for "handles" are an excellent choice. Or try apple slices, cherries, or pineapple chunks.

2 Dip your fruit into the chocolate just part of the way. Use a small fork or your own very clean, freshly washed fingers. Don't get your fingers hot and sticky by trying to cover the whole fruit with chocolate. Let extra chocolate drip back into the pan.

3 Arrange waxed paper on a plate. Lay each chocolate-dipped fruit chunk onto the paper, and refrigerate for a few minutes (or longer) so that the chocolate hardens.

Now You Have Your Own Chocolate-Covered Fruit.

Serve immediately, or keep in the refrigerator.

A FLAVOR-YOUR-OWN POPCORN PROJECT

Popcorn pops because of the explosion of the molecules of water inside the kernel. So you can expect that fresh popcorn will pop best, and so will popcorn that you have kept tightly sealed so that air doesn't dry out the kernels and remove their valuable exploding moisture.

To make the very best popcorn, pop your corn in a machine that uses air rather than oil. Plain popcorn, without salt or butter, is a fine snack. But you can also add a little creativity.

You Decide How to Flavor Your Fresh Popped Popcorn.

Here are three ways to give your popcorn extra flavor:

1 Mix your popcorn with peanuts and raisins.

2 Melt cheese. An easy way to melt cheese is to put cheese in a covered glass dish and heat it in the microwave at low temperature for about two minutes. Then ooze delicious cheese over your popcorn.

3 Mix 1 cup peanut butter and ½ cup honey in a glass dish, and heat the mixture in the microwave at low temperature for about two minutes. Or heat the mixture on the stovetop at very low heat, stirring often.

Pour the peanut mixture over about six cups (1½ quarts) popcorn. Press the peanut popcorn into a rectangular oiled baking pan. Cut into squares for eating.

Store your peanut popcorn squares in the refrigerator to keep them crisp.

A Stir-Up-Your-Own Salad Dressings Project

Fresh is best for salad dressings. Make salad dressing just before you fix your salads.

Here's what you need:

2 tablespoons vinegar
1 tablespoon lemon juice
¼ teaspoon salt
¼ teaspoon pepper
6 tablespoons vegetable or olive oil

Here's what you do:

1 Pour the vinegar and lemon juice into your blender or food processor.

2 Add salt and pepper.

3 Now's the fun part. Slowly, carefully add the oil. Most blenders and food processors have a tube or hole so that you can safely add a liquid while the machine is running. If so, turn on the machine and get it going steadily. Then *carefully* add the oil. Otherwise, add the oil one tablespoon at a time, and turn the machine on and off as you go.

4 You are creating an emulsion. The oil does not dissolve into the vinegar, and if you just poured these two liquids together, you'd find that they separated right away.

You decide how to dress up your salad.

Consider blending in *ONE* of these flavorings:

1 ½ teaspoon Dijon-style mustard
2 A pinch of parsley and a pinch of thyme
3 ¼ teaspoon basil and ¼ teaspoon oregano
4 A pinch of tarragon
5 1 clove crushed garlic
6 ¼ teaspoon grated lemon peel

> **Now You Have ½ Cup Of Your Own Salad Dressing.**

Serve immediately.

A MAKE-YOUR-OWN MAYONNAISE PROJECT

Mayonnaise making is the most fun of all, almost as much fun as eating a smooth creamy dollop of mayonnaise atop fat red tomato slices.

Here's what you need:

1 tablespoon vinegar
1 tablespoon lemon juice
1 large egg
½ teaspoon salt
1 cup vegetable oil

Here's what you do:

1 Pour the vinegar, lemon juice, egg, and salt in a blender or food processor. Cover and blend.

2 If your blender or food processor has a special tube or hole for adding liquids, then add the oil slowly and carefully while the machine is running. Otherwise, add the oil a little at a time, and turn the machine on and off as you go.

3 You are creating an emulsion. The egg and vinegar must absorb the oil as you blend. Otherwise, the oil would separate right away, and you'd be left with a mess.

Hint: This recipe works best if the egg is at room temperature. Warm a refrigerated egg for just a few minutes in a bowl of hot water.

Hint: If your mayonnaise is not thick enough, beat an egg yolk in a separate bowl. Then gradually blend the beaten egg yolk into your mayonnaise.

Important: *Store your mayonnaise in a jar with a good tight lid. Keep it refrigerated.*

You decide how to flavor your mayonnaise.

1 Blend in 1 tablespoon Dijon-style mustard.

2 Or blend in 1 clove crushed garlic.

3 Or try ½ teaspoon dry mustard with ¼ teaspoon paprika.

4 For a luscious green dressing, blend in ½ cup chopped ripe avocado, along with one tablespoon lime juice.

5 Blend in ½ cup pineapple juice, along with 1 teaspoon grated orange rind. You'd like this type of mayonnaise best with fruit salads.

6 Blend in 1 cup sour cream or yogurt. You'd like this type as a dip for vegetables and crackers.

NOW YOU HAVE 1½ CUPS OF YOUR OWN SPECIAL MAYONNAISE.

A STIR-UP-YOUR-OWN CRUNCHY GRANOLA PROJECT

Wash your hands before every project and especially wash your hands before you begin stirring up your own granola. You might want to mix your granola with your fingers.

Here's what you need:

- 2 cups old-fashioned oatmeal
- ½ cup shredded coconut
- ½ cup peanuts
- ½ cup wheat germ
- ½ cup hulled sunflower seeds
- ¼ cup honey
- ¼ cup vegetable oil
- 1 teaspoon vanilla extract
- ½ cup raisins

Here's what you do:

1 Thoroughly mix the oatmeal, shredded coconut, peanuts, wheat germ, and sunflower seeds.

2 Mix the honey, oil, and vanilla in a separate bowl, and then work the mixture into the dry ingredients. You can use your fingers if you feel like it.

3 Spread your mix on an oiled baking sheet. Then roast at 325°F (170°C) for 20 to 30 minutes. Stir after 15 minutes or so, and add the raisins just for the last five to ten minutes of roasting.

Here's how to make granola in a microwave oven:

1 Use a three-quart, heatproof glass bowl and microwave on medium heat for six minutes. Stir after three minutes or so.

2 Stir in the raisins, and microwave on medium heat for two more minutes.

NOW YOU HAVE ABOUT FIVE CUPS OF YOUR OWN CRUNCHY GRANOLA.

Store in a tightly covered container. Serve as a cereal, or use it to top fruit or ice cream.

A BAKE-YOUR-OWN MUFFINS PROJECT

Plain muffins are good. Or you can decide on your own special way to make your muffins fancy. Try blueberry, apple, or cranberry muffins, raisin, date, or bran muffins.

Here's what you need:

1 cup all purpose or unbleached flour
1 cup old-fashioned oatmeal
3 tablespoons sugar
4 teaspoons baking powder
1 teaspoon salt
1 large egg
¼ cup vegetable oil
1 cup milk

Here's what you do:

1 Preheat the oven to 400°F (200°C).

2 Combine flour, oatmeal, sugar, baking powder, and salt in a large bowl.

3 Break one egg into a separate bowl, and beat it slightly with a fork. Then stir in the vegetable oil and milk.

4 Add the egg mixture to the dry ingredients in the large bowl.

5 With a large spoon, mix only about 25 times, just enough to get the dry ingredients wet. ***The dough is supposed to be lumpy.*** If you mix too much, your muffins will not puff up right and will get strange tunnels in them.

6 Carefully spoon the batter into paper muffin cups in a muffin pan. Fill each cup about ⅔ of the way full.

7 Bake for 20 minutes, or until golden brown.

8 This recipe makes 12 good plain muffins. Cool them on a wire rack.

. . . .
A BAKE-YOUR-OWN FANCY MUFFINS PROJECT
. . . .

You decide if you want to make your muffins fancy instead.

Consider one of these choices:

1 *For blueberry muffins,* wash and drain 1 cup blueberries. Then mix them in with the dry ingredients before you add the egg, oil, and milk.

2 For *cranberry muffins,* increase the sugar in the recipe to ¼ cup. Wash and drain cranberries, and then carefully chop them until you have 1 cup chopped cranberries. Then mix them in with the dry ingredients before you add the egg, oil, and milk.

　　If you want, stir in ¼ cup chopped walnuts or chopped pecans.

3 *For apple muffins,* pare, core, and chop one large apple until you have about ¾ cup apple pieces. Stir the apple pieces into your dry ingredients, along with 1 teaspoon cinnamon and ½ teaspoon nutmeg. Then add the egg, oil, and milk.

　　If you want, stir in ¼ cup chopped walnuts or chopped pecans.

4 *For raisin or date muffins,* just stir in 1 cup raisins or 1 cup chopped dates.

5 *For oat bran or raisin bran muffins,* add 1 cup oat bran cereal or 1 cup raisin bran cereal in place of the 1 cup oatmeal. Stir in 1 cup oat bran or 1 cup raisin bran with the flour, sugar, baking powder, and salt. Then add 2 tablespoons molasses along with the egg, oil, and milk.

> **NOW YOU HAVE A DOZEN OF YOUR OWN FANCY MUFFINS.**

A CREATE-YOUR-OWN YOGURT PROJECT

Yogurt is a living organism. When you make yogurt, you are "growing" yogurt from a small amount of starter yogurt. The live yogurt bacteria ferment within milk to create more yogurt.

Fortunately, the yogurt bacteria are good for us—and yogurt is a delicious treat, becoming more popular every day.

Here's what you need:

4 cups (1 quart) whole milk or 2%-fat milk

3 tablespoons plain yogurt to use as a starter

Hint: Look at the label to make sure the yogurt you want to use for a starter is "live" or "active." Or use yogurt from another homemade batch. Some grocery-store yogurt brands have been treated and flavored so that they won't do to start new yogurt.

Here's what you do:

1 Warm the milk.

You can pour the milk into a one-quart, heatproof glass container and heat it at low temperature in the microwave oven for about two minutes. Or heat it at low temperature on the stovetop.

2 Put a kitchen thermometer into the warm milk, and let the milk cool until it is 95°F to 100°F (35°C to 38°C).

3 Remove any skin that forms on top of the milk.

4 Gently whisk the yogurt with a spoon or fork, and pour it into the milk.

5 Now beat the yogurt mixture with an egg beater until it is thoroughly mixed.

6 You will need four or five one-cup jars for your yogurt. (Electric yogurt makers come with them.) Make sure the jars for your yogurt are very clean. Before you use the jars, wash them in very hot water or in a dishwasher.

. . . .
CREATE-YOUR-OWN YOGURT
continued

Heat the yogurt with one of these methods:

1 Use an electric yogurt maker. Pour the yogurt mix into the jars that come with the machine. Cover, and set them into the machine for about six hours. (Of course, follow the instructions that come with the machine.)

2 Use an electric frypan. Set the pan for about 100°F (38°C). Fill it with warm water. Pour the yogurt mix into one-cup jars. Cover, and set them into the warm water. Cover the frypan and let them sit for about six hours (or overnight). Your yogurt is finished when it is creamy and almost firm. Chill before eating.

You decide how to flavor your yogurt.

Gently stir *ONE* of these flavorings into each jar.

1 A couple of drops of vanilla extract and a sprinkle of cinnamon.

2 1 tablespoon of fruit preserves.

3 Pieces of chopped fruit. (Especially try strawberries, blueberries, raspberries, or peaches. Or stir in chopped apple, with a sprinkle of cinnamon.)

4 1 tablespoon pure chocolate syrup.

5 1 tablespoon maple syrup.

6 Try frozen yogurt treats (see the next recipe).

> **NOW YOU HAVE MORE THAN FOUR CUPS OF YOUR OWN SPECIAL YOGURT.**

Cover each jar, and keep refrigerated.

Hint: Don't worry if the yogurt is still a little runny. It will firm up in the refrigerator. But if your finished yogurt is really runny, here is what to do. Soften 1 tablespoon (1 envelope) unflavored gelatin into ¼ cup cold water. Then heat the gelatin on high power in the microwave oven for about 30 seconds until the gelatin dissolves. Stir and add that mixture to the yogurt.

A FREEZE-YOUR-OWN YOGURT PROJECT

Freeze a creamy yogurt treat, and then flavor it with fruit or chocolate. It's better than ice cream!

Here's what you need:

2 cups plain yogurt
⅓ cup light corn syrup
2 teaspoons vanilla extract

Here's how to freeze yogurt:

1 Freeze yogurt for about two hours, or until the yogurt is a soft mush. Your own yogurt will do just fine. Freeze it in an airtight container.

2 Remove the yogurt from the freezer, and use a spoon to mix in corn syrup and vanilla. Then add your own special flavoring.

Finish freezing your yogurt.

3 Return your flavored yogurt to the freezer. Freeze until firm, and scoop it out whenever you want a frozen yogurt treat.

Here's how to freeze yogurt with an ice cream maker:

1 Freeze the small ice cream maker can. Then put the frozen "inside" can into the larger "outside" can of the ice cream maker.

2 Mix the yogurt, corn syrup, vanilla extract, and the flavoring you choose. Pour into the frozen can.

3 Crank according to the instructions that come with the machine. You will have frozen yogurt in just a few minutes.

You decide what flavors you want for your frozen yogurt.

Try mixing in *ONE* of these flavorings:

1 Stir in 1 or 2 cups pure fruit preserves or 1 to 2 cups of your own blended fruit. Mix thoroughly.

   You can make your own blended fruit by using your blender or food processor to make smooth strawberries, raspberries, peaches, or banana.

   Or just use a fork to mash strawberries or bananas.

2 For delicious chocolate frozen yogurt, stir in ¼ cup chocolate syrup.

> **NOW YOU HAVE TWO TO FOUR CUPS OF YOUR OWN FROZEN YOGURT.**

· · · · · · · · · · ·
A FREEZE-YOUR-OWN POPSICLES PROJECT
· ·

Freezing your own popsicles really is easy and fun. Your little sister or brother may want to help.

You decide the basic flavors for your popsicles.

Here are some suggestions:

1 Try fruit-flavored yogurt.

2 Try chocolate-flavored yogurt.

3 Try chocolate or butterscotch pudding.

4 Try blended fresh fruit.
   You can blend your own fruit in a blender or food processor. Try strawberries, raspberries, peaches, or bananas. Or just use a fork to mash strawberries or bananas.

5 Try pure fruit juice.

You decide the popsicle molds:

1 You can buy plastic molds.

2 Or you can use small paper cups. For the sticks, use plastic spoons. Or you can buy wooden popsicle sticks.

3 Or use ice cube trays. The kind that make large, square cubes are best. For the sticks, use plastic stirrers.

Freeze your popsicles halfway at first.

1 Pour your yogurt, fruit, or juice into the molds. Freeze for a short time. Wait to put in the sticks until the pops are half frozen and the sticks can stand upright.

2 Then freeze solid.

Unmold the pops to eat.

Peel away the paper cups. Or dip molds in hot water for a few seconds to loosen the pops.

: **NOW YOU HAVE YOUR OWN**
: **SPECIAL POPSICLES.**

A Bake-Your-Own Brownies Project

You can bake brownies or blondies with the same basic recipe—then mix and match for your own special treats.

Here's what you need:

½ cup (1 stick) unsalted butter, softened

1 cup sugar

1 teaspoon vanilla extract

2 large eggs

2 ounces unsweetened chocolate

¾ cup all purpose or unbleached flour

½ teaspoon baking powder

¼ teaspoon salt

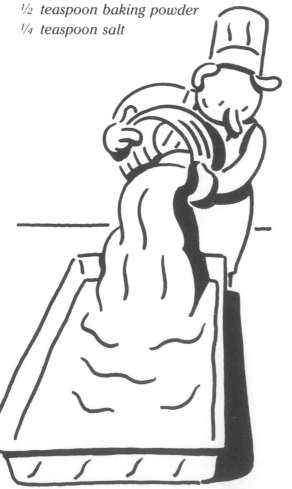

Here are three ways to melt the chocolate:

1 Melt the chocolate squares in the top of a double boiler over simmering water.

2 Or put the chocolate squares into a small heatproof glass dish. Cover the dish and heat in the microwave for two minutes at low heat. Then stir gently.

3 Or put the chocolate squares into a small custard cup and leave the cup in a bowl of hot water until the squares melt.

Here's what you do next:

1 Preheat oven to 350°F (180°C).

2 With an electric mixer, beat butter and sugar. Add vanilla extract, eggs, and melted chocolate. Mix well.

3 In a separate bowl, stir together flour, baking powder, and salt. Add to the batter, and mix well with the electric mixer.

4 Butter an 8-inch square baking pan. Spread the batter into the pan.

5 Bake for 30 minutes.

Now You Have 24 Warm Brownies.

Let them cool in the pan for at least one hour before you cut them. Then store them in a tightly covered container.

A BAKE-YOUR-OWN-BLONDIES PROJECT

Instead of chocolate, use peanut butter for a different flavor.

Here's what you need:

¼ cup unsalted butter, softened
1 cup brown sugar, well packed
1 teaspoon vanilla extract
½ cup peanut butter
2 large eggs
¾ cup all purpose or unbleached flour
½ teaspoon baking powder
¼ teaspoon salt

Here's what you do:

1 Preheat the oven to 350°F (180°C).

2 With an electric mixer, mix butter and brown sugar. Add vanilla extract, peanut butter, and eggs. Mix well.

3 In a separate bowl, stir together flour, baking powder, and salt. Add to the batter, and mix well with the electric mixer.

4 Butter an 8-inch square baking pan. Spread the batter into the pan.

5 Bake for 30 minutes.

NOW YOU HAVE 24 WARM BLONDIES.

Let them cool in the pan for at least one hour before you cut them. Then store them in a tightly covered container.

AN ADD-TO-YOUR-OWN BROWNIES OR BLONDIES PROJECT

You decide what to add to your brownies or blondies.

Choose *ONE* of these special additions *BEFORE* you bake the brownies or blondies:

For special chocolate chip delights: Bake the plain brownies or blondies for 5 minutes at 350°F (180°C). Then add 1 cup chocolate chips. Swirl the chocolate chips through the batter with a table knife. Put the pan back in the oven and bake for another 25 minutes.

Or use the same method to bake peanut butter chip or butterscotch chip brownies or blondies.

For nutty flavor: Before you start the baking, stir in ½ cup walnut pieces.

For an unusual apple flavor: Before you start the baking, stir in ½ cup chopped apple pieces.

You decide how to top your brownies or blondies.

Choose *ONE* of these toppings:

Make a brown sugar glaze.

Mix 2 tablespoons melted butter and ¼ cup well packed brown sugar.

After you cool the brownies or blondies, spread on the butter-sugar mixture. Carefully broil the pan for three minutes. Be sure to leave the oven door open when the broiler is on, and use thick oven mitts to protect your hands.

Make peanut butter frosting.

Combine ¼ cup unsalted butter and ¼ cup honey in a heatproof glass dish. Cover and microwave on high power for three minutes. Stir in ½ cup peanut butter.

After you cool the brownies or blondies, spread on the peanut butter frosting. Carefully broil the pan for three minutes. Be sure to leave the oven door open when the broiler is on, and use thick oven mitts to protect your hands.

Make chocolate-mint topping.

Put 1 cup chocolate-covered mints in a heatproof glass dish. Cover and microwave at low power for two minutes, until candy melts.

After you bake and cool the brownies or blondies, spread on the melted mint topping.

MAKE YOUR OWN FAVORITE RESTAURANT FOODS

Create a restaurant in your own kitchen. Concoct your own favorite eating-out foods. Rate the all-time hits in restaurant foods with your own pizza, hamburgers, chicken nuggets, and salad bar. You can even stuff your own baked potatoes, crank up your own ice cream, and create a Chinese "take-in" dinner.

A CONCOCT-YOUR-OWN MILKSHAKE PROJECT

Whisk up a milkshake with your own special ingredients.

Here's what you need for your basic good milkshake:

1 cup milk

½ teaspoon vanilla extract

½ cup (about 3 or 4 scoops) ice cream or frozen yogurt

1 Blend on low speed until your milkshake is frothy and smooth—and ready to drink.

2 Or use an egg beater.

3 Or just shake up your milkshake in a very tight container.

Hint: *Try making your milkshake extra cold. Blend in two crushed ice cubes.*

You decide how to flavor your milkshake.

Try adding one of these. Or try an elegant combination:

1 Try a fresh or frozen fruit:
   ½ banana, sliced
   or 10 or 12 strawberries, washed, hulled, and cut up
   or 1 peach, peeled and sliced
   or ½ cup frozen fruit

2 Try a fruit juice combination:
   ½ cup orange juice
   or ½ cup pineapple juice

3 Try a flavoring:
   2 tablespoons chocolate syrup
   or 2 tablespoons black (brewed) coffee

4 Try something unusual in your milkshake:
   ¼ cup chocolate chips
   or 2 tablespoons butterscotch syrup
   or 2 tablespoons peanut butter
   or ⅔ cups carrots, sliced and cooked
   or 1 tablespoon molasses, with 1 pinch cinnamon and 1 pinch nutmeg
   or ⅛ teaspoon almond extract

NOW YOU HAVE ABOUT TWO CUPS OF YOUR OWN SPECIAL MILKSHAKE.

Drink immediately.

PIZZA PECULIARS

Did you know that pizza wasn't really Italian at the beginning? Greeks invented a sort of pizza more than two thousand years ago.

But the Italians deserve credit because the Italians are the ones who first made pizza popular.

One man who helped make pizza famous was an Italian chef who loved his country. In 1889, this patriotic chef, Raffaele Esposito, created a red, yellow, and green pizza to celebrate the colors of the flag of Italy.

He used tomatoes for the red, mozzarella cheese for the yellow, and basil for the green.

How could you make an American pizza? Would anybody want to eat a red, white, and blue pizza?

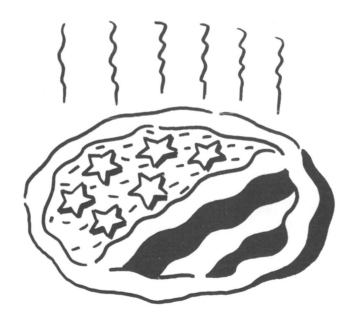

A MAKE-YOUR-OWN PIZZA PROJECT

If you plan to make your own pizza for dinner, be sure to allow enough time—a bit less than two hours, start to finish.

Pizza Dough

Here's what you need to make the pizza dough:

- *1 tablespoon dry yeast*
- *1 cup very warm water*
- *1 teaspoon sugar*
- *2 tablespoons olive or vegetable oil*
- *3½ cups all purpose or unbleached flour*
- *1 teaspoon salt*

Here's how to mix the ingredients:

1 In a large bowl, dissolve yeast in warm water.

Hint: Use warm water, not boiling water. Yeast is a living organism, and boiling water will kill it. But yeast "grows" and rises in warm water.

2 Next add the sugar and oil, along with two cups of the flour and the salt. Use a large spoon to beat until the mixture is smooth.

3 Stir in the rest of the flour.

Here's how to knead the dough:

1 Be especially sure to wash your hands before you knead the dough.

2 Sprinkle flour onto a good solid clean surface, something like a cutting board.

3 Turn the dough onto the surface. Work the dough, pushing it with the palms of your (clean) hands and then turning over a new surface to push again.

4 Knead the dough for five to ten minutes until your ball of dough becomes smooth and elastic.

MAKE YOUR OWN PIZZA
continued

Here's how to make your dough rise:

1 Lightly grease a large bowl, and put your kneaded ball of dough into the bowl.

2 Then roll your ball of dough over so as to grease the top very lightly.

3 Cover the bowl with a clean dishtowel or a piece of foil.

4 Now set the bowl in a warm place, such as over a pan of warm water or in an oven with a pilot light.

5 Let rise for 45 minutes.

Here's how to finish your dough:

1 Give your dough a good punch, and divide it in two.

2 Knead for just a minute to create two smooth balls.

3 Grease two pizza pans, and put one ball of dough in the center of each.

4 Now push out and flatten the dough with the palms of your hands until you form 12-inch circles.

5 Let your two pizza shells rise for a few minutes while you prepare the topping.

Hint: *If you're in a hurry, you can use frozen pizza dough—and still have the fun of creating your own toppings.*

Hint: *If you don't have round pizza pans, use rectangular baking sheets. Or for a really giant pizza, spread all the dough into a jelly roll pan.*

Non-Hint: *Can you twirl your dough in the air as if you were working for a pizzeria? That's fun, but we don't recommend it. You never know where it might land.*

PIZZA TOPPINGS

Here's what you need for basic pizza topping:

- *1 8-ounce can tomato sauce*
- *½ cup grated Parmesan cheese*
- *½ teaspoon pepper*
- *1 tablespoon minced garlic*
- *2 teaspoons oregano*
- *½ teaspoon basil*
- *¼ cup onion, very finely diced*
- *1 8-ounce package shredded mozzarella cheese (OR try shredded Romano cheese or a package of combined "pizza" cheeses)*

Here's what you do:

1 Preheat oven to 400°F (200°C).

2 Spread tomato sauce on each pizza with the back of a spoon.

3 Sprinkle on the Parmesan cheese, pepper, minced garlic, oregano, basil, and onion.

4 Arrange shredded mozzarella cheese on each pizza.

: **NOW YOU HAVE TWO**
: **12-INCH CHEESE PIZZAS**
: **READY TO BAKE.**

You decide what else you want on your pizzas:

Hint: *Put on any of these toppings before you arrange the mozzarella cheese.*

½ pound ground sausage, fried, and drained on a paper towel

or ½ pound (1 stick) precooked pepperoni, cut into thin slices

or ½ pound lean ground beef, browned and drained

or 1 can (2 ounces) anchovies
or sliced vegetables such as green pepper, olives, or dried tomato strips

Bake, one at a time, for about 25 minutes each. Or before you bake them, decide if you want to add other toppings.

: **NOW YOU HAVE TWO**
: **12-INCH PIZZAS THAT YOU**
: **DESIGNED AND DECORATED**
: **YOURSELF.**

. . . .
ALL-TIME HITS
. . . .

Is pizza your favorite food?

Most American kids rank pizza right at the top.

But chances are your great-grandparents didn't like pizza. When the first Italian pizza restaurant opened in New York City in 1939, pizza was a flop. The restaurant had to close because there just weren't enough people who liked pizza.

So how did pizza get so popular? When soldiers went to Europe to fight in World War II, they got their first good taste of pizza. And they liked it. When the soldiers came home in the mid-1940s, they were ready to keep on eating pizza.

You can do your own survey of favorite foods.

A MAKE-YOUR-OWN TACOS PROJECT

In Spanish, "taco" means a light meal or a snack. And that's exactly what these tacos are.

When you can't get out to your favorite Mexican restaurant, you can make your own tacos at home.

Here's what you need for basic tacos:

- 1 pound ground beef
- 1 small onion, chopped
- ¼ teaspoon cumin
- ½ teaspoon oregano
- ½ teaspoon garlic powder
- 10 taco shells
- 2 cups shredded Monterey Jack or packaged "taco" cheese
- 1 cup lettuce, washed and shredded

(Plus take your choice of options to serve with your tacos. Suggestions below.)

Here's how to make the taco filling:

1 In a large skillet, brown the ground beef with the chopped onion.

2 Stir in the cumin, oregano, and garlic powder.

Here's how to fill the taco shells:

1 Heat the taco shells according to the directions on the package.

2 Spoon about ¼ cup of your taco filling into each shell.

Here's how to top the taco shells:

Top with the shredded cheese and lettuce.

You decide what else to serve with your tacos:

Bottled taco sauce
or Chopped green chilies
or Diced tomatoes
or Sour cream

NOW YOU HAVE TEN OF YOUR OWN TACOS WITH SPECIAL TOPPINGS.

Serve immediately.

A MAKE-YOUR-OWN CHICKEN NUGGETS PROJECT

You don't have to get chicken nuggets from a package. You can be the first cook you know to make your own chicken nuggets.

Here's what you need:

4 chicken thighs or 4 boneless chicken breasts
Nonstick spray or vegetable oil
Seasoned bread crumbs

Here's how to prepare the chicken nuggets:

Preheat the oven to 375° F (190°C).

If you are using chicken thighs:

1 Remove the skin, and cut the meat off the bone in one piece.

> *Caution: You need an adult's help to cut off the chicken meat.*

2 Pull off any excess fat and cut thighs into one-inch pieces, as evenly as possible.

3 Spray the chicken pieces with nonstick spray.

If you are using boneless chicken breasts:

1 Remove excess fat or skin.

2 Cut into one-inch pieces, as evenly as possible.

3 Brush the chicken pieces with vegetable oil.

Here's how to roast chicken nuggets:

1 Roll each piece in seasoned bread crumbs.

2 Spray a large baking pan with nonstick spray.

3 Arrange the chicken pieces in the baking pan so that they do not touch each other.

4 Bake for ten to 15 minutes.

5 Turn over each piece, and bake for another ten to 15 minutes. Check one of the thicker pieces to see that it is roasted throughout. If not, put back for another five to ten minutes.

6 Serve with your choice of sauces.

> **NOW YOU HAVE ABOUT 32 OF YOUR OWN HOMEMADE CHICKEN NUGGETS.**

HAMBURGER HISTORY

More than two hundred years ago, the French people took a fancy to chopped beef imported from the German port city of Hamburg. Americans liked the idea of chopped (or ground) beef, too, and for years the Americans called it "Hamburg steak." Now we have more or less forgotten that hamburgers once arrived from Hamburg. These days hamburgers are all-American—and people from all around the world like to eat American-style hamburgers.

···········

A MAKE-YOUR-OWN SUPER BEEF BURGER PROJECT

· ·

This hamburger tastes lots better than the fast-food quarter-pounder.

And you don't need to grill or fry your hamburger. You can make your super beef burger in the microwave oven.

Here's what you need for the basics:

¼ pound lean ground beef
1 toasted hamburger bun

You Decide What You'd Like On Your Hamburger. Here are the options:

½ teaspoon Worcestershire sauce
1 thin slice cheddar or American cheese
1 thin slice tomato
1 thin slice Spanich onion
1 lettuce leaf
1 tablespoon mayonnaise
1 teaspoon Dijon-style mustard
1 tablespoon ketchup

Here's how to make your hamburger—easy:

1 Form the ground beef into a patty. Place on a white paper towel on a microwave-safe plate.

2 If you want Worcestershire sauce on your hamburger, sprinkle on ¼ teaspoon before you cook it. (The Worcestershire sauce will help brown the hamburger).

3 Cover your hamburger with another paper towel or with a piece of waxed paper.

4 Microwave your hamburger on high power for one to 1½ minutes, until one side is done. (The color may not be the brown you are used to. Make sure the hamburger is cooked through.)

5 Then turn your hamburger, and microwave it again on high power for one to 1½ minutes, until both sides are well done.

6 If you want a slice of cheese on top, put it on as soon as you take the hamburger out of the microwave oven. The heat will be enough to partly melt the cheese.

7 Place your hamburger on a toasted bun. Top with tomato, onion, lettuce, mayonnaise, and ketchup.

: NOW YOU HAVE YOUR OWN
: SUPER BEEF BURGER.

A Concoct-Your-Own Subs, Grinders, and Heroes Project

Shape this sandwich like a submarine. Open your jaws wide, and use your best grinders to eat it. And you're a hero if you can eat it all.

Here's what you need:

A submarine roll

You decide what kind of spread you want on the roll:

Mayonnaise
or Relish
or Butter

You decide what meat you want to add:

Lean deli ham slices
or Corned beef round slices
or Roast beef slices
or Smoked turkey slices

You decide what cheese you want to add.* Or add more than one type of cheese:

American
or Cheddar
or Provolone
or Swiss

You decide what veggies you want to add:

Lettuce
or Green pepper slices
or Tomato slices
or Olive slices
or Pickle wedges

> Now You Have Your Own
> Special Submarine,
> Grinder, Or Hero
> Sandwich.

Eat your sandwich right away, or wrap it in plastic and save it for your next lunch.

· · · · · · · · · ·

A CREATE-YOUR-OWN CHINESE RESTAURANT PROJECT

· ·

Do you like Chinese restaurant food? Here's a chance to create your own Chinese stir-fry chicken dinner.

Fix this dinner step by step. It's much easier than it looks. You can even use a microwave oven to cook the vegetables.

Here's what you need first:

2 boneless, skinless chicken breasts
Cut the chicken crosswise into very thin ⅛-inch slices.

Hint: *Before you start, gather all the ingredients. The first step is to slice chicken and mix it with delicious flavorings. Flavorings that soak into meat (or chicken or fish) are called a marinade.*

Here's what you need for the marinade:

3 tablespoons soy sauce
2 tablespoons water
1 tablespoon cornstarch
1 tablespoon rice vinegar
1 teaspoon sesame oil
½ teaspoon sugar
¼ teaspoon ginger
1 clove garlic, minced

Here's how to mix the marinade:

1 In a large bowl, stir together the soy sauce, water, cornstarch, rice vinegar, sesame oil, sugar, ginger, and minced garlic.

2 Add the sliced chicken, and turn over so that the marinade coats all of the slices.

3 Refrigerate the chicken, covered, while you fix the rice and vegetables.

Here's what you need for cooking the rice:

1 cup long-grained rice
1⅔ cups water

Here's how to cook the rice:

1 Combine rice and water in a large saucepan. Bring to a boil.

2 Stir with a fork to separate the rice grains.

3 Then turn the heat to low. Cover and simmer the rice for at least 20 minutes until the water is absorbed. (Some brands of rice call for simmering for as long as an hour.)

4 While the rice is simmering, prepare the rest of your Chinese dinner.

. . . .
CHINESE RESTAURANT PROJECT
continued

Here's what you need next:

3 *large celery stalks*

2 *medium carrots*

½ *cup blanched whole almonds*

Here's how to get the vegetables ready:

1 Scrub the celery stalks with a brush.

2 Scrape and scrub the carrots.

3 Slice the celery and carrots into thin ¼-inch pieces.

Here's how to cook the vegetables:

1 Put your sliced celery in the bottom of a small heatproof glass dish. Top the celery with the carrot slices.

2 Cover and microwave for four to six minutes. Turn the dish after two to three minutes.

3 Now leave the dish in the microwave oven until you are ready to use the celery and carrots.

Here's how to complete your dinner:

1 If you have a wok, this is the time to use it. Otherwise, use a large skillet.

2 Heat two tablespoons peanut oil over high heat.

3 Add the chicken mixture.

> *Caution: You need adult help when cooking with hot oil.*

4 Stir-fry the chicken for about five minutes, until it looks brown.

5 Add the carrots, celery, and almonds. Stir in gently.

6 You're finished. Turn off the heat. Pour the rice into a large casserole dish, and spoon your chicken, vegetables, and almonds on top. (Or you can serve the almonds in a separate dish.)

Hint: *Perhaps you would like to garnish your Chinese chicken dinner with a traditional tomato rose.*

> **NOW YOU HAVE YOUR OWN CHICKEN DINNER FOR FOUR, IN TRUE CHINESE RESTAURANT STYLE.**

. . . .
THE CHINESE CONNECTION
. . . .

Much of the food we think of as Italian may really have been Chinese in the beginning. The story is that, nearly 700 years ago, during the Middle Ages, the Italian explorer Marco Polo traveled to the mysterious Orient. Among the many discoveries he brought back to Italy from China may have been new recipes for wonderful pastas and dumplings. The Italians (and now the Americans) call the dumplings ravioli.

Marco Polo also brought back recipes for a delicious new frozen dessert he had tried in China, a sort of fruit-flavored ice that was the great beginning of the idea of ice cream.

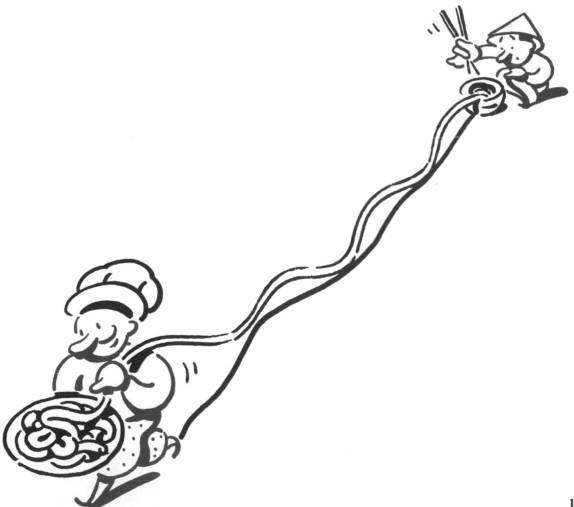

A CHINESE TOMATO ROSE GARNISHING PROJECT

Chinese chefs specialize in serving food with artistic flair. Here is a way to add art to your dinner with the garnish of an elegant tomato "rose."

Here's how to cut a tomato rose:

1 Use a small tomato or a cherry tomato for each tomato rose.

2 You need a serrated knife. (That's a knife with sharp notches along the edges.)

3 Carefully cut off the tomato stem.

4 To form the rose petals, stand the tomato straight up. Use slight sawing motions, and cut down through from the top in four square cuts.

Warning: Do not cut all the way through. The petals need to remain attached.

5 For "rose leaves," decorate your tomato rose with a few sprigs of parsley, celery leaves, or a spinach leaf.

NOW YOU HAVE A CHINESE TOMATO ROSE.

BE SURE TO TAKE YOUR KETCHUP

In the 1830s, a traveling salesman went about the western United States selling a medicine that he claimed would cure any illness.

He called his cure-all "Dr. Miles's Compound Extract of Tomato." The magical extract was ketchup.

A MAKE-YOUR-OWN SALAD BAR PROJECT

Restaurants have to install glass "sneeze shields" over their salad bars. Let's hope you won't need one for your own at-home salad bar.

Put out a line-up of veggies and other good salad fixings. Then let everyone choose. How many choices can you get into your salad bar?

You decide the salad bar choices.

1 Try as many of these options as you like: Begin with lettuce, washed and torn into leaves.

Hint: Try more than one variety of lettuce. Try iceberg, Boston, Bibb, or romaine. A red-leafed lettuce is fun for a change.

2 Then try other greens such as: Endive, escarole, cabbage, or spinach, washed and torn into leaves.

3 Prepare other vegetable choices, such as carrots, cauliflower, celery, cucumbers, green beans, peppers, olives, peas, radishes, or tomato wedges.

4 Put in yet more fixings for your salad, such as bacon bits, cheese cubes, chicken chunks, chow mein noodles, croutons, hard-cooked eggs, sprouts, sunflower seeds, meat or tuna chunks.

5 You can sprinkle on seasonings, too. Choose basil, celery salt, garlic powder, pepper, or tarragon.

6 Serve with a choice of salad dressings.

7 To save leftover salad fixings, wrap in plastic bags and put them in the refrigerator.

: **NOW YOU HAVE YOUR OWN**
: **SALAD BAR.**

A STUFF-YOUR-OWN BAKED POTATOES PROJECT

Who'd ever guess how creative you can get with a plain baked potato? You can use the microwave oven to bake potatoes. Then stuff them.

Here's what you need:

 4 medium-size baking potatoes

 ½ cup sour cream or plain yogurt

 ½ cup milk

 2 tablespoons butter or margarine

 2 tablespoons chopped fresh chives
   OR 1 tablespoon dried chives

 ¼ teaspoon salt

Pinch of pepper

 ½ cup grated cheddar cheese

 2 tablespoons bacon bits

Here's how to bake the potatoes:

1 Scrub each of your potatoes. Then use a fork to prick each potato several times.

2 Fold a white paper towel in the microwave oven. Arrange the potatoes on the towel in a circle.

3 Microwave the potatoes on high power for 12 to 14 minutes. Pinch them. They should still be slightly firm.

4 Let stand for five to ten minutes.

> *Warning: Be careful when you take the hot potatoes (with sometimes even hotter topping) out of the microwave oven. Use oven mitts to protect your hands.*

Here's how to stuff the potatoes:

1 Cut each potato lengthwise. Scoop the centers out into a large mixing bowl. Do your best to leave the skins whole.

2 Mash the potatoes with a fork.

3 Add the sour cream or yogurt, the milk, butter, chives, salt, and pepper. Beat with an electric mixer until smooth and fluffy.

4 Spoon the mixture back into the potato skins.

You decide how to top off your stuffed potatoes. Here's one way:

1 Top each with grated cheese and bacon bits.

2 Microwave again on high power for two minutes until the cheese is melted.

> **NOW YOU HAVE FOUR OF YOUR OWN STUFFED BAKED POTATOES, JUST LIKE THE RESTAURANTS.**

. . . .

A MAKE-YOUR-OWN ICE CREAM PROJECT
(With a Microwave Oven and an Ice Cream Freezer)

. . . .

Are you ready to start your own ice cream parlor?

Vanilla Ice Cream

Here's what you need:

½ cup sugar

½ tablespoon all purpose or unbleached flour

⅛ teaspoon salt

1 cup milk

1 egg

1 cup heavy cream

2 teaspoons vanilla extract

Here's how to mix and microwave your ice cream:

1 In a one-quart glass measure, mix together the sugar, flour, and salt.

2 Keep stirring, and pour in ¼ cup milk.

3 Then blend in ¾ cup milk.

4 Microwave on high power for two minutes. Stop and stir.

5 Microwave on high power for three more minutes. Stop and stir. Your mixture ought to be smooth and very slightly thickened.

6 Beat the egg lightly in a separate bowl. Pour a little of the hot milk mixture over the egg, and stir to combine.

7 Then pour the egg mixture into the rest of the hot milk.

8 Microwave on high power for 30 seconds. Stop and stir. If the mixture is not yet beginning to boil, microwave on high power for another 30 seconds.

9 Cover and refrigerate for about half an hour.

Here's how to finish your ice cream:

1 Stir in the heavy cream (unwhipped) and the vanilla extract.

2 Crank according to the instructions that come with your ice cream maker.

: **NOW YOU HAVE ABOUT ONE**
: **PINT OF YOUR OWN VANILLA**
: **ICE CREAM.**

ICE CREAM PROJECT
continued

Chocolate Ice Cream

1 Look back at the recipe for vanilla ice cream. Make this recipe just the same way. ***But add these ingredients:***

1 square (1 ounce) melted unsweetened chocolate

2 extra tablespoons sugar

2 Add the chocolate and the extra sugar to the milk mixture before you begin microwaving.

3 Freeze and crank just the same as the vanilla ice cream.

: NOW YOU HAVE ABOUT ONE
: PINT OF CHOCOLATE ICE
: CREAM.

Fruit-Flavored Ice Cream

1 Look back at the recipe for vanilla ice cream. Make this recipe *just* the same way. ***But change the ingredients:***

Only ¾ cup milk (not 1 cup)

Only ¾ cup heavy cream (not 1 cup)

2 After you have finished mixing and heating the ice cream mixture (but before you crank your ice cream in the ice cream maker), add 1 cup chopped, mashed fruit.

3 Freeze and crank just the same as the vanilla ice cream.

: NOW YOU HAVE ABOUT ONE
: PINT OF YOUR OWN
: FRUIT-FLAVORED ICE
: CREAM.

A MAKE-YOUR-OWN ICE CREAM PROJECT (WITH JUST A BLENDER)

You can make ice cream even without an ice cream maker. Here's a simple way to make your own homemade ice cream in a blender.

Here's what you need:

½ cup cold milk

1 envelope unflavored gelatin

½ cup milk, heated to the boiling point

¾ cup sugar

¼ teaspoon vanilla extract

3 cups chopped fruit

2 cups heavy cream

Here's how to mix your ice cream:

1 Pour ½ cup cold milk into the blender container. Sprinkle unflavored gelatin over the milk, and let stand for four to five minutes.

2 Add hot milk. Cover and blend at low speed until the gelatin is completely dissolved. This takes about two minutes.

3 Beat in the sugar and vanilla extract.

4 Add the fruit a little at a time. Blend at high speed after each addition until the mixture is smooth.

5 Pour into a large bowl and refrigerate. Stir occasionally until the mixture creates a mound when you drop a bit from the spoon.

6 Use an electric mixer to whip the cream. Whip on high speed until the cream forms soft peaks.

7 Using a spoon, gently fold the cream into the fruit mixture. Do not beat or whip at this point.

8 Pour your ice cream into two freezer trays or into a 8-inch square baking pan. Cover with plastic wrap.

9 Freeze until firm.

> **NOW YOU HAVE 1½ QUARTS OF YOUR OWN HOMEMADE ICE CREAM.**

A GIANT CHOCOLATE CHUNK COOKIE PROJECT

Instead of buying giant cookies at the shopping mall, make your own big and better cookies.

Here's what you need:

2 cups all purpose or unbleached flour

¼ teaspoon baking soda

¼ teaspoon salt

1 cup (2 sticks) butter or margarine, softened

1 cup granulated sugar

½ cup dark brown sugar, well packed

1 teaspoon vanilla extract

5 tablespoons unsweetened cocoa powder

¼ cup milk

1½ cups semisweet chocolate chunks

1 cup coarsely chopped walnuts, if you wish

Here's what you do:

1 Preheat the oven to 325°F (170°C). Line a baking sheet with foil.

2 Mix together the flour, baking soda, and salt in a bowl.

3 Use an electric mixer to cream the butter or margarine together with the white sugar, brown sugar, and vanilla extract. Beat at medium-high speed.

4 Then add the cocoa and the milk and beat at low speed. Gradually add the flour mixture, and beat at low speed.

5 With a large spoon, fold in the chocolate chunks and chopped walnuts.

6 Use ¼ cup batter for each giant cookie. Drop batter for four to six cookies onto one foil-lined baking sheet. Be sure the cookies are at least three inches apart.

7 Bake for 20 minutes, or until the tops look dry.

8 To cool, place the baking sheet on a wire rack for about five minutes. Then remove the cookies from foil and place on rack to finish cooling. You can use the same foil for baking more cookies.

NOW YOU HAVE ABOUT TWO DOZEN GIANT GOURMET CHOCOLATE CHUNK COOKIES.

FOODS TO PUNCH, TWIST, SHAPE, AND DESIGN

Here are projects that let you really do something. You can experiment with colors, get silly with shapes, and dash off your own designs. Punch out yeast rolls. Twist up pretzels. Shape sandwiches, cookies, or cakes. Design anything from butter to chocolate, from cheese to gelatin.

. . . .

A PARTY PUNCH DESIGN PROJECT

. . . .

What color would you like your fizzy party punch? What decorations do you imagine?

For party punch, you need four basic elements:

1 A fruit drink
2 A bubbly beverage
3 A frozen addition such as ice cubes or scoops of sherbet
4 Decorations floating on top of the punch bowl (the kind you can eat, of course)

Now comes the creative part. What sort of fruit drink do you want? *You design your own colors and your own flavor combinations.* Here are a few good party choices. Stir into the punchbowl one or two quarts of cranberry drink, grape juice, orange juice, or pineapple juice.

What sort of special taste effects do you want to create? *You decide the extra flavor for the punchbowl. Try ¼ cup lemon juice, lime juice, or orange juice.*

You decide which bubbly beverage. Stir into the punchbowl one or two liters of seltzer water or ginger ale.

You decide the frozen addition:

A tray full of ice cubes.
Scoops of fruit-flavored sherbet
Scoops of fruit-flavored frozen yogurt

You decide how to decorate the punchbowl. Float on thin slices of fresh fruit, such as lemon, lime, or orange.

You might even bounce in a few pitted cherries or float some strawberry halves.

> **NOW YOU HAVE ONE BOWL OF FIZZY PARTY PUNCH.**

The party starts immediately.

. . . .

A MINI-PIZZA DESIGN PROJECT

. . . .

Create instant mini-pizza, and design the topping however you like.

Begin with:

An English muffin, split in two

Add a basic pizza topping:

1 If you want your mini-pizza extra quick, spread on about ½ cup prepared pizza sauce.

2 If you want to decide yourself, spread and sprinkle on a basic pizza topping:

Tomato sauce, about 2 tablespoons per muffin
Oregano, a light sprinkling
Basil, a light sprinkling
Pepper, a light sprinkling
Shredded cheese, to cover the muffin

You decide the other toppings you want.

1 Use leftovers if you wish:

Chopped onion, about 1 tablespoon per muffin
  OR
Sliced pizza sausage or pepperoni
  OR
Green pepper or tomato strips

2 Or try something unusual like bacon bits or a combination of cheeses.

Toast your mini-pizza:

1 Toast in a toaster oven. Or bake in the regular oven for five to six minutes until hot and bubbly.

2 Or heat in the microwave oven for two to three minutes on full power, until hot and bubbly.

: **NOW YOU HAVE YOUR OWN**
: **DESIGN OF MINI-PIZZA.**

A SANDWICH DESIGN PROJECT

Get your sandwiches into good shape. Make sandwich ribbons, sandwich pinwheels—or everything else sandwiches. Your sandwiches can even stand up straight.

Be especially sure to wash your hands before you make sandwiches.

Here's what you need for your sandwiches:

Wholewheat bread

White bread

You decide the fillings: For deviled ham filling, mix:

1 can (2¼ ounces) deviled ham

1½ teaspoons prepared mustard

1 tablespoon chopped pickle relish

For egg salad filling, mix:

4 chopped, mashed hard-cooked eggs

2 tablespoons mayonnaise

1 teaspoon prepared mustard

½ teaspoon salt

Or use another soft filling, such as cream cheese or peanut butter.

Sandwich Ribbons

1 Spread one slice of wholewheat bread with deviled ham mixture (or other soft filling).

2 Top with a slice of white bread. Spread egg salad mixture (or other soft filling) on that slice. Top with a slice of wholewheat bread. Spread first filling on that slice. Top with a last slice of white bread. Each sandwich finishes with four slices of bread and three separate fillings.

3 Wrap each stacked sandwich as you make it, and chill in the refrigerator.

4 Wait till your sandwiches are completely chilled. Then, using a long bread knife, cut off the crusts from each sandwich.

: *Caution: You need adult help*
: *with slicing.*

Slice each sandwich into ribbons, as shown:

SANDWICH DESIGNS
continued

Pinwheel Sandwiches
Now make curled-up sandwiches.

1 For four small pinwheels, cut off the crusts from one slice of bread. Spread on filling.

2 Carefully roll the slice of bread into a pinwheel shape.

3 You may need to butter the edge of the rolled bread to help it to stick together.

4 Wrap each sandwich roll as you make it, and chill for at least 30 minutes.

5 Using a long bread knife, slice each sandwich roll into four pinwheels each.

Everything Else Sandwiches
You can cut any number of sandwich shapes; keep the design basic and simple.

1 Spread on the filling first.

2 *You decide how to shape the sandwiches.* Carefully cut your sandwiches into shapes. Use a cookie cutter, if you wish, but you will also need a knife so that you can cut all the way through.

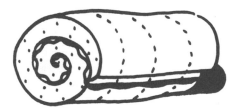

Stand-Up Sandwiches
Make these sandwiches just like the shaped sandwiches, but put them together so that they can stand up straight (or almost straight).

1 Put together three slices of bread with two layers of filling.

2 Now cut your stand-up sandwiches into simple shapes. Be sure to use a shape that's flat on the bottom.

NOW YOU HAVE YOUR OWN
SHAPE AND DESIGN OF
PARTY SANDWICHES.

129

A Cheese Ball Project

Here's a chance to design a party cheese ball with three kinds of cheese. The fun part is using the blender or food processor to mix the ingredients.

Here's what you need:

1 cup walnut pieces
½ cup fresh parsley leaves
1 package (8 ounces) cream cheese
½ cup blue cheese
1 cup cheddar cheese
¼ cup plus 2 tablespoons milk
2 teaspoons Worcestershire sauce

First get your ingredients ready:

1 Chop the walnut pieces in the food processor by pulsing just once or twice. Pour the pieces out onto a large sheet of waxed paper. (You will be shaping the cheese ball on this piece of waxed paper.)

2 Chop the parsley in the blender or food processor by pulsing just once or twice. Empty onto the walnuts. Mix the parsley and walnuts a little with your fingers.

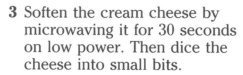

3 Soften the cream cheese by microwaving it for 30 seconds on low power. Then dice the cheese into small bits.

4 Crumble the blue cheese.

5 Dice the cheddar cheese into small bits.

Now use the blender or food processor to make a cheese blend:

6 Put milk and Worcestershire sauce into the blender or food processor. Cover the container, and blend.

7 Carefully drop cheese bits into the midst of the whirlpool. If you lose the whirlpool effect, stop the machine and use a rubber spatula to rearrange or stir the mixture. Continue blending until smooth.

8 Stop the machine. Carefully scrape out the cheese blend onto the waxed paper (on top of the ground nuts and parsley).

9 Slide your hands under the waxed paper and shape the cheese mixture into a ball. Coat the ball with nuts and parsley as you shape it.

10 Wrap the ball in plastic wrap or aluminum foil, and chill for three to four hours or overnight.

NOW YOU HAVE YOUR OWN SHAPED CHEESE BALL.

A POPCORN BALL PROJECT

Shape your own popcorn balls just the way you like them best. Be especially sure to wash your hands before you begin.

First pop about two quarts of popcorn:

1 For two quarts of popcorn, begin with ½ cup unpopped corn.
2 To make the best popcorn, pop your corn in a machine that uses air rather than oil.
3 Have your popcorn ready in a large bowl.

Here's what you need to make the syrup for your popcorn ball:

1 cup brown sugar, well packed
½ cup light corn syrup
¼ cup (½ stick) butter or margarine
½ cup water
1 cup cold water in a small bowl (for testing your syrup)

Here's how you make the syrup:

1 Stir the brown sugar, corn syrup, butter or margarine, and ½ cup water in a large saucepan.
2 Stir well and bring your syrup to a boil.
3 Turn the heat down and simmer your syrup for several minutes. Keep stirring.
4 Set the one cup cold water near you, so that you can test to see when your syrup is done.

Here's the fun part, testing your syrup:

1 Drop a small spoonful of syrup into your cup of cold water. The water will cool the syrup so that you can handle it.
2 Now try forming the syrup into a soft ball. As soon as the syrup can form a ball, remove the pan from the stove, and let the syrup cool for about ten minutes.

Here's how to make the popcorn balls:

1 Pour the syrup over the popcorn. Stir gently so that the syrup coats all the popcorn.
2 Put out a sheet of waxed paper for your popcorn balls.
3 Now use your (clean) hands, and shape your popcorn balls.

: **NOW YOU HAVE EIGHT TO**
: **TEN OF YOUR OWN SHAPED**
: **POPCORN BALLS.**

A Twist of Pretzels Project

Nothing is more fun that twisting and shaping your own pretzels.

Be sure to plan ahead, and allow time for the pretzel dough to rise. (You need at least four hours, but you can let the dough rise overnight, if you wish.)

Here's what you need:

- 2 cups very warm water
- 2 tablespoons (or two packages) dry yeast
- ½ cup sugar
- 2 teaspoons salt
- 2 tablespoons butter or margarine, softened
- 1 egg
- 6½ to 7½ cups unsifted all purpose or unbleached flour
- 1 egg yolk
- 2 tablespoons water
- Coarse (or kosher) salt

Here's how to mix pretzel dough:

1 If you wish, you can use an electric mixer for part of the mixing. First measure the warm water into a large mixer bowl.

Hint: Warm the bowl first by dipping it in warm water. Yeast rises best in a warm environment.

2 Sprinkle the yeast on the water, and stir to dissolve.

3 Add the two teaspoons salt, softened butter or margarine, egg, and three cups of the flour. Beat on medium speed until smooth.

4 Use a large spoon to mix in more flour, about one cup at a time. Keep mixing and adding flour until you have a stiff dough. Do not use the electric mixer for this part.

5 Cover the bowl tightly with plastic wrap, and refrigerate for at least two hours. (You can refrigerate this dough for as long as 24 hours, if you wish.)

A TWIST OF PRETZELS
continued

Here's how to twist and shape the pretzel dough:

1 Turn the dough onto a floured board. Divide in half. Cut each half into 16 equal pieces. (That's 32 in all.)

2 Between your hands, roll each piece into a thin strip about 20 inches long.

3 Here's the fun part: Twist and shape each long strip into a pretzel shape.

4 Arrange your pretzels on lightly greased baking sheets.

5 Use a fork to beat the egg yolk with two tablespoons water. Brush each pretzel with the egg yolk mixture. Sprinkle each with coarse salt.

6 Cover the pretzel sheets lightly with clean dish towels, and put in a warm, draft-free place. Let rise about 25 minutes, until doubled in size.

7 Heat the oven to 400°F (200°C). Bake the pretzels for 15 minutes, or until lightly browned.

8 Cool on wire racks.

> **NOW YOU HAVE 32 OF YOUR OWN SOFT TWISTED PRETZELS.**

A YEAST-ROLLS-IN-FANCY-SHAPES PROJECT

You can shape your rolls into braids, coils, figure 8's, or knots—or any number of even fancier shapes. Then watch the shapes puff up in the oven.

Here's what you need:

2½ cups very warm water

2 tablespoons (or 2 packages) dry yeast

1 tablespoon sugar

1 tablespoon salt

2 tablespoons butter or margarine, softened

6½ to 7½ cups unsifted all purpose or unbleached flour

1 egg

1 tablespoon milk

Here's how to mix the roll dough:

1 If you wish, you can use an electric mixer for part of the mixing. Measure the warm water into a large warm bowl.

Hint: *Warm the bowl first by dipping it in warm water. Yeast rises best in a warm environment.*

2 Sprinkle the yeast on the water, and stir to dissolve.

3 Add the sugar, salt, butter or margarine, and three cups of the flour. Beat on medium speed until smooth. (Or beat with a large wooden spoon.)

4 Using a large spoon, mix in more flour, about one cup at a time. Keep mixing and adding flour until you have a stiff dough. Do not use the electric mixer for this part.

Here's how to knead the roll dough:

Turn the dough onto a floured board, and knead for eight to ten minutes. Knead with the palms of your hands, pushing the dough again and again. Be patient! Knead until your dough is smooth and elastic.

....
YEAST ROLLS
continued

Let the dough rise:

1 Place the dough in a greased bowl, and turn the dough over so that it is lightly greased all around.
2 Cover the bowl with a clean dish towel, and place in a warm, draft-free place for about one hour, until the dough is doubled in size.

Here's the fun part, shaping the rolls:

1 Punch the dough down with your fist. Divide the dough in half. Then cut each half into 18 equal pieces. That's 36 in all.
2 Shape each roll.

Here are five ideas for shapes:

1 Between your hands, roll a piece of the dough into a strip about nine inches long. Fold the roll back on itself and twist into a braid.
2 Roll the nine-inch-long roll into a coil. Tuck the tail end underneath.

3 Form the nine-inch roll into a figure 8. Use your fingers to seal the ends together.
4 Form the nine-inch roll into a loose knot.
5 Twist the nine-inch roll, and then circle it into a wreath. Use your fingers to seal the ends together.

Suggestion: *See what other shapes you can create with pieces of dough. Keep it simple. The shape will puff up and may end up not looking much like its beginnings. (But that's part of the fun.)*

Here's how to finish the rolls:

1 Place the rolls on lightly greased baking sheets. Line them up about two inches apart. Cover each baking sheet with a clean dish towel. Let rise in a warm, draft-free place for about one hour, until doubled in size.
2 With a fork, beat the egg and milk together. Brush each roll with the egg mixture.
3 ***You decide if you would like seeded rolls.*** You can sprinkle the rolls with sesame seeds, poppy seeds, or caraway seeds.
4 Heat the oven to 400°F (200°C). Bake the rolls for about 15 minutes, or until lightly browned.
5 Cool on wire racks.

Suggestion: *For other creative ways to have fun with this dough, look at the bread basket project and the doughy face project in FOOD THAT LOOKS LIKE SOMETHING (OR SOMEONE).*

NOW YOU HAVE 36 OF YOUR OWN SHAPED ROLLS.

A FANCY BUTTER PROJECT

Why put up with ordinary butter when you can design your own fancy butter three ways.

Here's an easy way to make butter etchings:

1 Cut a stick of butter into ¾-inch pats. Lay the pats down flat, and use a knife (carefully) to etch in a design. Make a snowflake or a face—or whatever you decide.

Hint: You can buy butter stamps to stamp on a ready-made design. Of course, etching your own designs may be just as much fun.

2 Refrigerate your etched butter pats, covered, in a bowl of ice water.

Here's how to make butter curls:

1 To make butter curls, you need a butter curler or vegetable peeler, along with a dish of hot water and a dish of ice water—and a stick of butter.

2 Let the butter curler or vegetable peeler sit in the bowl of hot water for about five minutes.

3 Now pull the hot curler across a stick of butter.

4 As you finish each curl, drop the curl into the bowl of ice water. And dip your curler into the hot water once more.

5 When you are finished, refrigerate your butter curls, covered, in the dish of ice water.

Here's how to make butter balls:

1 To make butter balls, you need two flat spatulas or a pair of flat knives, along with a bowl of hot water and a bowl of ice water— and a stick of butter.

2 Let the spatulas sit in the hot water for about five minutes.

3 Cut a stick of butter into one-inch squares.

4 Stand a butter pat upright on one spatula. Place the second spatula on top, and move it around and around until you see a butter ball forming.

5 As you finish each ball, drop it into the bowl of ice water. And dip your spatulas into the hot water once more.

6 When you are finished, refrigerate your butter balls, covered, in the bowl of ice water.

NOW YOU HAVE YOUR OWN FANCY BUTTER DESIGNS.

Serve on holidays and other important occasions.

Hint: You can buy wooden sticks especially designed for shaping butter. But you can probably find utensils around your kitchen that will work just about as well.

· · · · · · · · · ·

A GELATIN CUBES PROJECT

· ·

Create shimmering, shining gelatin cubes that you can eat with your fingers.

Here's what you need:

2 envelopes unflavored gelatin

2 cups fruit juice
(You Decide The Flavor.)

Here's what you do:

1 In a small heatproof glass bowl, sprinkle the unflavored gelatin over one cup fruit juice. Stir.

2 Heat in the microwave oven on high power for two to three minutes. The mixture ought to be just short of boiling, and the gelatin should be completely dissolved.

: *Caution: You need adult help*
: *with boiling juice.*

3 Stir in 1 more cup fruit juice.

4 Pour into an 8-inch square glass baking dish.

5 Refrigerate overnight.

Here's how to make your cubes:

1 Your gelatin ought to be firm after a night in the refrigerator. Cut it into one-inch cubes. Or you can use a small cookie cutter to cut the gelatin into hearts, stars, or triangles.

2 To get the cubes out, hold the pan in warm water for ten seconds. Then try getting the cubes out with a spatula or wide knife. If the first try doesn't work, hold the pan in warm water for another ten seconds.

: **NOW YOU HAVE ABOUT 64**
: **GELATIN SHAPES.**

A COOKIES-FOR-EVERY-HOLIDAY DESIGN PROJECT

Shape and decorate these sugar cookies for holidays and other important occasions.

Here's what you need:

- ½ cup (1 stick) butter or margarine
- ¾ cup sugar
- 1 egg
- 1 tablespoon milk
- ½ teaspoon vanilla extract
- 1¾ cups all purpose or unbleached flour
- 1 teaspoon baking powder
- ¼ teaspoon salt

Here's how to mix the dough:

1 In a large mixing bowl, cream together the butter or margarine and sugar at medium speed of an electric mixer.

2 Add the egg, milk, and vanilla extract, and beat together.

3 In another bowl, stir together the flour, baking powder, and salt. Beat into the batter.

4 Chill your dough, covered, for an hour or more.

Here's how to cut out the cookies:

1 Preheat the oven to 350°F (180°C).

2 Sprinkle a pastry cloth with flour. Roll out your cookie dough very thin, between ⅛ and ¼ inch.

3 You decide what shapes you want your cookies. Dip the cookie cutter in flour, and cut out your cookies.

4 Carefully lift the cookies onto ungreased baking sheets, and line them up about one inch apart.

Hint: *You can buy cookie cutters for almost any holiday or season, but if you don't have what you want, use a knife to cut out shapes. Cut out a paper pattern first, and then use the paper as a guide.*

· · · · · · · · · · ·
HOLIDAY COOKIES
continued

Here's how to bake your cookies:

1 Bake for eight to ten minutes. Pay attention so that they don't burn.

2 Bake just one tray at a time.

3 Cool on the baking sheets for two minutes. Then remove to wire racks and cool completely.

Here's the fun part, decorating your cookies:

1 You can sprinkle on colored sugar crystals before or after you bake the cookies. The crystals tend to stick better if you put them on before. Very gently, use your finger to press the sugar crystals into each cookie.

2 Or frost your cookies in different colors. Use a separate small dish for each color. For each color, mix about ½ cup of white frosting with a few drops of food coloring. Experiment, one drop at a time, until you get the right color.

Hint: To make basic white frosting, look at the cake-for-every-occasion recipe in this section.

3 You can create designs and faces from your choice of decorating materials:
Pecan and almond pieces
   or Shoestring licorice
      (Cut them up for excellent hair and eyelashes.)
  or Silver dragees
      (Silver dragees make good eyes and buttons, but they are hard and not safe for small children.)
  or Nonpareils
  or Chocolate chips or chunks
  or Gumdrops, candy corn, and small holiday candies
  or Chow mein noodles
      (Create unusual hair.)

4 Be sure to allow enough time for decorating your cookies—or ask friends to help. And be sure to clean up as you go.

NOW YOU HAVE ABOUT 60 OF YOUR OWN DESIGNER COOKIES.

A CAKE-FOR-EVERY-OCCASION DESIGN PROJECT

You can shape a cake for each season: spring, summer, fall, and winter.

Choose one of our four cake designs for this project—or design your own cake. Begin with a basic cake and basic frosting, and go on from there.

BASIC CAKE

You can use almost any cake recipe to start your career in cake designing, shaping, and decorating.

For ideas, look at the make-your-own cake mix project in the FOOD FACTORY section. You can use your own cake mix to make yellow, white, spice, orange, or chocolate cakes.

Decide how you will cut your design:

If you are making a spring bunny cake, then use two 8-inch or 9-inch round pans.

If you are making a winter snowbaby, then use one 8-inch or 9-inch round pan plus one 8-inch square pan.

If you are making a summer sailboat or an autumn owl, then use one 9 × 13-inch baking pan.

Here's how to bake your cake:

1 Bake your cake according to the recipe directions.

2 Let cool in the pans for ten minutes. Then carefully invert onto a wire cooling rack to finish cooling.

3 When the cake is cool, carefully transfer it to a large cutting board where you can do the cutting and shaping.

4 Then assemble the cake on a tray or plate large enough to hold the final shape. Do the frosting and decorating right on that tray or plate. Remember that your own designs are probably going to be larger than ordinary cakes.

NOW YOU HAVE A BASIC CAKE READY TO SHAPE, DESIGN, FROST, AND DECORATE.

· · · · · · · · · · ·
BASIC FROSTING
· ·

This is simple white frosting. You can ice a large cake with this frosting, and you ought to have some left over for decorating the cake.

Here's what you need for frosting:

⅓ cup butter or margarine, softened
3 cups sifted confectioner's sugar
3 tablespoons hot milk
1½ teaspoon vanilla extract
¼ teaspoon salt

Here's how to mix the frosting:

Use an electric mixer. In the small mixer bowl, mix the butter or margarine, confectioner's sugar, hot milk, vanilla extract, and salt. Beat on medium speed until smooth and creamy.

Hint: If your frosting seems too stiff, mix in one more tablespoon milk. If your frosting seems too liquid, mix in one more tablespoon confectioner's sugar. You can balance out your frosting by adding just a very little extra milk or sugar at a time.

To color the frosting for small decorations: Use a spoon to mix about ¼ cup of frosting in a small dish with three or four drops of food coloring. To get a deeper color, add food coloring only one drop at a time. Use a separate dish and separate spoon for each different color.

Suggestion: *For decorating icing, look at the gingerbread house project in HOLIDAY SURPRISES. For a honey frosting recipe, see the cupcakes project in FUN FOOD WITH SECRET MESSAGES.*

> **NOW YOU HAVE WHITE FROSTING, ENOUGH FOR A LARGE CAKE PLUS FROSTING DECORATIONS.**

A SPRING BUNNY CAKE

Here's a design for a spring bunny cake—complete with floppy ears and a bow tie.

Here's what you need for a spring bunny cake:

Basic cake baked in two 8-inch or 9-inch round pans (and cooled)

12 × 18-inch piece of heavy cardboard covered with aluminum foil

Basic white frosting

Red food coloring

Grated coconut

Pink gumdrops

6 clean pipecleaners

Here's how to put the bunny together:

1 Set one whole round layer at one end of the foil-covered cardboard. This is for the bunny's head.

· · · · · · · · · · ·

A SPRING BUNNY CAKE
continued

2 Cut the second round layer at outer edges to form two curved ears. Then cut the center piece between the ears into a bow shape, like this:

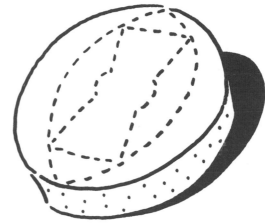

3 Place the ears and bow like this:

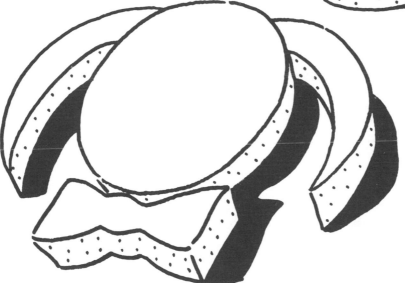

Here's how to frost and decorate the spring bunny cake:

1 Use about ¾ of the basic white frosting to frost the bunny's face and ears. Use frosting to cover the seams.

2 Mix two or three drops of red food coloring into the remaining ¼ of the frosting, only enough to tint the frosting pink.

3 Frost the tie and the inside of the ears in pink.

4 Place two pink gumdrops for the eyes and one pink gumdrop for the nose.

5 Place three pipecleaners for whiskers on each side of the bunny's nose. Or use pink frosting if you want edible whiskers.

6 Sprinkle the bunny's head and ears with grated coconut.

: **NOW YOU HAVE YOUR OWN**
: **SPRING BUNNY CAKE.**

A Summer Sailboat Cake

Here's a design for a sailboat cake to celebrate the arrival of summer.

Here's what you need for a sailboat cake:

Basic cake baked in a 9 × 13-inch pan (and cooled)

12 × 3-inch piece of aluminum foil or wrapping paper

12 × 18-inch piece of heavy cardboard covered with aluminum foil

Basic white frosting (See page TK)

Blue food coloring

Red food coloring

Shoestring licorice

A small paper American flag (or you can draw and cut out a paper flag)

Here's how to put the sailboat cake together:

1 Cut two triangular sails and a base for your sailboat, like this:

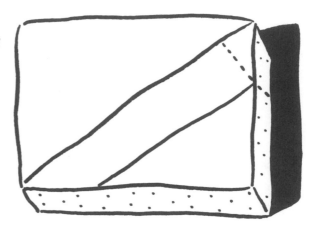

2 Roll up the 12 × 3-inch piece of foil or wrapping paper to serve as a 12-inch-long mast for your sailboat cake.

3 Arrange the base, sails, and mast on the foil-covered cardboard. Put together your summer sailboat like this:

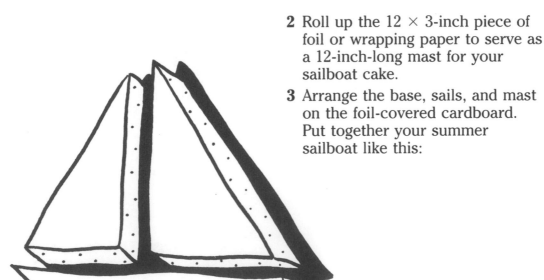

· · · · · · · · · · ·

A SUMMER SAILBOAT CAKE
continued

Here's how to frost and decorate the summer sailboat cake:

1 Use about ¾ of your basic white frosting to frost the two sails.

2 Mix about ¼ cup of the remaining frosting in a separate small dish with two or three drops red food coloring. Continue adding red food coloring, one drop at a time, until you get a bright red color.

3 Mix all the rest of the frosting with four or five drops of blue food coloring. Continue adding blue food coloring, one drop at a time, until you get a bright blue color.

4 Frost the base of your sailboat in bright blue.

5 Use the red frosting to decorate the boat. You might use toothpicks, a very small spoon, or a decorating tip to put on the finishing touches. Decorate the sails with red frosting stiches and sail rings. Decorate the hull with racing stripes. If you have a decorating tip, you might even be able to frost in a name for your boat.

6 Use shoestring licorice for ropes along your sails.

7 Top the mast with a small paper flag.

Suggestion: *Does your family have a flag of its own? You might want to design a family flag on paper and use it to "fly" over your sailboat cake.*

: **NOW YOU HAVE YOUR OWN**
: **SUMMER SAILBOAT CAKE.**

AN AUTUMN OWL CAKE

Here's a design for an owl cake for autumn (and perfectly spooky for Halloween).

Here's what you need for an owl cake:

Basic cake baked in a 9 × 13-inch pan (and cooled)

12 × 18-inch piece of heavy cardboard covered with aluminum foil

Basic white frosting (See page TK)

Yellow food coloring

Red food coloring

1 ounce (1 square) unsweetened chocolate

Two short flat casserole-dish candles

Here's how to put the owl cake together:

1 Cut the owl's head and body in one piece, and use the corners for owl wings, like this:

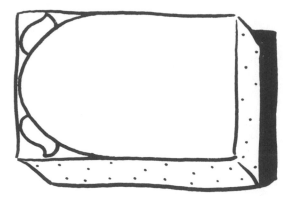

2 Arrange owl and wings on the foil wrapped cardboard. Put together your owl like this:

. . . .

AN AUTUMN OWL CAKE
continued

Here's how to frost and decorate the owl cake:

1 Mix an orange-colored frosting for the owl. Use only about ¾ of the basic white frosting. (Save the rest for other owl colors.) Mix the frosting with three drops yellow food coloring and two drops red food coloring. If you want a darker orange color, add three more drops yellow food coloring and two more drops red food coloring.

2 Frost the owl's body and wings. Use frosting to cover the seams.

3 To frost a little red beak and perhaps some creepy red claws, mix 2 tablespoons of the remaining basic frosting with one drop red food coloring. You might want to add another drop for a bright red color.

4 Frost a beak and claws for the owl.

5 Now get ready to frost in some black feathers. Put 1 ounce (1 square) unsweetened chocolate in a heatproof glass dish. Cover and melt in the microwave on low power for two minutes. Stir gently.

6 Stir the melted chocolate into the remainder of the basic frosting.

7 Use toothpicks, a very small spoon, or a decorating tip to frost chocolate feathers for your owl. Be sure to decorate the wings. And fix up feather chocolate ears and tiny grouchy-looking eyebrows.

8 Now finish with spooky eyes for the owl. Set in the two short flat casserole candles. Now you light up really spooky owl eyes, like this:

NOW YOU HAVE YOUR OWN SPOOKY OWL CAKE.

A Winter Snowbaby Cake

Here's a design for a winter snowbaby cake.

Here's what you need for a snowbaby cake:

Basic cake baked in one 8-inch round pan and one 8-inch square pan (and cooled)

12 × 18-inch piece of heavy cardboard covered with aluminum foil

Basic white frosting

Red food coloring

1 ounce (1 square) unsweetened chocolate

The tip of a tiny real carrot (for the nose)

Chocolate chips or chunks (for buttons)

Here's how to put the snowbaby cake together:

1 Arrange the round layer on the foil-covered cardboard for the snowbaby's body.

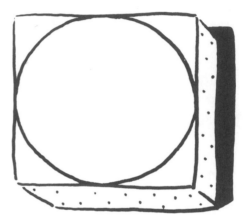

2 Cut the square layer for head, arms, and hat, like this:

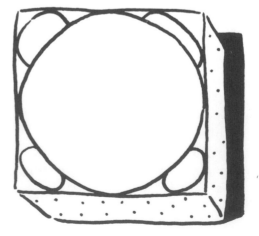

· · · · · · · · · · ·

A WINTER SNOWBABY CAKE
continued

3 Put together your snowbaby like this:

Here's how to frost and decorate your snowbaby:

1 Frost the snowbaby's body and head in basic white frosting. Use only about ¾ of the basic frosting. (Save the rest for other snowbaby colors.) Use frosting to cover the seams.

2 To frost a red mouth, red mittens, and a red decoration for the snowbaby's hat, mix two tablespoons of the remaining frosting with one drop of red food coloring. You might want to add more, one drop at a time, until you achieve a good bright red color. Use a separate dish and spoon for each color frosting.

3 Now get ready to frost black eyes, hat, and belt. Put one ounce (one square) unsweetened chocolate in a heatproof glass dish. Cover and melt in the microwave oven on low power for two minutes. Stir gently.

4 Stir the melted chocolate into the remainder of the basic frosting.

5 Use toothpicks, a very small spoon, or a decorating tip to frost chocolate eyes, hat, and belt for the snowbaby.

6 Use the tip of a tiny real carrot for the nose.

7 Put on chocolate chips or chunks for buttons.

> **NOW YOU HAVE YOUR OWN SNOWBABY CAKE.**

BASIC CAKE DECORATIONS

You can create designs and faces from your choice of decorating materials. (Decorate your cake only after it is shaped and frosted.) You might want to try:

Chocolate chips or chunks
or Chow mein noodles
or Coconut flakes
or Gumdrops, candy corn, and small holiday candies
or Lemon, lime, and orange slices
or Lollipops
or Marshmallows
or Mint wafers and other thin cookie pieces
or Nonpareils and sugar crystals
or Pecan and almond pieces
or Shoestring licorice
or Silver dragees

. . . .

CREATE OTHER CAKE DESIGNS

. . . .

Here is how to cut your own unique cake designs. Each of your cakes can be one-of-a-kind.

1 Begin with sketches on paper. Keep your sketches simple. Begin with an easy shape.

2 Decide the best way to bake the cake to get the design you want:
   • In one 8-inch round pan and one 8-inch square pan
   • In one 9 × 13-inch rectangular pan
   • In two 8-inch round pans
   • In two 8-inch square pans

3 Then on fresh pieces of paper, draw cake layers the exact size. Measure carefully, and figure out how you will cut the cake, and how you will put it back together. Use a pencil so that you can erase mistakes.

4 Try to design your shapes so that you don't waste cake pieces.

Repeat: Keep your design simple.

Suggestion: *To try a Christmas tree cake or a patriotic flag cake, look at HOLIDAY SURPRISES.*

> **NOW YOU CAN CREATE**
> **YOUR OWN UNFORGETTABLE**
> **CAKES.**

A PURE CHOCOLATE DESIGN PROJECT

This project is one of the easiest and one of the most fun at the same time. You can create pure chocolate candies in any color or shape you can dream up.

Here's what you need:

Chocolate "buttons" in the colors you want

Candy molds in the designs you want

Hint: *Chocolate is still chocolate even if it's not brown. You can buy chocolate "buttons" in about a dozen colors.*

Here's what you do:

1 Melt the chocolate buttons. Put them in a heatproof glass dish. Use a separate dish for each color, and melt just a few at a time. Cover and microwave on low power for one minute. Stir gently.

2 Carefully spoon your melted chocolate into the candy molds.

3 Gently, gently tap the mold on the counter to get rid of air bubbles.

4 Put your mold into the freezer for about five minutes—or into the refrigerator for about 30 minutes. You can tell when your candy is hard by checking to see that no dark spots remain in the bottom of the mold.

5 Spread out a sheet of waxed paper, and gently turn the mold out onto it. Tap out the candies.

You decide how to make your candy fancy:

1 Swirl two colors into the mold. Gently stir the two colors in each mold, and then freeze.
   OR

2 Create layers of colors. Spoon in one color, enough to fill half of each mold. Freeze for about three minutes or refrigerate for about 15 minutes—until the candy is partly hardened. Then gently spoon in a second color. Freeze for about five minutes or refrigerate for 30 minutes the second time.
   OR

3 Make chocolate popsicles. Use a popsicle mold. Lay in popsicle sticks, and spoon your melted chocolate over each. Then freeze or refrigerate.

: **NOW YOU HAVE YOUR OWN**
: **DESIGN OF PURE**
: **CHOCOLATE CANDIES.**

· · · · · · · · · ·

A CHOCOLATE STORY

· ·

When Christopher Columbus first came to the New World, he was quite delighted with the people he met there.

The native Central American people talked to Columbus and his men by sign language. They brought gifts. And they shared their food.

The New World people served hot chocolate, corn on the cob, and fried iguana.

Columbus and his men loved corn on the cob.

They did not much like the hot chocolate.

And they positively hated fried iguana.

You can imagine why they did not like fried lizard. But what was wrong with the hot chocolate?

The original hot chocolate was unsweetened. The Europeans just couldn't stand the bitter taste. (Try unsweetened baking chocolate. You'll get the point.)

When Columbus returned from his fourth voyage in 1502, he did bring back a few cocoa beans, just as curiosities.

Within a few years, however, the Europeans finally discovered the value of the cocoa beans—just as soon as they figured out that they needed to add a little sweetening.

Soon almost all the people of Europe were enjoying their favorite New World discovery: sweet hot chocolate.

But Christopher Columbus himself was sticking with wine, water, and dreams of gold.

A CHOCOLATE STORY FROM A DIFFERENT PERSPECTIVE

Cocoa beans may have been just another foreign curiosity to the Europeans.

But that's not how cocoa beans looked to the native Americans who were there to greet Columbus.

The native Americans, without the sweet tooth of Europeans, liked their bitter chocolate drink so much that they drank it several times a day.

And they prized cocoa beans so much that they traded them back and forth like money.

While Columbus dreamed of gold across the seas, the people of America found their gold at home. Plain cocoa beans were already as good as gold to them.

FOODS THAT LOOK LIKE SOMETHING (OR SOMEONE)

Do you prefer to eat food that looks like boats, ants, elephants, porcupines, or people? Here's your chance. You'll especially like the cheese eyeballs.

A PORCUPINE MEATBALLS PROJECT

These meatballs don't exactly look like porcupines, but they do have bristles—rice bristles.

Be especially sure to wash your hands before you begin shaping meatballs.

Here's what you need:

1 egg
2 tablespoons finely chopped onion
1 tablespoon Worcestershire sauce
½ teaspoon nutmeg
½ teaspoon salt
1 pound lean ground beef
¼ cup uncooked long-grain rice
2 cups beef bouillon

Here's how to make the meatballs:

1 Break the egg into a large bowl. Beat it slightly with a fork.

2 Add chopped onion, Worcestershire sauce, nutmeg, and salt. Stir together.

3 Add the ground beef and uncooked rice. Stir all together with a large fork. (A large fork helps to work all the other ingredients into the ground beef.)

4 Shape into about 20 small meatballs.

Here's how to roast the meatballs:

Heat the oven to 400°F (200°C). Line up the meatballs in a baking pan. Bake, uncovered, for 25 minutes. Turn once during roasting.

: *Caution: You need adult help*
: *with turning the hot meatballs.*

Here's how to serve the meatballs:

Heat the beef bouillon and pour it over the meatballs just before you serve them.

: **NOW YOU HAVE 20**
: **PORCUPINE MEATBALLS,**
: **PERFECTLY GOOD FOR**
: **DINNER.**

A TURKEY IN THE STRAW PROJECT

You can shape up four turkey-in-the-straw salad plates from turkey leftovers. And just taste the delicious curry in the salads.

Here's what you need:

 3 cups cold turkey, already roasted and cut into bite-sized pieces

⅓ cup diced celery

¼ cup mayonnaise

½ teaspoon curry powder

Lettuce leaves and tomato wedges

Potato sticks

Here's how to mix the turkey salad:

In a large bowl, combine the cut-up turkey pieces with diced celery, mayonnaise, and curry powder.

Here's how to serve the turkey salad:

1 On each of four plates, fan out a bed of washed lettuce leaves. Decorate the edges with tomato wedges.

2 Now make the "straw." Sprinkle the lettuce leaves with plenty of potato sticks.

3 Flatten out a small center for each "turkey." Scoop on three large spoonfuls of the turkey salad mixture.

4 Use your (clean) hands to shape the mixture into a "turkey." Don't worry if the shape doesn't look exactly like a turkey. Here's how it might look:

NOW YOU HAVE FOUR TURKEY IN THE STRAW SALAD PLATES.

....

A Pumpkin Face Sandwiches Project

....

Construct a "pumpkin" face for your sandwiches.

Here's what you do:

1 Make a sandwich. Faces show up well on round "party" bread that's a dark color (such as rye or pumpernickel).

2 Spread the *outside* surface of the sandwich (where the face will go) with mayonnaise, peanut butter, or softened cream cheese. That's the "glue" for your pumpkin face.

Hint: *Soften cream cheese in the microwave oven, unwrapped, for 30 seconds on low power.*

Here are some face-decorating choices:

1 For eyes, try stuffed olive slices or raisins.

2 For eyelashes and eyebrows, try parsley or dill leaves.

3 For green hair, try parsley or celery leaves.

4 For yellow hair, try carrot curls.

Suggestion: *Look at the veggie lookalike projects for a way to make carrot curls.*

5 For a nose, try a carrot tip.

6 For a mouth, try a slice of red pepper.

7 For arms and feet, try carrot sticks and celery sticks.

Here's another way to make a face on your sandwich:

Color mayonnaise or cream cheese with a drop or two of food coloring. Then "paint" on a face.

Suggestion: *Look back at the sandwich-shaping projects in FOODS TO PUNCH, TWIST, SHAPE, AND DESIGN. You could make faces on your sandwich shapes.*

YOU'LL FIND THAT PUMPKIN FACE SANDWICHES ARE VERY GOOD TO EAT.

A CHEESE EYEBALLS PROJECT

Can you stand these eyeballs looking up at you? Can you pop one in your mouth?

Here's what you need:

- ½ pound grated Cheddar cheese
- ½ cup (1 stick) butter or margarine, softened
- ½ teaspoon salt
- 1 teaspoon paprika
- 1 cup all purpose or unbleached flour
- 1 6-ounce bottle of small stuffed olives

Here's what you do:

1 Preheat the oven to 400°F (200°C).

2 In a small bowl, combine the cheese with the butter or margarine. Blend thoroughly with a large wooden spoon.

3 In a separate dish, combine the flour, paprika, and salt.

4 Blend the flour mixture into the cheese mixture until they are thoroughly combined.

5 Measure one teaspoon of the mixture and form an "eyeball" around an olive. Turn the olive so that it is "staring" outward. You can form about two dozen "eyeballs" from this recipe.

6 Line up the "eyeballs" on ungreased baking sheets.

7 Bake for 15 minutes.

Hint: If you want to make them ahead of time, freeze them on baking sheets, UNBAKED. As soon as they are frozen, put them in plastic bags, and keep them frozen. Just thaw and bake them when you're ready.

NOW YOU HAVE ABOUT 24 CHEESE EYEBALLS, READY TO SERVE AT YOUR NEXT PARTY.

VEGGIE LOOKALIKE PROJECTS

Here are five ways to make vegetables look like something—including very edible.

Ants Crossing a Bridge

1 Wash celery stalks, and cut off the leaves.

2 Fill each celery stalk with peanut butter or cream cheese.

3 Line up raisin ants on your celery bridge.

Cucumber Wheelies

1 Peel a cucumber up and down so that you make stripes, like this:

2 Slice into very thin "wheels" (½ inch thick or less).

3 Wrap your cucumber wheels in plastic wrap, and freeze for half an hour or more.

4 Serve and eat frozen.

Carrot Curls

1 Scrape a large carrot, and cut it into sticks.

2 Use a vegetable peeler to shave off long strips of carrot. Or peel thin curly slices from each end toward the center, and leave the center uncut.

3 Drop each cut carrot stick into ice water to open and curl.

Suggestion: *Use carrot curls for "hair" or other veggie decorations.*

MORE VEGGIE LOOKALIKES

Radish Roses

1 Hold the radish upright, and use a knife to make overlapping lengthwise slices from top to stem. Be careful not to cut through the stem end.

2 Drop radishes in ice water to open up like a rose.

3 Here's how your radish roses ought to look:

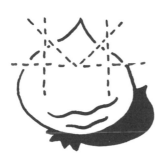

Green Pepper Cages

1 Cut a large green pepper in half, and clean out the seeds and membranes, so the pepper looks like this:

2 Cut the edge of each half into a zigzag shape, like this:

3 Fill each green pepper cage with carrot sticks, carrot curls, celery sticks, cauliflower buds, and radish roses.

> ALL OF THESE ANTS, WHEELIES, CURLS, ROSES, AND CAGES ARE VERY GOOD TO EAT.

A FRUIT FACE PROJECT

Here's how to make fruit look back at you.

1 Peel and cut in half a large peach or pear.
2 Lay the fruit half on a "bed" of cottage cheese and lettuce—and then decorate it into a fruit face.
3 Spread plain yogurt or cream cheese on your fruit-face choices (the raisins, currants, and so on). That's the "glue" for the face.
4 Now "glue" on a fruit face.

Here are some fruit-face choices:

1 For eyes, use raisins, currants, fresh blueberries or pieces of grapes.
2 For eyebrows and eyelashes, use parsley or dill leaves.
3 For green hair, use parsley or celery leaves.
4 For yellow hair, use carrot curls.

Suggestion: *Look at the veggie lookalike projects for a way to make carrot curls.*

5 For a nose, use a piece of banana, of course.
6 For a mouth, use pieces of dried fruit or bits of fresh red strawberries or cherries.
7 For arms and legs, use carrot sticks or celery sticks.

NATURALLY, FRUIT FACES ARE GOOD TO EAT.

A MELON BOAT PROJECT

A honeydew melon (or watermelon) boat makes a beautiful centerpiece at summer parties. And just about nothing tastes any better. Here's how to make one.

1 Cut a honeydew melon in half. Or if you're ambitious (and have some help), cut a watermelon in half lengthwise. Carve the edges in a zigzag pattern.

2 Remove the seeds.

3 Scoop out melon balls into a bowl. Use a one-inch melon scoop. Scoop out the melon "meat" until the shell is empty.

4 Fill your melon boat with melon balls. And combine with your choice of fresh fruit:
   Cantaloupe balls or chunks
   or Fresh pineapple chunks
   or Strawberries
   or Blueberries
   or Grapes
   or Pitted cherries
   or Peach, pear, or plum wedges
   or Banana slices

5 Sprinkle lemon or lime juice over the fruits so they will retain their color.

6 Fill the melon shell. Cover with plastic wrap, and refrigerate until ready to serve.

7 *You decide how to top the melon boat.* If you wish, top with scoops of fruit sherbet just before you serve the melon boat. Or garnish with mint or basil leaves.

> NOW YOU HAVE A
> FRUIT-FILLED PARTY MELON
> BOAT.

Hint: Just for fun, you can scoop a variety of sizes of melon balls, by also using a large ice cream scoop and different sizes of spoons.

Hint: If you use banana slices, be especially sure to dip them in lemon juice so that they won't turn brown.

. . . .

A RAINBOW SALAD PROJECT

. . . .

Here's how to create three very fancy layers of gelatin rainbow. You need a large ring mold for the three layers.

Rainbow Ring
Here's what you need:

- 3 envelopes unflavored gelatin
- 1½ cups cranberry juice
- 1 8-ounce can (1 cup) cranberry sauce
- 1 11-ounce can mandarin orange sections
- 2 cups chopped walnuts
- 1 8¼-ounce can crushed pineapple
- 1 cup cottage cheese
- 1¾ cups unsweetened grape juice
- 2 cups fresh or frozen blueberries

Here's how to make the first layer:

1 In a large bowl, sprinkle one envelope unflavored gelatin into ½ cup cranberry juice. Let it stand a couple of minutes until the gelatin is soaked through. Heat in the microwave oven on high power for 30 to 45 seconds, until the gelatin dissolves.

2 Stir in one cup more cranberry juice.

3 Refrigerate for a half hour or so, until the mixture mounds when you drop it from a spoon.

4 Stir in cranberry sauce.

5 Drain the can of mandarin orange sections, and save the juice in a separate dish.

6 Stir the orange sections and one cup of chopped walnuts into the gelatin mixture.

7 Pour into the bottom of the mold, and refrigerate until set, between 30 minutes and one hour.

....

RAINBOW SALAD
continued

Here's how to make the second layer:

1 Mix together juice from the can of mandarin oranges and juice from the can of crushed pineapple. The combination ought to make 1¾ cups of juice. If not, add water to make up the difference.

2 Pour ½ cup of the combined orange-and-pineapple juice into a large bowl. Sprinkle one envelope unflavored gelatin over the juice. Let it stand until the gelatin is soaked. Heat in the microwave oven for 30 to 45 seconds, until the gelatin dissolves.

3 Stir in the 1¼ cups of remaining juice.

4 Let set until the mixture creates mounds when you drop it from a spoon, about half an hour.

5 Stir in the crushed pineapple, one cup chopped walnuts, and the cottage cheese.

6 Pour this second layer into the mold on top of the first layer. Refrigerate until set, between 30 minutes and one hour.

Here's how to make the third layer:

1 In a large bowl, sprinkle one envelope unflavored gelatin over ½ cup grape juice. Let it stand until the gelatin is soaked. Heat in the microwave oven for 30 to 45 seconds, until the gelatin dissolves.

2 Stir in 1¼ cups more grape juice.

3 If you plan to add frozen blueberries, stir them in at this point.

4 Let set until the mixture forms mounds when you drop it from a spoon, about half an hour. If you plan to add fresh blueberries, stir them in at this point, when the mixture is partially set.

5 Pour this third layer into the mold on top of the second layer. Refrigerate until solidly set, about one hour.

Here's how to unmold your gelatin rainbow:

1 Set the mold in a pan of warm water for three minutes (or more).

2 Hold a large plate on top of the mold, and quickly turn over mold and plate together.

> *Caution: You may want to ask for adult help with unmolding.*

> **NOW YOU HAVE A RAINBOW RING.**

. . . .

A CUPCAKE CONES PROJECT

. . . .

Here's an easy way to make cupcakes that look like ice cream cones.

Here's what you need:

Basic cupcake batter

(For ideas, look back at the cake mix projects in THE FOOD FACTORY.)

12 flat-bottomed wafer ice cream cones

Here's what you do:

1 Make batter for cupcakes.

2 Preheat the oven to 350°F (180°C).

3 Spoon the cake batter into about a dozen flat-bottomed wafer ice cream cones. Fill each about ⅔ full.

4 Line up the cones on a large baking dish or jelly roll pan.

5 Bake for 20 minutes. They'll puff up and look like ice cream cones.

6 Let your cupcake cones cool before you frost and decorate them.

: **NOW YOU HAVE ABOUT A**
: **DOZEN CUPCAKE CONES.**

. . . .

A CARNIVAL CONES PROJECT

. . . .

Here's how to decorate ice cream cones to look as if they came from a carnival.

Here's what you need:

16-ounce package semisweet real chocolate pieces or 6 ounces (6 squares) semisweet chocolate

About 12 ice cream cones

Nonpareils or flaked coconut

Here's what you do:

1 Melt the chocolate, and stir gently.

2 Using a pastry brush, brush the melted chocolate inside each cone and around the edge.

3 Before the chocolate hardens, lightly roll the edge of each cone in colored nonpareils or flaked coconut.

: **NOW YOU HAVE ABOUT A**
: **DOZEN CARNIVAL CONES**
: **READY TO FILL WITH ICE**
: **CREAM.**

....
A BREAD BASKET PROJECT
....

Look back at the braided yeast rolls project in FOODS TO PUNCH, TWIST, SHAPE, AND DESIGN. Here's a handsome edible basket that you can make from that same dough.

Here are the supplies you need:

Two ovenproof bowls (about 8 or 9 inches in diameter and 4½ inches deep)

Hint: *Large stainless steel mixer bowls would be ideal.*

Two 10 × 10-inch wire racks

Heavy-duty aluminum foil

Prepare the yeast dough:

1 Prepare the dough just as in the braided yeast rolls recipe. Let the dough rise for about one hour, just as if you were going to make rolls. But, of course, this dough will get a whole different shape.

2 While your dough is rising, prepare a basket form for it.

Here's how to create a basket shape for the dough:

1 Cut four strips of heavy-duty aluminum foil, each ten inches long by 2½ inches wide. Grease the strips thoroughly, and place them around the edge of one 10-inch wire rack, grease side up.

2 Grease the outside of a bowl thoroughly. Turn the bowl upside down on the foil strips on the wire rack.

3 Do just the same with the other bowl and the other rack.

. . . .

BREAD BASKET
continued

Here's how to shape the dough:

1 Punch the dough down with your fist. Divide the dough in half. Then cut each half into 12 equal pieces. That's 24 in all.

2 Set two of the pieces aside.

3 Between your hands, roll each of the 22 pieces into 30-inch-long rolls. Your 22 dough pieces will be shaped like long, thin pencils.

4 Twist two together to form a twisted rope. Continue until you have eleven twisted ropes.

5 Wrap the ropes around one of the bowls, beginning at the place where the foil touches the bowl.

6 Whenever you start a new rope, pinch together the ends of each rope. Continue wrapping until the whole outside of the bowl is covered with the twisted ropes of dough. At the top (actually the upside-down bottom of the bowl), pinch together the last ends.

Here's how to shape a handle for the basket:

1 You have two dough pieces left over for the basket handle. Roll each one into a 24-inch strip. Twist the two together into a rope.

2 Place this long rope over the other bowl from one side to the other, so that each end touches the foil strip.

Here's how to finish the basket:

1 Cover each basket-bowl with clean dish towels. Let rise in a warm, draft-free place for about 30 minutes, until doubled in thickness.

2 Preheat the oven to 400°F (200°C).

3 With a fork, beat together an egg and 1 tablespoon milk. Carefully brush the mixture over the basket and handle.

4 Carefully place each wire rack directly on the oven racks. That will allow the hot oven air to circulate inside and outside the bowls.

: *Caution: You may need adult*
: *help in placing the wire racks*
: *and aluminum foil in the hot*
: *oven.*

5 Bake for 20 minutes, until your basket is golden brown. Check during the 20-minute baking, and make sure that your basket is browning evenly. If any part seems to be too dark, cover it with aluminum foil to keep it from burning.

6 Remove the basket and handle from the bowls and cool on wire racks.

7 Fasten the handle to the basket with toothpicks or skewers. (Do not try to hold this basket by its handle.)

: NOW YOU HAVE A FINE
: BREAD BASKET.

· · · · · · · · · ·
AN ELEPHANT'S EARS PROJECT
· ·

Sometimes you see elephant's ears for sale at fairs and carnivals as "fried dough." But this dough isn't fried. It's baked. And baking makes elephant's ears all the more delicious (for you, not for the elephant).

Here's what you need:

¼ cup (½ stick) butter or margarine

1 cup all purpose or unbleached flour

3 tablespoons sugar

½ teaspoon baking powder

½ teaspoon salt

⅓ cup milk

3 tablespoons brown sugar, well packed

1 teaspoon cinnamon

Here's how to mix the dough:

1 Place the butter or margarine in a heatproof glass dish. Cover and melt in the microwave oven for about one minute on low power.

2 In a large bowl, combine the flour, sugar, baking powder, and salt.

3 Mix this dough by hand. Stir three tablespoons of the melted butter or margarine into the flour combination. Stir in the milk, and stir until you have a smooth dough.

Here's how to roll the dough:

1 Preheat the oven to 400°F (200°C).

2 Lightly sprinkle a large cutting board with flour. Pat or roll out the dough to a rectangle, about 5 × 9 inches.

3 Brush the remaining tablespoon of butter or margarine onto the rectangle.

4 Combine the brown sugar and cinnamon in a small dish and sprinkle onto the rectangle.

5 Now begin at the narrow end, and roll the rectangle up tightly. Pinch at the end to seal.

6 Using a sharp knife, cut the roll into four pieces.

Here's how to bake the elephant's ears:

1 Place the four circles on a baking sheet. Use your hand to flatten each circle and pat it into shape.

2 Bake for 10 to 12 minutes.

3 Cool on wire racks.

: **NOW YOU HAVE FOUR**
: **ELEPHANT'S EARS.**

A DOUGHY FACE PROJECT

Look back at the braided yeast rolls project in FOODS TO PUNCH, TWIST, SHAPE, AND DESIGN. Here's an easy, funny face you can make from that same dough.

The doughy face uses only about ⅓ of the dough. So you can make a doughy face—and still have dough left over for rolls.

Be especially sure to wash your hands before you shape the face (and the other rolls).

Here's how to make a doughy face:

1 When you have the yeast roll dough risen and ready to shape, begin a doughy face along with the rest of the rolls.

2 The recipe for braided yeast rolls asks you to cut the dough into 24 pieces. Take three of those pieces and form them into one large, round "face."

3 Now take four more pieces of dough. In your fingers, roll each to a nine-inch pencil shape. Twist two shapes together into a sort of braid. Use your fingers to seal the "braids" to the doughy face. Or you can use "braids" to make hair and beard for a Santa Claus roll.

4 Take one more piece of dough. Cut it into small pieces, and use it to form tiny eyes, eyebrows, nose, ears, and mouth. Use very tiny pieces of dough to make bulgy pupils for the eyes. Gently seal the features onto the face, and very carefully place the doughy face on a baking sheet with the other rolls.

5 If you'd like your doughy face to have a dark complexion, brush on melted butter. Or if you'd like a comic look (and a glazed expression), brush melted butter on only the nose and eyeballs.

6 Now let rise and bake along with the other rolls. The fun part is to watch all the features puff up as the rolls bake.

NOW YOU HAVE A FUNNY PUFFY FACE WITH BRAIDS OR BEARD—READY TO ADMIRE AND EAT.

A GINGERBREAD PEOPLE PROJECT

These gingerbread people are good and soft.

Here's what you need for gingerbread people dough:

- ¾ cup (1½ sticks) butter or margarine
- 1 cup molasses
- ½ cup honey
- 1 cup sour milk or buttermilk
- 6½ cups all purpose or unbleached flour
- 2 teaspoons ginger
- 4 teaspoons baking powder
- ¾ teaspoon baking soda
- ½ teaspoon salt
- 1 tablespoon lemon or orange extract

Here's how to mix the dough:

1 Place the butter or margarine in a heatproof glass dish. Cover and microwave on low power for about 70 seconds.

2 In a large bowl, mix the melted butter or margarine, molasses, and honey until smooth. Use a large wooden spoon. Stir in the sour milk or buttermilk.

3 In a separate bowl, combine the flour with the ginger, baking powder, baking soda, and salt. Stir into the butter-molasses mixture.

4 Add the lemon or orange extract and mix until you have a smooth, stiff dough.

Here's how to shape gingerbread people:

1 Preheat the oven to 350°F (180°C).

2 Sprinkle a pastry cloth with flour. Roll out the dough to ¼ inch thick. Cut with floured gingerbread-people cutters.

Here's how to bake and decorate gingerbread people:

1 Before baking, decorate the gingerbread people with raisins, currants, or bits of dried fruit. Very gently push the dried fruit pieces into the cookie dough.

2 Bake on ungreased baking sheets for eight to ten minutes.

3 Mix frosting. Stir together one cup sifted confectioner's sugar with one tablespoon warm milk and ½ teaspoon vanilla extract. If the frosting is too thick, add 1 more tablespoon warm milk.

4 Finish decorating with frosting.

NOW YOU HAVE ABOUT 48 GINGERBREAD PEOPLE.

KITCHEN ART (NOT FOR EATING)

Yₒu can be an artist in the kitchen. Create beautiful ornaments and decorations for almost any holiday or important occasion.

A DOUGH ORNAMENTS PROJECT

You can make your own Christmas tree ornaments. Or create door-knob ornaments for other holidays and for events like birthdays and graduations.

Be sure to write your name and the date on the bottom of each ornament. You'll want to keep these ornaments to show to your grandchildren!

Cooked Dough Ornaments

Cooked dough takes longer to make, but cooked dough is really a great deal better than uncooked. The dough shapes more readily, and the ornaments hold up better.

Here's what you need:

2 cups all purpose or unbleached flour

2 cups water

1 cup salt

2 tablespoons cream of tartar

Food coloring
About 6 loops of string or wire (for hanging the ornaments)

Here's how to fix the dough:

1 In a medium saucepan, mix together the flour, water, salt, and cream of tartar.

2 Heat on medium heat and stir constantly until the mixture is thick and satiny.

3 Let cool to room temperature.

4 Divide your dough into two parts, and place into two plastic bags.

Here are two ways to color the dough:

(1) You decide what food coloring you want to add. Put about ten drops food coloring into each bag. Then squeeze the dough inside the bag until it is evenly colored. You can add more food coloring, two drops at a time, until the color is as deep as you want.

(2) OR leave the dough uncolored, and later you can paint the finished ornaments with tempera or watercolor paints.

DOUGH ORNAMENTS
continued

Here's how to shape the ornaments:

(1) Mold into shapes with your hands.
(2) OR flatten the dough, and cut out the shapes with cookie cutters.
(3) Either, way be sure to mold the dough around a looped string or wire so that you will be able to hang the finished ornament.

Here's how to finish the ornaments:

1 Let the dough ornaments dry thoroughly, 24 hours or so. If the weather is damp and the ornaments are not drying properly, then you may want to dry them in the oven. In that case, dry the ornaments at 200°F (95°C) for 30 minutes.

2 Paint the ornaments with tempera or water colors. (Even if you colored the dough, you may want to paint in details.)

3 If you plan to keep the ornaments for more than a few weeks, finish by brushing them with clear shellac.

Fast Uncooked Dough Ornaments

Use this recipe if you want a simple play dough for little kids.

Here's what you need for uncooked dough ornaments:

2 cups all purpose or unbleached flour

1 cup salt

1 cup water

1 teaspoon vegetable oil

Food coloring

About 6 loops of string or wire (for hanging the ornaments)

Here's how to fix the dough:

1 Stir together the flour, salt, water, and oil.

Hint: *If the dough seems too sticky to handle, add more flour, a tablespoon or two at a time.*

2 Add food coloring a few drops at a time, until you get the right color.

3 Now go ahead with shaping, drying, and painting your ornaments.

NOW YOU HAVE EIGHT TO TWELVE HAND-MADE ORNAMENTS.

AN EGGSHELL ORNAMENTS PROJECT

Every time you use eggs, save the shells, and soon you'll have plenty to make into ornaments. Eggshell ornaments are traditional for celebrating Easter and the arrival of spring.

Here are the supplies you need:

For blowing out the eggshells:
Raw eggs
A short skewer
For each egg color you want:
¾ cup hot water
¼ teaspoon food coloring
1 tablespoon white vinegar

For decorating the eggs:
White glue (plain or fabric-type)
A long tapestry needle
Scraps of fabric, gift wrap, old holiday cards or prints
Rickrack, ribbon, and gold and silver braid
8-inch strands of yarn or fancy twine for each egg ornament

Here's how to blow out the eggs:

1 With a skewer, carefully make a small hole in each end of a fresh egg.
2 Hold the egg over a bowl. Put the egg against your mouth, and blow as hard as you can.
3 The egg will come out of the shell into the bowl. (The eggs are perfectly all right. Save the eggs, and use them.)
4 Let the eggshells drain and dry for half an hour or longer.

Here's how to color the eggs:

1 Use a bowl or cup (such as a custard cup) large enough to hold an egg. Use a separate cup and separate spoon for each color.
2 For each color you want, mix ¾ cup hot water with ¼ teaspoon food coloring and 1 tablespoon white vinegar. If you want a darker shade, stir in more food coloring, one drop at a time.
3 Carefully dip and turn eggshells to get an even color.
4 Let the eggshells dry before you decorate them.

Hint: *You may want to leave some (or all) of the eggs their natural color.*

EGGSHELL ORNAMENTS
continued

Here's how to decorate the eggs:

1 Carefully glue on designs with fabric or plain white glue. Work with cotton swabs or toothpicks, and hold each egg securely in a kitchen towel.

2 Let the glue dry completely before you go on to the next steps.

3 If you're really ambitious, you could fix your eggshell ornaments on a tree. Either use a small plastic tree, or break off a real branch and bring it inside to decorate.

You decide the designs. Of course, all your decorations must be small and light. Here are a few design options:

* Small pictures cut from old holiday cards or gift wrap
* Tiny bows
* Rick rack and ribbon
* Small braiding (available in gold and silver)
* Lace
* Sequins

Here's how to fix the eggshell ornaments for hanging:

1 Thread a tapestry needle with an eight-inch length of yarn or twine.

2 Run the needle up through the center of the egg, from the bottom of the egg to the top and back again, so that you have a loop at the top. At the bottom of the egg, tie the ends and glue the yarn in place. To hold the loop in place at the top, also drop a bit of glue just where the yarn comes through the top hole.

NOW YOU HAVE EGGSHELL ORNAMENTS.

A BIRD NEST PROJECT

You can make these bird nests for Easter, to celebrate the arrival of spring—or just for fun.

Here's what you need:

For the nests:
1 egg white
3 cups sifted confectioner's sugar
1 tablespoon milk or light cream
Food coloring

For the grass:
1 cup grated coconut
1 teaspoon water
Green food coloring

Here's how to make the bird nests:

1 In the small bowl of an electric mixer, beat the egg white at high speed until it is stiff.

2 Gradually add three cups sifted confectioner's sugar and one tablespoon milk or light cream. Keep beating.

3 Work food coloring into the dough, two or three drops at a time, until you get the best color. If you want two or more colors, divide the dough, and use a separate bowl to stir in each color.

4 Let the dough dry, uncovered, for 30 minutes.

5 Work with the dough until you have shapes you like for nests and baskets.

Now make the nest grass:

6 You can make this in a jar. Place one cup grated coconut, one teaspoon water, and five or six drops of green food coloring in the jar. Cover the jar tightly and shake, shake, shake.

Finish the bird nests:

7 Place the green coconut on top of the nest. Let dry for half an hour or so.

A JACK-O'-LANTERN STORY

Jack was an Irishman who was afraid of nobody.

To prove how brave he was, one night Jack invited the devil to have a drink with him at the local tavern. The devil is always on the lookout for a soul to snatch, so he was eager to accept Jack's offer.

But when the time came to pay for the drinks, Jack pleaded with the devil to turn himself into a sixpence coin. The devil obliged.

But as soon as the devil turned himself into a sixpence coin, Jack popped him into his pocket and refused to let him out.

Why didn't the devil just turn himself back into a devil, you may ask? Well, the devil couldn't do that because all Irish sixpence coins have a sign of the cross on them, and the devil can't move past a cross.

Soon the devil cried and whined and begged Jack to let him go.

Jack was a man who knew how to drive a good bargain. He told the devil he would let him go if the devil promised to leave him (and his soul) alone for a whole year. The devil agreed, and Jack had a happy, devil-may-care year.

But of course, at the end of the year, the devil came to grab Jack's soul.

Jack cheerfully told the devil that he'd be glad to go with him, but that he was very, very hungry. The devil rather likes to carry away a fat, well-fed soul, so he climbed right up an apple tree to get Jack one last apple.

Naturally, since he was dealing with clever Jack, climbing that tree was a big mistake. Jack quickly carved a cross on the trunk of the tree, and the devil didn't dare climb down.

Why didn't the devil just change himself into a bird, you may ask? We don't know. Maybe birds have souls too good for the devil.

This time Jack forced the devil to promise that he would leave him alone for ten long years. Jack went off, hoping for ten years of peace and quiet.

Unfortunately, before the ten years were over, Jack died. Now he couldn't go to heaven. And the devil couldn't take him.

Poor Jack is condemned to roam the earth forever, lighting his way with a burning coal inside a pumpkin.

And so that was the first Jack-o'-Lantern.

A JACK-O'-LANTERN PROJECT

You can make a fine traditional Jack-o'-lantern—or a different sort of Halloween pumpkin.

Here's how to pick a pumpkin in the first place:

Pick a pumpkin that's bright orange, without too many blemishes, and heavy for its size.

Here's how to cut a pumpkin face:

1 Use a long sharp knife to cut the top opening. Remember that the opening must be large enough for your hand to fit in—but small enough that it doesn't cut into the places where you will want to cut pumpkin eyes.

> *Caution: You need adult help with cutting.*

2 Scoop out the pumpkin pulp. Scrape the inside of the pumpkin. Patience! Cleaning out a pumpkin is a lot of work. When you are finished, be sure to clean up.

3 Draw ideas on paper before you cut the pumpkin face.

Here are guidelines for the pumpkin face:

1 Keep the design simple and easy to cut.

2 Don't cut too near the bottom of the pumpkin.

3 Think about how the candle will shine through. Big features look good because they let through more light.

4 But leave space between the features. You don't want them to cut into each other. The features need to be big but not too big.

Here's how to light your pumpkin:

1 Use short, fat, casserole-type candles.

Suggestion: *The record-holding world's largest pumpkin was grown by Robert Gancarz in 1986. That pumpkin weighed 671 pounds. You'll probably want something slightly smaller.*

> *Warning:* Take this job outside, and put down lots of newspapers. This job is messy!

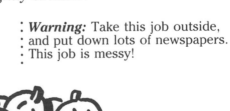

JACK-O'-LANTERN
continued

2 To create a place to stick your candle inside the pumpkin, try a glob of play dough at the bottom of the pumpkin.

3 OR light a candle, and hold it over the pumpkin so that the wax melts and creates a sticky place.

4 OR cut a candle-sized hole all the way through the bottom of the pumpkin.

> *Caution: You need adult help with lighting the candle inside the pumpkin.*

> **NOW YOU HAVE A TRADITIONAL HALLOWEEN JACK-O'-LANTERN.**

If you want a different sort of Jack-o'-lantern, here are six other ways to decorate the pumpkin face:

1. Cut two faces, one on each side.

2. Instead of cutting a pumpkin face, paint on a pumpkin face. The pumpkin will last longer when it's not cut. (But, of course, you won't be able to light it with candles.)

3. Dress up your pumpkin with vegetables (and other funny stuff):

For eyes: apples, cranberries, marshmallows, mushrooms, potato pieces

For nose: carrot, celery stalk, cucumber

For mouth: beans, carrot, celery

For teeth: candy corn, corn kernels, cranberries

For ears: apple halves, paper cups, potato halves

For eyebrows, eyelashes, hair, beard, mustache: apple peels, celery leaves, chow mein noodles, crepe paper, lettuce leaves, macaroni, orange peels, pipecleaners, spaghetti

For glasses and pipes: pipecleaners

For hats: crepe paper, a knitted cap

4. Dress up your pumpkin face with clay or play dough.

5. Dress up your pumpkin with paper ties, ruffles, and hats.

> *Caution: If you dress your pumpkin in paper, you can't light candles in it. But on a painted, uncut pumpkin, paper decorations look impressive.*

6. Make a pumpkin person. Stuff old clothes with newspapers or rags, and seat them under a pumpkin head. You don't necessarily need to create a bum. Try dressing a pumpkin head as Dracula—or see if you can dress a pumpkin person in a Halloween costume like your own.

> *Another Caution: If your pumpkin is anywhere near paper or rags, you can't light a candle in it.*

> **NOW YOU HAVE A DIFFERENT SORT OF JACK-O'-LANTERN.**

A MICROWAVE FLOWER DRYING PROJECT

When you pick flowers, don't let them wilt away. Instead, put your microwave oven to use.

You need to allow three to five days between the time you dry the flowers and the time you fix them for arranging.

Here are the supplies you need:

Garden or wild flowers (fresh, firm, and about half open)

Silica gel (available at florists and hobby shops)

Cardboard shoeboxes (with no metal staples)

Toothpicks

Metal or plastic containers with lids

Florist's wire (available at florists)

Florist's tape (available at florists)

A soft artist's brush

Aerosal hair spray or artist's fixative spray

Hint: *The hair spray is safer and less potentially toxic than the artist's fixative. Whichever you use, be sure you do not aim at yourself or at another person, and make sure you are in a well ventilated room. (Or take this job outside.) Non-aerosol spray is too heavy for this use.*

Here's how to dry flowers:

1 Pour about two inches of silica gel into the bottom of a shoebox.

2 Cut flower stems to a length of two inches.

3 Insert flower stems into the silica gel, right side up and so they don't touch each other or the sides of the box. Gently use a toothpick to separate the petals.

. . . .

MICROWAVE FLOWER DRYING
continued

4 Slowly and gently, sift the silica gel to cover the flowers. Use a toothpick to work the silica gel in between the petals. You want to be sure that all parts of the flower are in contact with the silica gel. Gently tap the edge of the box to be sure the grains of gel settle around all of the flower parts.

5 Place the container of flowers into the microwave oven. Set a cup of water in with the container. (The water keeps the flowers from becoming brittle.)

6 Use high power to dry the flowers.

Here's how long to dry each type of flower:

Daisies . . . . . 3 minutes
Roses . . . . . . 1½ minutes
Violets . . . . . 2½ to 3 minutes
Pansies . . . . 2½ to 3 minutes
Carnations . . 1 minute
Daffodils . . . 2½ minutes
Asters . . . . . . 2½ minutes

7 Leave the box in the microwave overnight so as not to disturb the gel's contact with the flowers. The best time to dry flowers is in the evening when the microwave oven is not needed for cooking. It's important not to disturb the flowers until they have set.

8 The next morning, check for dryness by carefully removing enough gel so that you can touch the petals. If the petals are not completely dry, cover them with gel again, and reheat on high power for one minute.

9 When the flowers are dry, carefully pour off the gel crystals. When you have poured off all that you can, carefully remove each flower. Slide two fingers under the flower. Lift it and very gently shake it to get rid of excess crystals.

10 Place the flowers in a dry container (metal or plastic) with about an inch of silica gel in the bottom. Just insert the stems in the gel, and let the flowers sit on top of the gel. Cover with a tight lid and leave for two to five days.

Here's how to prepare the flowers for arranging:

1 When the two to five days of waiting have passed, use a soft artist's brush to brush off the remaining crystals of silica gel.

2 Cut a piece of florist's wire. With floral tape, bind each flower to the wire. Stretch and wind the tape around the base of the flower and down the wire.

3 Spray the flowers lightly with aerosol hair spray or with artist's fixative.

NOW YOU'RE READY TO MAKE FLOWER ARRANGEMENTS WITH YOUR OWN DRIED FLOWERS.

HOLIDAY SURPRISES

Some holiday foods are supposed to bring you holiday good luck. Some are supposed to tell you about why we celebrate the holiday. Some are just for fun.

This year you might even try celebrating some holidays you've never celebrated before.

BEGIN YOUR NEW YEAR WITH SPECIAL FOODS

New Year's Day is not always January 1st. People around the world celebrate new year at different times. But they always celebrate with special foods.

Long ago, the Seminoles of ancient Florida celebrated their New Year in midsummer when the corn harvest came in. Their year began when they once again had fresh foods to eat.

Just as long ago in Europe, New Year's arrived in April with the first warm spring air.

On Chinese New Year, usually in February, the Chinese smeared honey on their paper pictures of the gods so that when the gods went up to heaven to report, they would have only sweet things to say about the people here below.

Rosh Hashanah, the Jewish New Year, falls in September. Rosh Hashanah is a time for sweet foods (carrot coins and apples dipped in honey) and a time to wish friends a sweet New Year.

Scottish children celebrate Hogmanay, the last day of the old year, by going door to door collecting fruit and nuts and special coins from their neighbors. Hogmanay for Scottish children is a bit like trick-or-treating at Halloween is for us.

In the American South, children used to hop around the table at New Year's (and sometimes still do). Then they sat down to eat cornbread and "Hoppin' John," a dish of dried red peas, rice, and ham.

The French eat pancakes for New Year's.

The Swiss eat whipped cream for good luck.

The English drink a wassail.

What will you make for your good luck New Year's food?

· · · · · · · · · ·

A VALENTINE STORY

· ·

Legends tell of eight saints named Valentine, and Valentine's day honors all of them.

The most famous of the Valentines, however, is Bishop Valentine of Interamna.

Bishop Valentine lived in the third century, during the decline and before the fall of the Roman Empire, when people (at least according to some of the stories) were not really civilized.

The Roman emperor at the time, Claudius II, was particularly uncivilized. He wanted his people to think only of war and never of love.

He wanted the men of his empire to be soldiers, not sweethearts—and certainly not husbands or fathers.

And so he issued orders forbidding marriages. The cruel emperor made even the mere thought of love against the law.

Bishop Valentine took pity on the lovers of the time (for there were still a few good people around). He even performed secret marriage ceremonies for them.

For the crime of encouraging love, the emperor threw Bishop Valentine into prison.

There are several stories about the months Bishop Valentine spent in prison. Perhaps he was a very old man at the time, and the jailer's daughter was kind to him.

Or perhaps Valentine was a young man, and perhaps he fell in love with the jailer's daughter.

In some stories, the jailer's daughter is blind, and so she loves Valentine with her heart, even though she cannot see him.

In some of the stories, Valentine cures her, and she can see again.

But in the end, the cruel emperor condemns Valentine to death, and the two friends are torn apart.

On that last morning, Valentine writes a love letter and signs it, "From your V."

Valentine's letter is the first Valentine.

And the day that poor Valentine died might have been February 14th in the year 269 A.D.

Now Valentine's Day is a good time for a marriage proposal, a wedding, or maybe just a paper Valentine or a candy kiss. And today Valentine's Day is not only for sweethearts but for family and friends.

Bishop Valentine would not have wanted it any other way.

Who is your Valentine?

A FROZEN YOGURT VALENTINE SURPRISE PROJECT

For your Valentine, try a meringue shell filled with frozen strawberry yogurt. You'll need a heart-shaped cake pan for the meringue shell—or else small heart-shaped molds. Or you can shape the meringue yourself.

Here's what you need for the meringue shell:

3 egg whites, room temperature

¼ teaspoon cream of tartar

¼ teaspoon salt

¾ cup sugar

1 to 2 drops red food coloring (if you want a pink meringue shell)

Here's how to make the meringue shell:

1 Preheat the oven to 275°F (135°C).

2 Use butter or margarine to lightly grease the bottom and sides of a heart-shaped cake pan. Or you can use about eight small heart-shaped molds.

3 Use an electric mixer to beat the meringue. In the small mixer bowl, beat the egg whites at high speed with the cream of tartar and salt. Your mixture is ready when you see soft peaks form. If you want a pink meringue, this is the time to mix in one or two drops of red food coloring.

Hint: To get the egg whites to room temperature in just minutes, set a small bowl of egg whites into a larger bowl of warm water.

4 Gradually beat in the sugar, two tablespoons at a time. Beat well after each addition. Continue beating until stiff peaks form.

5 Spread about ⅔ of the meringue on the bottom of the heart-shaped cake pan. Use the remaining third to fill around the sides of the pan. Or divide the meringue among the small heart-shaped molds.

6 Bake for one hour.

7 Cool in the pans.

· · · · · · · · · ·
FROZEN YOGURT VALENTINE SURPRISE
continued

Here's what to do if you want to shape the meringue yourself:

1 You'll need heavy brown wrapping paper or brown paper bags (the kind you get at the grocery store). Cut the paper to fit two baking sheets.

2 Use a pencil to draw eight outlines of hearts, about four inches across and three inches apart, on the paper.

3 Spoon heaping tablespoons of meringue directly onto the brown paper, in the center of each of the hearts. Form eight mounds.

4 Use the back of a spoon to push down the center of each meringue mound. Then follow your heart outline, and use a knife and spoon to form each mound into a heart shape.

5 Bake for one hour.

6 Turn off the oven, and let the meringues remain in the oven until they are cool.

Frozen Strawberry Yogurt
Here's all you need:

4 cups strawberry yogurt
OR
4 cups plain yogurt plus ½ cup strawberry all-fruit spread

Topping of ¾ cup fresh or frozen strawberries

1 Use four cups of strawberry yogurt. OR begin with four cups of plain yogurt, and stir in ½ cup strawberry all-fruit spread.

2 Freeze the yogurt in an airtight container until firm.

3 OR make frozen yogurt in an ice cream maker. Mix and crank according to the instructions that come with the machine.

4 Just before serving, scoop frozen strawberry yogurt into the meringue.

5 If you wish, top with fresh strawberries (if you have any fresh strawberries in February), or use packaged frozen strawberries. Let the frozen strawberries thaw before you use them.

> **NOW YOU HAVE A BEAUTIFUL FROZEN YOGURT SURPRISE FOR VALENTINE'S DAY.**

Serve to your Valentine immediately.

VALENTINE DREADFULS

Is Valentine's Day only for love and kindness?

Sometimes Valentine Day can get nasty.

The decade of the 1870s was a time when you could find real lace Valentines. Or you could buy your sweetheart a "mechanical" Valentine, the type that today we call "pop-up" cards. Some of these gorgeous Valentines were so splendid that now they are displayed on the walls of museums.

Then a New York printer, John McLaughlin, decided to turn Valentine's Day around, from love to hate.

With the help of cartoonist Charles Howard, he invented the first insult Valentine cards. He called them "vinegar Valentines," and he sold them (on cheap paper) for only a penny apiece.

The other name for the cards was "penny dreadfuls," because they really were dreadful.

The rude Valentines were immensely popular. People liked to insult their enemies and tease their friends—and often they did it without signing their names to the cards.

Kids used them to hassle their teachers. You wouldn't have wanted to be an unmarried teacher in those days. Every Valentine's Day, your students would let you know all about how you were too ugly for marriage—and too stupid to lead a classroom.

More than a hundred years have passed, but vinegar Valentines are always around, in one form or another.

And now they cost a lot more than a penny.

A President's Day Non-Story

When George Washington was a little boy, he took his shiny little hatchet, and he chopped down his father's favorite cherry tree.

His angry father roared, "Who did this deed?"

And perfect little Georgie replied, "I did it, Father, with my own little axe. I cannot tell a lie."

Did this really happen? Could such a boy grow up to become the much-loved first president of the United States?

Take heart. The story is a lie.

Mason Locke Weems (usually called Parson Weems, because he claimed to have been Washington's clergyman in Virginia) made up the story and then wrote it as if it were real.

He knew it wasn't true. He just thought it might be the sort of thing we'd like to hear about the first president.

So now we fix up cherries on Presidents' Day just for fun.

These days, Presidents' Day is not only to celebrate George Washington's birthday. (George Washington was born on February 22nd in 1732.)

Now we celebrate Presidents' Day on the third Monday in February for all the presidents of the United States.

Who is your favorite president?

Most kids in surveys say that their favorite president is John F. Kennedy or Abraham Lincoln.

In whatever year people ask kids about their favorite president, a close second is always the current president. Presidents Reagan and Bush are among the favorites.

And small children often like President Teddy Roosevelt when they hear that teddy bears were named after him.

Take a survey yourself, and see who the favorite presidents are now.

And enjoy a spectacular cherry dessert in honor of all our favorite presidents.

A VERY CAREFUL FLAMING CHERRIES JUBILEE PROJECT FOR PRESIDENTS' DAY

In honor of your favorite presidents, fix a cherry dessert and scoop on your favorite ice cream. Then make it all light up.

Here's what you need:

½ cup sliced almonds

½ cup cherry preserves

⅛ teaspoon cinnamon

Almond or orange extract

6 sugar cubes

Ice cream **(You decide your favorite ice cream for Presidents' Day.)**

Here's what you do:

1 Toast the sliced almonds in a skillet over medium heat. Stir until lightly browned. Or toast in the microwave oven on high power for 1½ minutes. Set aside.

2 Melt the cherry preserves in a small, heavy saucepan over low heat. Stir frequently. Or melt them in the microwave oven on high power for two minutes.

3 Mix in the cinnamon.

: *Caution: You need adult help*
: *with the rest of the project.*

4 Pour almond or orange extract over the sugar cubes. Use about one teaspoon per sugar cube.

5 Dish out scoops of ice cream in six dessert bowls.

6 Pour the hot cherry preserves mixture over the ice cream (about 1½ tablespoons for each).

7 Sprinkle with toasted almonds.

8 Place an extract-soaked sugar cube on top of each serving of ice cream.

9 Have an adult light each sugar cube with a match.

10 Serve your spectacular flaming dessert immediately.

: **NOW YOU HAVE SIX**
: **SERVINGS OF A VERY**
: **CAREFUL FLAMING CHERRY**
: **JUBILEE DESSERT FOR**
: **PRESIDENTS' DAY.**

Perhaps a future president would like to try some.

. . . .

St. Patrick

. . . .

Did you know that St. Patrick was not Irish?

St. Patrick came from Scotland.

Patrick was a wealthy teenager in Scotland when his troubles began (that would have been about the year 400 A.D.), and at that time his name was "Maewyn Succat."

When Maewyn Succat was 16 years old, Irish pirates arrived in primitive cowhide boats. They captured the poor boy and took him away to Ireland to sell him as a slave.

Back then, the Irish people were ignorant, savage, and miserably poor.

St. Patrick lived through slavery, and eventually he escaped.

But he decided to return. The Irish people needed his help. In dreams, they called to him to come back.

He came back, as they had hoped, and he brought glorious things to the Irish people. For 30 years, St. Patrick worked in Ireland. He taught Christianity. He founded a new kind of farming so that the Irish people were no longer so poor. He taught the Irish people to read and write and to create works of art and poetry and music.

(He may have died on March 17th about the year 463 A.D.)

Along with all his good works, St. Patrick may have driven the snakes out—along with the toads and what the ancient Irish people remembered as "disgusting blind worms."

At least, that's what the storytellers say. And it is true that Ireland has no snakes.

Except perhaps just one. Irish legend has it that one monster serpent is left swimming forever in a deep mountain lake.

St. Patrick was so busy throwing smaller snakes out of Ireland that he had to tell the monster to wait. He just didn't have time, and he told the monster he would get around to banishing him "tomorrow."

And now in Ireland, on a very spooky evening, sometimes, from a distant lake, you can hear a monster wailing, "Is it tomorrow yet?"

A GREEN MILKSHAKE PROJECT FOR ST. PATRICK'S DAY

This milkshake is just right for St. Patrick's Day because it's just naturally green.

Here's what you need:

- 1 cup honeydew melon or kiwi fruit, cut up
- ½ cup milk
- 1 tablespoon lemon juice
- 1 to 2 tablespoons sugar (if you want)
- 2 large scoops lime sherbet

Here's how to shake up your milkshake:

1 In a blender, combine the melon or kiwi fruit pieces, milk, lemon juice, and sugar (if you want). Cover, and blend on high speed for ten seconds.

2 Turn the blender down to lowest speed. Remove the cover, and with the blender still running, add the two scoops lime sherbet. Blend until thick and smooth.

3 Pour into frosted glasses, and serve immediately.

> NOW YOU HAVE TWO TALL
> FROSTY GLASSES OF GREEN
> MILKSHAKE FOR ST.
> PATRICK'S DAY.

. . . .

THE STORY OF RACING PANCAKES

. . . .

In the Middle Ages, Lent meant giving up favorite foods. For all of the forty days before Easter, Christian people ate no meat, no eggs, and no butter.

Naturally, just before Lent began every year, the people were eager to use up their rich food—and they always wanted a last good carnival.

(In fact, the word "carnival" comes from the Latin words, "carne" and "vale." Put the two words together, and they mean "Farewell, meat.")

The very last day before Lent is always a Tuesday. The French call the day "Mardi Gras."

(That translates to "Fat Tuesday," and that's when Carnival is going on in New Orleans every year.)

The English call the day "Shrove Tuesday," because on this day people often go to church to "shrive"—or confess—their sins.

That's where the story begins.

In Olney, England, long ago in 1445, a Christian cook was making pancakes on Shrove Tuesday. She needed to use up all the butter in the house before Lent began.

Suddenly, the church bells rang, and the good woman realized that she was late for church.

She dashed out the door and ran all the way to the church—still holding her skillet of pancakes.

Now women in Olney carry on the tradition. Each runner must wear a dress (no slacks or shorts), an apron, a scarf, and a hat. Each must carry a skillet, and, as she runs, she has to succeed in flipping a pancake at least three times.

Occasionally, women from the United States challenge the women of Olney.

The prize can be a prayer book, a blessing from the vicar and perhaps a kiss from some high official—or a trophy shaped like a frying pan.

If you want, you can make racing pancakes without racing all the way to church.

. . . .
A RACING PANCAKES PROJECT FOR LENT
. . . .

Some people can flip pancakes in the air (even while racing to church). We don't recommend it, though.

Here's what you need:

2 cups all purpose or unbleached flour

2 tablespoons sugar

1 teaspoon baking soda

1 teaspoon salt

2 eggs

2 cups buttermilk
(OR substitute 4 tablespoons dry buttermilk powder and 2 cups water)

2 tablespoons melted butter, margarine, or vegetable oil

Here's how to make your racing pancakes:

1 In a large bowl, mix together the flour, sugar, baking soda, and salt.

2 In a separate bowl, beat the eggs slightly. Add the buttermilk (or dry buttermilk powder and water) along with the melted butter, margarine, or oil.

3 Pour the egg mixture into the flour mixture. Stir just until moistened. The batter will be slightly lumpy.

4 Lightly grease a griddle. Heat until drops of water thrown off your fingertips dance over the surface.

5 Use a ¼-cup measure to dip the batter. Pour it on the griddle. Cook each pancake until bubbles appear and break. Turn over and cook until golden.

6 Serve with butter and syrup.

Here's how to make blueberry pancakes:

For a change, just add 1 cup fresh or frozen blueberries to the pancake batter. Then, if you want, you can serve the pancakes with blueberry syrup.

> **NOW YOU HAVE ABOUT 12**
> **LARGE RACING PANCAKES**
> **TO SERVE ON SHROVE**
> **TUESDAY, BEFORE RACES,**
> **OR JUST ABOUT ANY TIME.**

. . . .
BAD HAMAN, GOOD HATS
. . . .

Haman had a fine hat. The hat was so big that he could keep things in it, as if it were a pocket.

When we bake Haman's hat cookies for Purim, we make them with three corners because Haman's hat had three corners.

Now, Haman was a thoroughly, completely, totally, absolutely bad man.

Whenever you hear Haman's name, we want you to imagine making as much noise as possible, just to show how very bad a man Haman was. You might hiss and boo. You might stomp your feet and whirl a noisemaker.

Haman's hat cookies and all that noise are part of celebrating Purim.

Purim comes in late February or early March. In the Jewish calendar, that's the 14th or 15th day of Adar.

Purim celebrates the downfall of the evil Haman. Here's how it came about.

Haman was the adviser to the great Biblical king and queen of Persia, King Ahasuerus and Queen Esther.

Haman often spent his time telling the king bad and false tales about the Jewish people of the kingdom. And he often bragged to the king of his own importance.

Finally, Haman became so convinced of his own importance that he ordered everyone in the kingdom to bow to him whenever he appeared.

As you can imagine, no one wanted to bow to Haman. One of the Jewish men, Mordecai, was brave enough to tell Haman that he would never bow to him.

Haman turned purple with rage.

He decided to kill Mordecai and all the other Jewish people by drawing lots from his hat. The Hebrew word for "lots" is Purim, and of course, that's how the holiday got its name.

Now Haman was not the wise man that he thought he was, because he didn't know two important facts.

He didn't know that Queen Esther was Jewish.

And he didn't know that Mordecai was Queen Esther's cousin.

. . . .

BAD HAMAN, GOOD HATS
continued

Queen Esther waited for the day the lots had determined. She prepared a grand feast for the king, and she waited until the king was in a very good mood—and until Haman was chortling and gloating over his evil plans.

Then she gently let the king know that, all along, Haman had been telling lies about the Jewish people, and that Mordecai no more deserved to die than Esther herself—for, she declared to her husband, she herself was Jewish.

King Ahasuerus listened with astonishment. But King Ahasuerus loved his queen, and he realized that he had been worng.

The king ordered Haman put to death that very day.

So, in the end, the day that Haman foretold for others to die was the day of his own death.

And all they had left of him (and all they wanted left of him) was his hat.

You don't have to wait until Purim to bake a few delicious Haman's hats.

A Haman's Hat Project for Purim

Here's what you need for Haman's hats:

For the dough:
- ½ cup (1 stick) butter or margarine
- ½ cup sugar
- ½ cup brown sugar, well packed
- 2 eggs
- 1 teaspoon vanilla extract
- 2½ cups all purpose or unbleached flour
- 1 teaspoon baking powder
- ½ teaspoon baking soda
- ½ teaspoon salt

For the filling:
- 6-ounce can of filling or 4-ounce jar of preserves
  (You decide what sort of filling. Traditional choices are prune filling, poppy seed filling, plum filling, or apricot or cherry preserves. We recommend all-fruit spreads.)
- 2 teaspoons grated lemon peel
- ¼ cup ground walnuts or pecans (if you wish)

Here's how to mix the dough:

1 In a large mixer bowl, cream together butter or margarine, sugar, and brown sugar.

2 Beat in eggs and vanilla.

3 In a separate bowl, combine the flour, baking powder, baking soda, and salt.

4 Now gradually beat the dry ingredients into the butter-sugar mixture. Beat until smooth.

Here's how to finish Haman's hats:

1 Preheat the oven to 350°F (180°C).

2 Lightly sprinkle a pastry cloth with flour. Roll the dough out until the dough is very thin, about ⅛ inch.

3 Cut a 4-inch circle for each cookie.

Hint: If you don't have a four-inch cookie cutter, use the rim of a big glass or of an empty coffee can.

4 Stir together a can of filling or a jar of preserves with grated lemon peel and ground walnuts or pecans (if you wish).

5 Place a heaping teaspoon of filling into the center of each cookie. Gently fold up two sides, and pull the third side across in a triangular shape. Pinch the edges together.

6 Carefully lift the cookies onto lightly greased baking sheets, and line them up about one inch apart.

7 Bake for 12 to 15 minutes, until they are golden brown.

8 Cool on a wire rack.

Now You Have About 20 Haman's Hats.

THE STORY OF PASSOVER

In ancient times, more than 3,000 years ago, the Jewish people were slaves in Egypt.

For centuries, the slaves had built pyramids for the pharaohs of Egypt.

The time of liberation came at last.

From a burning bush, God appeared to Moses. The time had come for Moses to lead his people out of Egypt.

Pharaoh would not let the people go, and so God struck Egypt with plagues, each plague more dreadful than the last. Locusts and frogs descended on Egypt. Fire and hailstorms destroyed the land.

Finally, Moses told Pharaoh that the worse plague of all was arriving. The Angel of Death would kill all the first-born sons of Egypt.

The Jewish people, however, were spared.

Each Jewish household sacrificed a lamb and sprinkled its blood on their doorposts, so that the Angel of Death would "pass over" those families and spare their children. (That's how Passover is named.)

Pharaoh's own first-born son died, and, in despair, Pharaoh let the Jewish people free.

The Jewish people knew that Pharaoh would soon change his mind and send his soldiers to capture them again. So they left in a great hurry.

God parted the waters of the Red Sea so that the people could escape— and Pharaoh's soldiers came thundering through. But the waters closed again. The soldiers perished. And the Jewish people were free at last.

Passover is a time to remember the exodus from Egypt and a time to celebrate freedom. And because Passover falls in March or April (the 15th to 22nd days of Nisan in the Jewish Calendar), Passover is also a time to celebrate the arrival of spring.

A Charoses Project for Passover

At the seder dinners of Passover, each food is symbolic of the freeing of the Jewish people. Charoses are symbolic of the mortar that the slaves used to build the pharaoh's pyramids. They do taste much better than mortar. You can make your own charoses for Passover this spring.

Here's what you need for charoses:

- ½ cup walnuts
- 1 apple
- ¼ cup raisins
- ¼ teaspoon cinnamon
- ⅛ teaspoon ginger
- 3 tablespoons Passover grape juice

Here's how to make charoses by hand:

1 Chop the walnuts (or buy them already chopped). Peel, core, and chop the apple into very small bits. Chop the raisins.

> : *Caution: You need adult help*
> : *with chopping.*

2 Stir together the chopped walnuts, chopped apple, chopped raisins, cinnamon, ginger, and Passover grape juice.

3 Chill in the refrigerator.

Here's how to make charoses in a food processor:

1 Put the walnuts in the food processor, and process them just until they are chopped. Take the walnuts out and get ready to chop the apple.

2 Peel, core, and cut the apple into small pieces. Process for one or two seconds until they are chopped. (Do not process long enough to make applesauce.) Take the apple pieces out and get ready to chop the raisins.

3 Process the raisins for a few seconds until they are chopped. (Do not make raisin juice!)

4 Add the chopped walnuts, chopped apple pieces, cinnamon, ginger, and Passover grape juice. Process for just a few seconds until you have a paste.

5 Chill in the refrigerator.

> : Now You Have About 1½
> : Cups Of Your Own
> : Passover Charoses.

Serve on matzoh.

. . . .

APRIL FOOLS DAY

. . . .

April Fools Day used to be New Year's Day.

There was a time when New Year's Day fell in the spring, just about April 1st. More than four hundred years ago, however, King Charles IX of France decided to change the calendar. Along with other changes, King Charles moved New Year's to January 1st, where it has stayed every since.

But back then people still remembered the old New Year's Day, and now the old holiday seemed a fine joke, a good time for a silly celebration.

What's the funniest April Fools joke you've every seen?

We found some old stories of April Fools jokes from times past.

Often the old tricks involved ridiculous errands. The tricksters tried to convince someone to run to the bookstore for a copy of *The Life and Adventures of Eve's Grandmother*. Or they sent someone to hunt for the gowp (another word for fool, so the person was really hunting for himself—or herself).

Sometimes the old tricks involved unappetizing foods. Tricksters lined doughnuts with wool, or filled a sugar bowl with salt.

Remember that even on April Fools Day, no one dares play tricks on a cook. There's an old proverb about that: "Only a fool argues with a skunk, a mule, or a cook."

AN APRIL FOOLS ORANGE CUSTARD "FOOL" PROJECT

In England, the word "fool" used to mean a stewed fruit and custard dessert—stewed and soft like the brain of a fool.

This April Fools Day dessert is a kind of "fool"—very delicious, not a trick to eat at all.

But since this "fool" has no eggs, it is not a true custard. Gelatin is the thickener. April Fool—sort of!

Here's what you need:

1½ cups orange juice
* 1 envelope unflavored gelatin*
* 2 tablespoons sugar*
* 1 cup whipping cream*
A small orange

Here's how to mix the fool:

1 Measure ½ cup orange juice into a heatproof glass bowl. Sprinkle the gelatin over the orange juice. Microwave for 30 seconds or more on high power until the gelatin is dissolved.

2 Stir in the sugar. Add the remaining cup of orange juice and stir thoroughly.

3 Refrigerate for about 30 minutes until the mixture is partly set, and a little dropped from a spoon forms a soft mound.

4 In the small bowl of an electric mixer, whip the cream until it forms soft peaks.

5 Gently fold the whipped cream into the orange juice mixture.

6 Pour the folded mixture into a mold or bowl. Refrigerate for at least one hour, until set.

Here's how to unmold and serve the fool:

1 To unmold, set the mold or bowl into a pan of warm water for two or three minutes. Wipe the outside dry.

2 Turn out onto a platter.

3 Garnish the fool with orange twists. Make orange twists by slicing a whole unpeeled orange crosswise. Cut more than halfway through each slice and twist the slice.

NOW YOU HAVE FOUR LARGE OR SIX SMALL SERVINGS OF ORANGE FOOL.

HOW TO FIGURE EASTER

Easter falls on a different date every year.

How can you tell when next Easter will be? Here's how:

1 Look at a calendar and find the spring equinox. That will be March 20 or 21.

2 Find the first full moon due after the spring equinox.

3 The next Sunday after that full moon is Easter Sunday.

Easter is always on a Sunday, and Easter is always sometime between March 22 and April 25. (But there are other complications. Some Eastern Christians celebrate Easter along with Passover. So there are really two Easters every year, somewhere or other in the world.)

AN EASTER EGGS PROJECT

If you want to make a very special Easter eggs bread, keep the eggs uncooked. If you want to roll, hide, hunt, and play games with Easter eggs, you'll be much happier with hard-cooked eggs.

You can color and decorate them the same either way. You just need to be extra careful with the raw eggs.

Here's what you need:

For the Easter eggs:

12 hard-cooked or uncooked eggs, in their shells

For each egg color you want:

¾ cup hot water

1 tablespoon white vinegar

Food coloring

Here's how to color the eggs:

1 Use a bowl or cup large enough to hold an egg. Use a separate cup and separate spoon for each color.

2 For each color you want, mix ¾ cup hot water with three or four drops food coloring and the white vinegar. If you want a darker shade, stir in more food coloring, one drop at a time.

3 Carefully dip and turn the egg to get an even color.

4 Let the eggs dry before you decorate them.

Suggestion: *For ideas on how to decorate Easter eggs, look back at the eggshell ornaments project in KITCHEN ART.*

Important: *If you plan to eat the hard-cooked Easter eggs, keep them in the refrigerator when you're not hiding and seeking and otherwise enjoying them.*

NOW YOU HAVE A DOZEN COLORED EASTER EGGS.

Use them for Easter fun, games, decoration, and egg salad. Or use your eggs for the Very Special Easter Eggs Bread on page 205.

EASTER FOOD TALES

Eat eggs at Easter, and you are celebrating new life at spring—and ancient superstition says that if you eat an egg at Easter, all the next year no snake will bite you.

Eat cake or candy bunnies at Easter, and you are reminding us that, like the rabbit, we are frail and need God to help us.

Eat pretzels at Easter, and you are recalling two arms crossed in prayer at Easter. (The original word for "pretzel" meant two arms.)

Eat pastry or candy lambs at Easter and you are reminding us of the sacrificial lamb of the Jewish Passover and that Jesus was crucified and arose during the Passover season in Israel.

Eat hot cross buns in the weeks before Easter, and you are reminding us of the Passover cakes and of the cross of Jesus. And ancient superstition says that is you eat hot cross buns at Lent, all year long your house will be safe from fire.

A Very Special Easter Eggs Bread Project

This is a gorgeous bread with Easter eggs nestled in it. Be sure to leave enough time for the bread to rise and bake.

Here's what you need for Easter eggs bread:

For the Easter eggs:
12 uncooked, dyed Easter eggs
For the bread:
½ cup milk
½ cup sugar
1 teaspoon salt
½ cup (1 stick) butter or margarine
2 tablespoons grated lemon peel
5 teaspoons (or 2 envelopes) dry yeast
½ cup very warm water
2 eggs, at room temperature
About 4½ cups all purpose or unbleached flour
For glaze and decoration:
1 egg, beaten
Colored nonpareils

Here's how to mix the dough:

1 Pour the milk into a large, heatproof glass dish. Cover and heat at high power in the microwave for one minute, or until the milk is almost boiling. Or heat in a pan on the stove.

2 Stir in the sugar, salt, butter or margarine, and grated lemon peel. Allow to cool until the mixture is lukewarm.

3 In a separate bowl, sprinkle the yeast on the water, and stir.

4 Add the yeast to the milk mixture. Slightly beat the eggs and add them to the milk mixture.

5 Beat in 2½ cups flour until the dough is smooth.

6 Stir in more flour, ½ cup at a time, until the dough pulls away from the side of the bowl.

Here's how to knead the dough:

1 Sprinkle flour onto a good solid surface, like a board or pastry cloth.

2 Turn the dough onto the surface. Work the dough, pushing it with the palms of your (clean) hands and then turning over a new surface to push again.

3 Knead the dough for five to eight minutes until your ball of dough becomes smooth and elastic.

EASTER EGGS BREAD
continued

Here's how to make the dough rise:

1 Lightly grease a large bowl, and put your kneaded ball of dough into the bowl. Then roll the ball of dough over to grease the top very lightly. Cover with a clean dish towel or a piece of foil.

2 Place the bowl in a warm place, such as over a pan of warm water or in an oven with a pilot light.

3 Let rise for one hour, or until doubled in size.

4 After one hour, give the dough a good punch, and let it rise again for about 30 minutes, or until nearly doubled in size again.

You decide which way to shape the Easter eggs bread:

Shape the dough into two large rings, each with six eggs.
OR shape the dough into 12 rings or nests, with an egg in the center of each.

Here's how to shape the dough:

1 To make two large rings, divide the dough into four pieces. Roll and roll each dough piece until it becomes a rope about 35 inches long. On a greased baking sheet, form two of the ropes into a braided ring. Create six openings in the braided ring, and place one egg in each. Repeat with the other two ropes and the rest of the eggs.

2 To make 12 small rings or nests, divide the dough into 12 pieces. Shape each piece into a small looped roll. Move each to a greased baking sheet, and place an egg in each center.

Here's how to finish the Easter eggs bread:

1 Cover the baking sheets with clean dish towels, and let the rolls rise about 30 minutes, or until doubled in size.

2 Preheat the oven to 375°F (190°C).

3 Brush each ring with the beaten egg. If you wish, sprinkle each with colored nonpareils.

4 Bake about 20 minutes for the large rings or about 15 minutes for the small rings. Serve warm.

NOW YOU HAVE 12 SERVINGS OF A VERY SPECIAL EASTER EGGS BREAD.

· · · · · · · · · · ·
MOTHER'S DAY
· ·

Back in Old England, working folk got a day off every May to "go a-mothering." They visited their mothers and took gifts of violets and "mothering cake."

"Mothering cake" in England could be a rich fruitcake or else small hard cookies. Though they were not at all alike, both treats for mothers had the same name, "simnel cake." In northern England and Scotland, children fried pancakes for their mothers and called them "carlings." Or sometimes children baked waffles for their mothers on special irons that they used only once a year.

In the United States, Anna Jarvis began to campaign for a special day for mothers in 1906 when her own beloved mother, Anna Reese Jarvis, died. Since Anna Reese Jarvis died on May 9, her daughter originally chose that day for Mother's Day. (And, of course, May was the traditional time to "go a-mothering.")

By 1914, the president had proclaimed the second Sunday in May as a national day for mothers.

Near the end of her long life, Anna Jarvis felt that Mother's Day had become too commercial. She felt that sons and daughters ought to pay real attention to their mothers on Mother's Day. She wanted people to go back to the old ideas of helping and honoring their mothers.

This Mother's Day, why don't you fix your mother a delicious French toast breakfast?

A French Toast Project for Mother's Day

Early in the morning on Mother's Day, put on your French beret and fix French Toast for your mother.

Here's what you need:

- 2 eggs
- ¼ cup milk
- ¼ teaspoon salt
- 2 slices (or more) white or wholewheat bread
- 2 tablespoons butter or margarine, optional

Here's how to make French toast:

1 Preheat the oven to 400°F (200°C). Or use a toaster oven.

2 Beat the eggs lightly with a fork. Stir in the milk and salt.

3 Dip the bread slices into the egg-milk mixture. (You ought to have plenty of the mixture left if you decide on more than two slices of French toast.)

4 Toast the bread in a toaster oven. Or toast in the oven for 12 to 15 minutes, until the bread is golden brown French toast.

5 OR melt two tablespoons butter or margarine in a large skillet. Then sauté the bread in the skillet at medium-high heat, until browned. Turn over and brown the other side. (Sauté means to cook briefly in a small amount of butter or oil.)

6 Serve with maple syrup.

> **Now You Have At Least Two Slices Of French Toast For Mother's Day.**

You may want to make more.

FATHER'S DAY

William Jackson Smart was the father behind Father's Day in the United States.

His daughter, Mrs. John Bruce Dodd, thought up Father's Day as she sat in church at a Mother's Day service in 1909.

Mrs. Dodd was a baby when her mother had died, leaving behind six children. Her father had worked hard by himself to bring up his five sons and one daughter. Mrs. Dodd thought that fathers like hers deserved a special day just like Mother's Day.

Previously, Father's Day had been celebrated only as a part of Mother's Day. Mrs. Dodd felt strongly that fathers are just as important as mothers and deserved their own holiday.

She began her campaign in 1909. Father's Day arrived (officially, at least) much more slowly than Mother's Day. A few states and many churches began celebrating Father's Day right away. But it wasn't until 1972 that the president finally proclaimed a national Father's Day for the third Sunday in June (the month of Mr. Smart's birthday).

You'll never guess the good Mr. Smart's nickname. We're lucky Father's Day isn't called "Billy Buttons Day."

Father's Day is a good time for family reunions. On Father's Day this year, why don't you make the salad? This is a salad you can make for a big family crowd—or just for Dad.

A PEA AND BEAN SALAD PROJECT FOR FATHER'S DAY

Be sure to leave enough time for the salad to marinate for a few hours or overnight.

Here's what you need:

For the salad:
1 16-ounce can kidney beans, drained
1 16-ounce can chick peas, drained
1 8-ounce can wax beans, drained
1 8-ounce can green beans, drained
1 small green bell pepper
½ small red bell pepper
½ Spanish onion

For the salad dressing:
¾ cup vinegar
⅔ cup honey
⅓ cup vegetable oil
1 tablespoon Dijon-style mustard
½ teaspoon salt
¼ teaspoon pepper

Here's how to mix the salad:

1 Rinse the kidney beans and chick peas. In a large bowl, combine them with the wax beans and green beans.
2 Chop the green pepper and red pepper.
3 Cut the Spanish onion into thin slices.
4 Toss all of these ingredients together.

Here's how to mix the salad dressing:

With a blender, blend together the vinegar, honey, salad oil, mustard, salt, and pepper.

Here's how to finish the salad:

1 Pour the dressing over the mixed beans and peas.
2 Cover and marinate for a few hours or overnight.
3 Drain the dressing from the salad before serving.

Hint: Save leftover dressing, and pour it over other vegetables. The dressing adds a delicious flavor.

NOW YOU HAVE EIGHT TO TEN SERVINGS OF PEA AND BEAN SALAD FOR A FATHER'S DAY FAMILY DINNER.

· · · · · · · · · · ·

PATRIOTIC HOLIDAYS

· ·

Fourth of July arrives, and we're ready with the red, white, and blue—for eating. The strawberries, cherries, and a few raspberries are in for the red. The blueberry harvest is ready for the blue. And the first new white potatoes of the season are on the table, not to mention a few crops of peas and tomatoes.

On the East Coast the salmon have just begun their run.

Today we can enjoy frozen foods all year. But the fresh foods are still the best.

We really ought to eat fresh cherry pie not on Washington's birthday but on the Fourth of July.

Picture the happy citizens of the newly formed United States of America celebrating the first years of independence. The traditional dinner was poached salmon along with the new potatoes and early peas.

Then they would have thought up a good red, white, and blue dessert.

We have three desserts to celebrate American holidays.

Choose Patriotic Ice Cream, Old Glory Cake, or a Red-White-and-Blue Cheese Pie.

And serve them for the Fourth of July—or for Labor Day, Veteran's Day, Memorial Day, Flag Day, or Election Day.

They all go well right after a parade.

PATRIOTIC ICE CREAM

For six servings of Patriotic Ice Cream, you'll need six parfait glasses or six sherbet glasses.

Here's what you need:

½ pint blueberry ice cream
½ pint vanilla ice cream
½ pint strawberry ice cream

Suggestion: *To make your own ice cream, look back at the make-your-own ice cream projects in FOODS TO PUNCH, TWIST, SHAPE, AND DESIGN.*

Here's how to design patriotic ice cream:

1 Scoop two or three tablespoons of blueberry ice cream into the bottom of each parfait or sherbet glass. Use the back of a spoon to press down the ice cream.

2 Be careful not to get ice cream on the edges of the glasses as you scoop it in. If you do, wipe it off with a damp paper towel. Do this each time you scoop in another layer.

3 Next scoop in two or three tablespoons of vanilla ice cream. Press it down with the back of a spoon.

4 Finally, scoop in two or three tablespoons of strawberry ice cream, and press it down with the back of a spoon.

5 Clean off the edges of the glasses one last time.

6 Serve immediately. Or cover each glass with plastic wrap, and set in the freezer until time to serve.

NOW YOU HAVE SIX SERVINGS OF YOUR OWN PATRIOTIC ICE CREAM.

AN OLD GLORY CAKE PROJECT

You can use almost any basic cake recipe for an Old Glory cake.
Then frost and decorate your cake to look like the stars and stripes of the American flag.

Here's what you need for an Old Glory cake:

Basic cake baked in a 9 × 13-inch pan

A 12 × 18-inch piece of heavy cardboard covered with aluminum foil

Basic white frosting

Blue food coloring

Red food coloring

A sheet of waxed paper 13 inches long

A ruler

Toothpicks

Very small white candies such as "Tic Tacs"

Here's how to get the cake ready:

1 Let the cake cool in the pan on a wire rack for 10 minutes. Then carefully move the cake onto the 12 × 18-inch cardboard wrapped in aluminum foil.

Hint: To remove the cake from the pan, cut around the edge with a table knife, and then put the cardboard base over the cake in the pan. Hold one hand under the pan, and one hand over the cardboard. Turn over in one motion. Lift the cake pan carefully off the cake. If the cake does not come out right away, put it back in the warm oven for one minute.

2 Let the cake cool completely. Brush off the crumbs.

3 Thinly frost the cake with about two cups of basic white frosting.

4 In a separate dish, mix about one cup of the remaining frosting with five drops of blue food coloring or a tiny dab of paste coloring. (Paste food coloring allows you deeper, brighter shades, so you might prefer that type for flag colors.) Add blue food coloring one drop at a time until you have the right blue color for the flag.

5 In a separate dish, mix about one cup of the remaining frosting with a tiny dab or five drops of red food coloring. Add red food coloring one drop at a time until you have the right color for the flag.

OLD GLORY CAKE
continued

Here's how to use the waxed paper to draw the stripes:

1 Fold the paper in half along the 13-inch length. Now you have a waxed-paper marker to help you draw the thirteen stripes on the flag cake.

2 Use a toothpick as your "pencil" to make 12 marks equal distances apart along the 9-inch edge of the cake.

3 Use the toothpick to draw stripes in the frosting at each guide mark. Use the cut paper as a "straight edge" as you draw each stripe. Now you have 13 stripes drawn.

Here's how to get your stars in the right place:

Use your toothpick "pencil" to mark off a square at the upper left corner of the cake. The square ought to measure down to the top of the seventh stripe. Do your best to make it square rather than lopsided. (You can always "erase" wrong toothpick marks.)

Here's how to put in the stars and stripes:

1 Fill in the square with blue frosting.

2 Frost in every other stripe with red frosting. Begin with a red edge stripe, and continue until you have seven red stripes and six white stripes.

3 Now all you need is to line up stars in the field of blue. For stars, use dabs of white frosting or line up very small white candies such as "Tic Tacs." Use your toothpick "pencil" to help line them up right.

NOW YOU HAVE A 9 × 13-INCH OLD GLORY CAKE.

A RED-WHITE-AND-BLUE CHEESE PIE PROJECT

Here's what you need:

For the crust:
 1 cup (2 sticks) butter or margarine
 1 cup graham cracker crumbs
 1 tablespoon sugar

For the filling:
 1 8-ounce package cream cheese
   OR 1 cup ricotta cheese
 1/3 cup sugar
 1 egg
 1 tablespoon lemon juice

For the topping:
 4 cups (1 quart) strawberries
 2 cups (1 pint) blueberries

Here's how to make the crust:

1 Use a heatproof glass pie plate. Place the butter or margarine in the pie plate and microwave on high power for 30 to 45 seconds. (Or you can melt the butter in a pan over low heat.)

2 Mix together the graham cracker crumbs and sugar.

3 Stir the crumbs into the melted butter.

4 Be especially sure to wash your hands before you start this step. Use your fingers to press the mixture over the bottom and up the sides of the pie plate.

5 Microwave on high power for two to three minutes. OR bake in the oven at 350°F (180°C) for ten minutes.

6 Set aside to cool.

Here's how to make the filling:

1 To soften the cream cheese, place it in a large glass mixing bowl. Cover and microwave on low power for 30 seconds. OR place the cream cheese on a small dish in a pan of warm water until the cream cheese is about room temperature. (Ricotta cheese is already soft.)

2 Use the electric mixer to make the filling. Beat together cheese, sugar, and egg until smooth. Stir in the lemon juice.

215

. . . .

RED-WHITE-AND-BLUE CHEESE PIE
continued

Here's how to finish the pie:

1 Pour the cheese mixture into the cooled crust.

2 Microwave on high power for 90 seconds. Turn the dish a half turn. Then microwave on high power again for another 60 to 90 seconds, or until the mixture is set about halfway between the crust and the center. Now let the pie sit for about ten minutes.

3 OR bake the pie in the oven at 350°F (180°C) for 20 to 25 minutes, or until, when you insert a knife about halfway between the crust and the center of the pie, the knife comes out clean.

4 Cool and refrigerate.

Here's how to put on the topping:

1 Wash and drain the strawberries and blueberries.

2 Cut the strawberries into halves or slices.

3 Use strawberries and blueberries to create a design on top of the pie.

Here are three design suggestions:

1 Try for a flag effect. Design stripes of red strawberries across about two-thirds of the pie, with a field of blueberries across the other third.

2 Or try for a flower effect. Slice the strawberries and fan them out, cut side up, in overlapping layers to form a flower design. Circle the strawberries with blueberries.

3 Or try for a star effect. Form a star of strawberries, circled by blueberries.

NOW YOU HAVE AN INDEPENDENCE DAY RED-WHITE-AND-BLUE CHEESE PIE.

A Carrot Coins Project for Rosh Hashanah

Rosh Hashanah is the New Year's celebration that falls in September or October. In the Jewish calendar, that's the first and second days of Tishri.

Carrot coins give you three wishes for a happy new year. First, they're sweet, and that's one way to wish God to inscribe you for a sweet New Year. Second, the carrot coins wish you prosperity (and many real coins) in the New Year.

And third, the Yiddish word *mehren* can mean either "increase" or "carrots." So carrot coins are a funny way of hoping that your merits increase in the New Year.

Here's what you need:

About 1 pound carrots

½ cup orange juice

2 tablespoons honey

2 tablespoons brown sugar, well packed

¼ teaspoon nutmeg

¼ cup golden raisins

1 medium orange

Here's how to make carrot coins:

1 Scrape the carrots and cut them into "coins," each about ½ inch thick.

2 In a large saucepan, combine the carrot coins with the orange juice, honey, brown sugar, nutmeg, and golden raisins.

3 Over medium-high heat, bring the liquid to a boil. Stir, and turn the stove down to low heat.

4 Simmer for about 30 minutes.

5 Peel and section the orange. Cut it into chunks, and put it into the pan for the last five minutes of simmering.

6 Serve your carrot coins warm.

Now You Have Four Or Five Servings Of Carrot Coins To Help Bring In A Sweet New Year.

PUMPKIN NAMES

Pumpkins aren't just pumpkins. Farmers grow pumpkins for particular purposes—and then probably lie awake nights thinking up funny names for the new pumpkins.

If you want to bake a pumpkin pie, for instance, try Winter Luxury, Yellow Cheese, or Early Sugar Sweets.

If you want a big orange Jack-o'-Lantern (or food for farm animals), try Triple Delights, Connecticut Fields, Big Moon, Big Max, or (naturally) Jack-o'-Lanterns.

If you want just a lot of pumpkin seed, try Lady Godiva or Naked Seeded pumpkins.

Or you can always join Linus at Halloween and wait for the Great Pumpkin.

A HALLOWEEN PUMPKIN COOKIES PROJECT

Here's what you need:

½ cup (1 stick) butter or margarine

1 cup pumpkin

1 cup sugar

1 egg, slightly beaten

1 teaspoon milk

1 teaspoon vanilla extract

2 cups all purpose or unbleached flour

2 teaspoons baking powder

1 teaspoon baking soda

1 teaspoon cinnamon

½ teaspoon salt

1 cup chocolate chips

½ cup nuts (if you wish)

Here's how to make pumpkin cookies:

1 Preheat the oven to 375°F (190°C).

2 Place the butter or margarine in a heatproof glass dish. Cover and microwave on high power for 30 seconds.

3 In a large bowl, mix together pumpkin, sugar, melted butter or margarine, beaten egg, milk, and vanilla extract.

Hint: You can use an electric mixer for this step, but when you add the flour, the dough will get stiff, and you can beat it better by hand.

4 In a separate bowl, combine the flour, baking powder, baking soda, cinnamon, and salt. Add to the pumpkin mixture, and mix until smooth.

5 Stir in the chocolate chips and nuts (if you wish).

6 Drop from a teaspoon onto a lightly greased baking sheet. Line up about 1½ inches apart.

7 Bake for ten to 12 minutes, until golden brown.

8 Cool on baking sheet for two minutes. Then remove to a wire rack to finish cooling.

NOW YOU HAVE ABOUT THREE DOZEN PUMPKIN COOKIES FOR HALLOWEEN.

Store them in an airtight container, and give them as treats.

A CRANBERRY RELISH PROJECT FOR THANKSGIVING

The fun of making cranberry relish is chopping each fruit, one at a time. Here are directions for chopping the fruit with a food processor, but you can also use a food grinder.

Here's what you need:

- 1 12-ounce bag fresh cranberries
- 2 medium oranges
- 2 Golden Delicious apples
- 1 lemon
- ¾ cup sugar

Here's how to make cranberry relish:

1 Wash the fruit and let it drain.

2 Put the cranberries into a food processor, and pulse the machine on and off until they are chopped. Put the chopped cranberries into a 1½-quart container.

3 Cut the oranges into quarters. Remove any seeds. Then cut each quarter into four to six pieces. Put the orange pieces into the food processor, and pulse the machine on and off until they are chopped. Place the chopped oranges into the container with the cranberries.

4 Cut the unpeeled apples into quarters, and cut out the cores. Then cut each quarter into three pieces. Put the apple pieces into the food processor, and pulse the machine on and off until they are chopped. Add to the cranberries.

5 Cut the lemon into quarters. Remove any seeds. Then cut each quarter into two pieces. Put the lemon pieces into the food processor, and pulse the machine on and off until they are chopped. Place into the container with the cranberries.

6 Pour the sugar over the mixture, and stir completely.

7 Cover, and refrigerate for at least two hours or overnight to blend the flavors.

NOW YOU HAVE ABOUT ONE QUART OF CRANBERRY RELISH FOR THANKSGIVING.

THE STORY OF HANUKKAH

Hanukkah is like another sort of Thanksgiving—and just as much fun.

This is the story.

In ancient times, the Jewish people of Judea rebelled against the Syrian tyrants.

The Judeans really didn't stand a chance. The Syrian army sat high atop warrior elephants, and they were powerful beyond belief. They were proud enough to make statues of gods using their own faces, as if they themselves were gods. They installed these ridiculous statues even in the sacred Temple of Jerusalem.

They were so sure of their power that finally they stopped paying attention.

That's when the Judeans rebelled.

And, against all odds, the Judean people won.

The Judean people reclaimed their own country, and at last they were able to return to their Temple.

On the first Hanukkah, Judah Maccabee entered the ruined Temple of Jerusalem to cleanse and purify it and bright it back alive again.

In the debris, he found one hidden vial of undefiled oil, still sealed and pure. During the eight days of the rededication of the Temple, these drops of oil burned brightly on and on, long past the time when the flame ought to have burned out.

For over 21 centuries, Hanukkah candles have shone in memory of the miracle.

A LATKES PROJECT FOR HANUKKAH

Potato pancakes fried in oil remind us of the Hanukkah miracle of the oil. But remember that at Hanukkah, a very small amount of oil goes a very long way.

Here's what you need:

For the pancakes:

- 4 *large baking potatoes*
- 1 *medium onion, finely chopped*
- 2 *eggs*
- ½ *teaspoon salt*
- ½ *teaspoon pepper*
- 2 *tablespoons flour, matzoh meal or cracker crumbs*

For the topping:

- 1½ *cups warm applesauce* OR
- 1 *cup sour cream*

Here's how to make the pancake batter:

1 Peel the potatoes. Use a grater or food processor to grate them. If you use a food processor, cut the potatoes into chunks, and use the grating blade. Put in the potato chunks, and pulse the machine only once or twice.

2 Scrape the grated potatoes into a strainer, and let them drain for a few minutes.

3 Crack the eggs into a large bowl. Beat lightly, and then add the salt, pepper, and flour (or matzoh meal or cracker crumbs).

4 Add the grated potatoes and chopped onion. Stir all together for potato pancake batter.

Here's how to fry potato pancakes:

1 Lightly grease a griddle. Heat until drops of water from your fingertips dance over the surface.

2 Use a ¼-cup measure to dip the batter. Pour it on the griddle. Cook each pancake about four minutes on each side, or until golden brown.

3 Serve with warm applesauce or sour cream.

NOW YOU HAVE ABOUT A DOZEN OF YOUR OWN HANUKKAH LATKES.

A BANANA BOAT PROJECT FOR KWANZAA

The holiday of Kwanzaa is a special holiday for African-Americans. Kwanzaa is a time for celebrating harvest, a time for family reunions, another sort of Thanksgiving.

Since Kwanzaa is the Swahili word for "first fruit," celebrate Kwanzaa with fresh fruit.

Here's what you need:

4 ripe bananas

Peanut butter, if you wish

1 fresh pineapple (or fresh pineapple chunks)

1 medium orange

You Choose the Topping:
whipped cream, ice cream, or frozen yogurt, plus a sprinkling of nuts.

Here's how to fix the bananas:

Peel each banana, and split it lengthwise. If you wish, spread with peanut butter and make banana "sandwiches." Wrap in plastic or foil, and freeze while you are preparing the other fruit.

Here's how to cut fresh pineapple:

: *Caution: You need adult help*
: *with cutting pineapple.*

1 Cut off the top and bottom of the pineapple.

2 Slice the pineapple into about one-inch slices. Then, *after* you've sliced it, take off the hard outer shell in pieces. Cut out the hard core of each pineapple slice, and cut the good pineapple fruit into small chunks.

Here's how to finish your banana boats:

1 Peel and section the orange, and cut it into chunks.

2 Arrange the frozen banana "boats" on banana split or other desert dishes. Scoop on pineapple chunks and orange chunks.

3 Top with your choice of whipped cream, ice cream, or frozen yogurt. If you wish, sprinkle on nuts.

: **NOW YOU HAVE FOUR**
: **BANANA BOATS FOR**
: **KWANZAA.**

CHRISTMAS FOODS TRIVIA QUIZ

1 What Christmas food was once against the law?

2 What humble food (just for Christians who were avoiding rich foods as a penance before the holidays) developed into a spectacular Christmas dessert?

3 By what date ought good Christmas cooks to have their plum puddings ready?

4 According to legend, what lucky Christmas food did Mary eat the evening before Jesus was born?

5 What was the menu for the first Christmas celebration in North America?

6 For what Christmas beverage did President George Washington use his own special recipe?

7 What president was host at the first Christmas dinner in the White House?

8 What unusual dinner did Fannie Farmer suggest for Christmas of 1909?

9 If you really have a lot to do, how busy are you?

. . . .

CHRISTMAS FOODS TRIVIA
continued

1 Mince pie was illegal in 17th-century New England.

Before that, mince pies were baked in an oval dish, the same shape as the manger in the stable at Bethlehem, and then topped with a tiny pastry baby.

This enraged the grim Puritans, as if the bakers were making a joke about the Christ Child.

The Puritans passed a law against mince pies.

Eventually, mince pie came to be tolerated but only if it was plain, round, and undecorated.

2 English plum pudding was once the humble frumenty.

Frumenty started as a sort of plain porridge made of hulled wheat boiled in milk.

Over the years, frumenty developed into a rich Christmas dessert, as people began to add spices, sugar, fruits and nuts—and a topping of blazing brandy.

3 The "deadline" for plum pudding was "Stir-Up Sunday," a Sunday in late November about four weeks before Christmas, when the morning service begins, "Stir up, we beseech Thee, O Lord, the wills of thy faithful people."

The puddings then had a chance to age nearly a month before Christmas.

4 Spinach

5 On Christmas of 1607, Captain John Smith and his companions celebrated their first Christmas in the New World "among the salvages." In spite of "extreme winde, rayne, frost and snow," they had a fine time, with warm fires, and plenty of food: "good Oysters, Fish, Flesh, Wilde Fowl and good bread . . . "

6 Eggnog

7 John and Abigail Adams hosted the first Christmas dinner in the White House. In the time of George Washington's spectacular Christmas dinners, the White House had not yet been built.

8 In the *Women's Home Companion* for 1909, the famous cook, Fannie Farmer, described an all red and green dinner.

9 According to an Italian proverb, if you really have a lot to do, then you're busier than an oven at Christmas time.

A GINGERBREAD HOUSE PROJECT FOR CHRISTMAS

Make a gingerbread house you can display all during Christmas. When Christmas is over, you can eat the gingerbread house and all its decorations.

Be sure to leave enough time to work on your gingerbread house. You may want to make the patterns one day, and fix the dough another day. And this is a good project to work on with parents and friends.

Gingerbread House Pattern

The first step is to cut the pattern for your gingerbread house.

Here are the supplies you need for cutting the patterns:

Sheets of graph paper

A straightedge, triangle, and compass

A sharp pencil

A pair of scissors

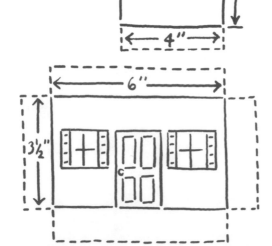

Here's how to cut the patterns:

1 For the front and back of your house, draw two 3½ × 6-inch rectangles. Make sure the two rectangles are just the same size.

2 For the sides of your house, draw 2 pentagons. (A pentagon is a figure with five sides. Look at the diagram and see how the sides of the house raise to a roof peak and form five sides.)

3 First draw a four-inch base for each. Then use your triangle to draw 3½-inch sides at right angles to the base (90 degrees). Then draw the roof peaks. Draw three-inch triangular roof peaks (at a 50-degree angle), rising to a point at the top. The two sides for the house should be the same.

4 In the paper models, cut out openings for the door and windows.

5 Draw a rectangular roof for the house, 6½ × 7 inches. Draw a line down the long center of the roof, 3½ inches on each side. **Look at the diagram to see how.**

GINGERBREAD HOUSE
continued

Cardboard "Under" House

Next step to cut posterboard (or cardboard) pieces for the house. These posterboard pieces go under the gingerbread pieces and hold your house together.

Here's what you need for the "under" house:

Posterboard (or cardboard)

Scissors or shears (heavy enough for cutting posterboard)

Glue (white, nontoxic)

Make sure the posterboard is clean. Wipe it with a damp cloth to make sure, and then let it dry.

Here's how to make the posterboard house pieces:

1 Use the patterns. Lay each pattern on the posterboard, and draw the outline.

2 Draw in a one-inch tab at each side of each piece.

3 Check your posterboard outlines *before* you cut. Make sure they are right while you can still change them easily.

> : *Caution: You may need adult*
> : *help with cutting posterboard.*

4 Carefully cut the posterboard into shapes for the front and back of the house and for the two sides—and for the tabs. (Do *not* cut out openings for door and windows.)

5 Fold the tabs inward. Use a straightedge to help make the fold straight.

Here's how to make the posterboard roof:

6 Lay the paper pattern for the roof on posterboard, and draw an outline.

7 Cut the posterboard for the roof.

8 Measure and draw a line down the long center of the roof, 3½ inches on each side.

9 Fold along the long center line of the roof. Use a straightedge to help make the fold straight. ***Look at the diagram to see how.***

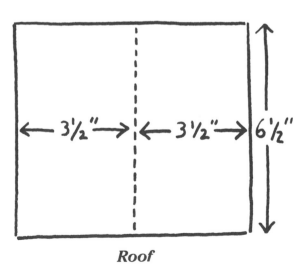

Roof

. . . .
GINGERBREAD HOUSE
continued

Here's how to assemble the posterboard "under" house:

1 Create a base to hold your gingerbread house. Use your heaviest posterboard or cardboard. Cut it 12 × 18 inches.

2 Put glue on each tab as you go. First use the tabs to glue together the four sides of the house.

3 Next glue the folded roof to the tabs at the tops of the house sides. The roof is supposed to jut out over the sides just a little. (Do not glue the bottom tabs to the base just yet. Save that step for later, when you have the gingerbread sides on.)

4 Let the glue dry.

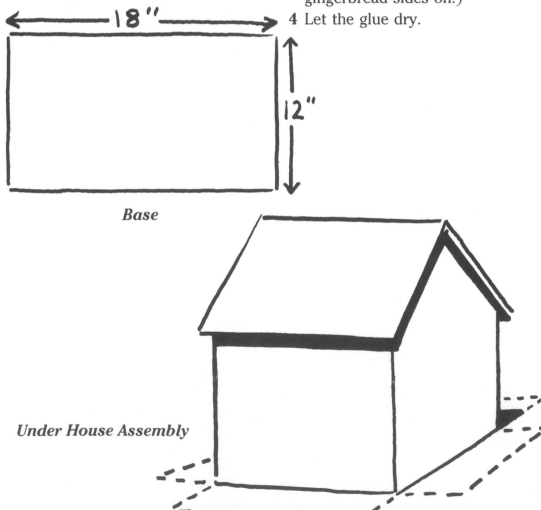

Base

Under House Assembly

· · · · · · · · · · ·
GINGERBREAD HOUSE
continued

Gingerbread House Dough

Here's what you need for the gingerbread dough:

⅔ cup brown sugar, well packed

⅔ cup molasses

1 teaspoon ginger

1 teaspoon cinnamon

½ teaspoon cloves

¾ teaspoon baking soda

⅔ cup butter or margarine

1 egg

5 cups all purpose flour

Here's how to make the dough:

1 In a heatproof glass one-quart bowl, stir together the brown sugar, molasses, ginger, cinnamon, and cloves. Heat in the microwave oven on high power for two to three minutes, until the mixture starts to boil. Stir in the baking soda.

2 Measure the butter or margarine into a large mixing bowl. Pour the hot mixture over the butter, and stir until the butter melts.

3 Beat the egg slightly, and stir into the butter-sugar mixture.

4 Add the flour gradually. Stir in each addition before you add more. Stir thoroughly until you have a stiff dough.

5 Knead dough and form into a ball.

6 Wrap the ball of dough in waxed paper and refrigerate until well chilled, at least an hour.

Here's how to shape the dough:

1 Preheat oven to 325°F (170°C).

2 Sprinkle flour onto a clean, solid surface, such as a cutting board or a pastry cloth.

3 Turn the dough onto the surface, and roll out to about ¼-inch thickness.

4 Lay each of your paper patterns on the dough, and cut out shapes by tracing around the patterns with a sharp knife.

5 Cut the paper pattern for the roof along the fold, and make your gingerbread roof in two pieces.

6 Use a knife or toothpick to trace the outlines for the door and windows onto the dough.

7 Roll up dough scraps. Use a cookie cutter to cut one or two gingerbread people to live at your gingerbread house.

8 Carefully place the gingerbread house pieces on greased baking sheets.

9 Bake the baking sheets one at a time. Bake for ten to 15 minutes, until the gingerbread pieces are firm and lightly browned.

10 Cool thoroughly on wire racks before you assemble your house.

. . . .

GINGERBREAD HOUSE
continued

Icing for the House
The next step is to fix ornamental icing for your house.

Here's what you need for the icing:

2 egg whites

½ teaspoon cream of tartar

Pinch of salt

About 2½ cups sifted confectioner's
  sugar

Red food coloring

Blue food coloring

Yellow food coloring

Here's how to mix the icing:

Hint: To see how to separate egg whites, look back at the white cake project in THE FOOD FACTORY.

1 Use an electric mixer. In the small mixer bowl, beat the egg whites, cream of tartar, and salt at high speed. Beat until stiff peaks form.

2 Gradually add confectioner's sugar. Beat well after each addition. Add enough confectioner's sugar to make the icing thick enough for decorating the house. This icing needs to be thicker than ordinary cake frosting.

3 Cover the bowl with a damp cloth until you are ready to use the icing.

Here's how to color part of the icing:

1 Measure ½ cup icing into a separate bowl. Mix with three or four drops of red food coloring. (Or for a more intense color, use food coloring paste.) Add red food coloring, one drop at a time, until you have a Christmas shade of bright red.

2 Measure ½ cup icing into a separate bowl. Mix with three or four drops of blue food coloring to make a shade of light blue.

3 Measure ½ cup icing into a separate bowl. Mix with two drops of blue food coloring and two drops of yellow food coloring. Add blue and yellow food coloring, two drops at a time, until you have a Christmas shade of bright green. (Or the food coloring paste will make an especially good shade of green.)

4 Cover each bowl with a damp cloth until you are ready to use it.

GINGERBREAD HOUSE
continued

Decorations for the House

The next steps are to decorate the gingerbread house pieces. (Decorate the gingerbread before you put it all together.)

Here's what else you need to decorate the house:

1 pound large red gumdrops
  OR 2 packages Necco-type wafers

½ pound green gumdrops

2 large oblong red jelly candies

1 pound grated coconut

Green food coloring

Large green gumdrops

Here's how to put in the door and windows:

1 First lay out the four gingerbread sides for the house.

2 Now ice in a red door. Use a small spatula or knife.

3 Next ice in light-blue windows.

4 Put green icing into a decorating tip or "fun gun." Use a small plain tip. Carefully draw the outline of green shutters at each side of the windows.

5 Fill in the shutters with green icing, and outline the windows and panes of window glass with green.

6 Let the icing dry.

7 Cover the leftover icing in the bowls with a damp cloth until time to use it again.

Here's how to decorate the gingerbread roof:

1 Use red gumdrops to make "tiles" to cover the roof pieces. Slice red gumdrops down the center to create four slices from each gumdrop. (Discard or cut the outer slices.)

2 Use a little plain icing to "butter" one side of each gumdrop slice. Stick the gumdrop slices, curved sides down, in rows on the roof. Begin at the bottom or eaves of the roof, and work upward. Then repeat on the other side of the roof.

3 OR use Necco-type wafers. Spread icing over one side of the roof. Cover with overlapping rows of wafers, starting at the bottom edge or eaves of the roof.

GINGERBREAD HOUSE
continued

The Finish

Here's how to put together the gingerbread pieces:

1 Now it's time to attach the gingerbread side pieces of the house to the cardboard "under" house. Use icing as your "glue."

> : *Caution: You may need adult*
> : *help with putting together the*
> : *gingerbread house.*

2 Spread icing on the back of one piece at a time. Press the piece tightly to the corresponding cardboard side.

3 Let each piece dry in place before you add the next piece.

4 Use real glue to finish gluing the posterboard "under" house to the base. Use the bottom tabs to glue each side the house to the center of the base. Let the glue dry.

5 Don't worry about spaces left over at the corners of the house. Fill them in with red or green icing as your "corner boards."

6 Spread icing on the backs of the roof pieces one at a time. Press each roof piece tightly onto the cardboard roof pieces. Let the eaves jut out over the sides.

Here's how to make the chimney:

1 Use icing to "glue" together the two long red jelly candies. Cut a wedge-shaped piece from one end (to fit the chimney over the peak of the roof). Slice the top edge off evenly (so the chimney will be flat on top).

2 Use red icing to fit the chimney on top of the roof.

GINGERBREAD HOUSE
continued

Here's how to make the garden:

1 Use large green gumdrops for shrubs. Place them at each side of the door and around the base of the house.

2 Save some grated coconut for snow. Color the rest green for grass. In a large bowl, mix one teaspoon water with a few drops of green food coloring. Toss the colored water and coconut together until the coconut is green.

3 Spread the green coconut around the house. Leave space for a walkway.

4 Make a walkway with slices of red gumdrops or jellies. Glue them in place with icing.

5 Stand one or two gingerbread people on the walkway. Prop them up with a gumdrop "stand" and some icing "glue."

Here's how to put in snow:

1 Sprinkle white coconut over the green grass to make snow.

2 Put bits of white icing on the green shrubs.

3 Spread a little white icing on the edges of the roof to look like snow.

> **NOW YOU HAVE YOUR OWN CHRISTMAS GINGERBREAD HOUSE.**

A CHRISTMAS TREE CAKE PROJECT

You can use almost any basic cake recipe for a Christmas tree cake. Then frost and decorate your cake to look like a Christmas tree. (And you don't need a special Christmas tree cake pan—although you can use one if you want.)

Here's what you need for a Christmas tree cake:

Basic cake baked in a 9 × 13-inch pan (and cooled)

A 10 × 14-inch piece of heavy cardboard, covered with aluminum foil

Basic white frosting

Blue and yellow food coloring

Red licorice ropes

Silver dragees

Red and green Christmas nonpareils or sprinkles

Small red birthday candles

Birthday candle holders

Here's how to get the cake ready:

1 Let the cake cool in the pan for ten minutes.

2 Then carefully move the cake onto a large cutting board.

Hint: *To remove the cake from the pan, cut around the edge with a table knife. And then put the cardboard base over the cake in the pan. Hold one hand under the pan, and one hand over the cardboard base. Turn over in one motion. You ought to be able to lift the cake pan (carefully) off the cake. If the cake does not come out right away, put it back in the warm oven for one minute.*

3 Let the cake cool completely.

Here's how to get the frosting ready:

Mix the basic white frosting with five drops of blue food coloring and five drops of yellow food coloring. Add blue and yellow food coloring, two drops at a time, until you have a Christmas shade of bright green. (Or green food coloring paste makes an especially intense shade of green.)

CHRISTMAS TREE CAKE
continued

Here's how to shape the Christmas tree:

1 Lightly cut a small mark in the center of the nine-inch side of the cake. Place a straightedge from the mark to one of the far corners. With a serrated knife, slice straight up and down along the straightedge. Repeat the process on the other side. **Look at the diagram to see how.**

2 Carefully move the two cut-off pieces onto the 10 × 14-inch cardboard covered with aluminum foil. Put the two cut-off pieces together so that they form a triangle. (They will be about the same shape and size as the piece from which you cut them. If you have studied geometric angles, you can see why.)

3 Then carefully move the two cut-off pieces onto the aluminum-covered cardboard.

4 Frost the two pieces. They will form the bottom layer of the Christmas tree.

5 Carefully move the other piece on top. It's the top layer of the Christmas tree.

Here's how to finish the Christmas tree:

1 Finish frosting the tree with the green frosting. Swirl the frosting around to give an idea of branches for the tree.

2 Loop licorice ropes to look like garlands.

3 Sprinkle with silver dragees and with red and green nonpareils or sprinkles.

4 Place candles in candle holders at points on the edges of the cake and in the center.

: **NOW YOU HAVE A**
: **TWO-LAYER CHRISTMAS**
: **TREE CAKE.**

Light the candles for a way to say "Happy Birthday" to the Christ Child.

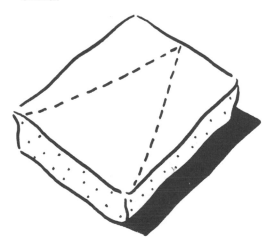

....
LUCKY CHRISTMAS FOODS
....

You will have one lucky month for each cook whose food you eat on Christmas day.

Don't refuse the dessert at Christmas, or you will lose a friend before the next Christmas.

If you eat a raw egg first thing Christmas day, you will be able to carry heavy weights.

For good health all year, eat an apple at midnight on Christmas Eve.

To frighten the devil away, threaten to bake him in a Christmas pie.

Leave a loaf on your table after Christmas dinner, and you will have bread all year.

To appease evil spirits, leave out a bit of porridge overnight on Christmas Eve.

For a good harvest, save some crumbs from Christmas dinner to sow with your seeds in the spring.

Wear some new clothing on Christmas day, or the "Christmas Cat" might sneak in and eat up your Christmas dinner.

For family luck, get everyone in the family, even the baby, to take a turn stirring the Christmas cooking.

To honor the Christ Child, share your Christmas bounty with the animals.

FOODS WITH SECRET STORIES

Can food help you be what you want to be?

Can the right recipes make you smart or beautiful, muscular or magical?

Would you like to drink a magic potion? Dine with a sports legend? Eat astronaut's food from outer space? Even swallow a few fried worms?

Here's your chance.

MAGIC POTIONS

A magic potion must truly be the most delicious drink in the universe.
But how would it taste?

Would it combine all the best flavors? That's what Lewis Carroll said when
he described the magic potion Alice drank in *Alice in Wonderland*. He said
Alice's drink mixed flavors of "cherry-tart, custard, pine-apple, roast turkey,
toffy, and hot buttered toast."

Of course, there is also the question of what the magic potion does to you
after you drink it. After she drank the magic potion, Alice found herself shut-
ting up like a telescope, until she was only ten inches high.

A "MAGIC" ICY TOFU COOLER PROJECT

This is the closest we could find to a magic potion. Icy tofu cooler is cold,
delicious, and just a little mysterious.

Here's what you need:

⅓ *pound soft tofu*
½ *cup fruit juice*
½ *ripe banana, sliced*
 2 *ice cubes*

You decide a juice you like best:
apple cider, grape juice, orange
juice, or pineapple juice.

Blend your beverage:

1 Blend the tofu, fruit juice, and
banana until very smooth.

2 Add ice cubes to make your drink
extra cold, and blend again.

You decide what else to add:

1 If you wish, add ½ cup dates or
½ cup fresh fruit, cut up.

2 Blend until smooth, or leave your
drink chunky.

> **NOW YOU HAVE TWO OR**
> **THREE GLASSES OF ICY**
> **TOFU COOLER.**

. . . .

TOFU TRIVIA

. . . .

Is tofu a strange, rare food?
  Not any more.

In what country do people like tofu best?
  Probably in China, Japan, or Korea. For thousands of years, people in Asia have eaten tofu as a basic, everyday food. Tofu is as important to them as milk or bread is to us.

Tofu is made from soybeans. Did you ever eat soybeans before?
  Yes.
  You have probably eaten soybean products
  ...if you like Chinese food
  ...if you eat foods made with cooking oil or shortening
  ...if you put salad dressing on your salads
  ...if you're a vegetarian
  ...if you were allergic to milk when you were a baby
  ...if people in your family bake with soy flour

What country grows the most soybeans?
  You'd think the answer would be China or Japan. No. The answer is the United States. In the United States, soybeans are mostly used to feed farm animals.

What can you make from tofu?
  You'd be surprised. Tofu is a soft, mild food. When you see tofu for sale at the grocery store, you might think it looks a little like a block of cheese.

Here are just a few of the recipes you can make with tofu:
  Carrot Salad, Cheese and Onion Casserole, Cheesecake, Chop Suey, Fruit Cocktail with Frozen Tofu, Korean Barbecue Sauce, Macaroni Salad with Deep-fried Tofu, Milkshakes with Tofu, Pineapple Sherbet with Tofu, Scrambled Eggs with Tofu, Tofu–Brown Rice Croquettes, Tofu Fondue, Tofu Guacamole Dip, Tofu Ice Cream, and Tofu–Peanut Butter Cookies.

. . . .

TEA PARTIES

. . . .

The tradition of tea parties is that you can invite anyone: your mother or father, your best friend, a dog or cat, dolls or teddy bears.

You can invite anyone, but all your guests must be on their very best behavior.

You must also make your tea party as elegant and fancy as you possibly can.

In Frances Hodgson Burnett's *The Secret Garden,* two cousins, Mary and Colin, and their friend Dickon hold secret tea parties in a walled-in garden that no one else can enter.

Now Mary and Colin are a very sad pair.

Mary's parents have just died in India, and she has had to travel from India to live at a gloomy manor house in England, with people she had never met before. Mary is a nasty, spoiled child who likes to throw temper tantrums when she doesn't get her way—and nothing is going her way.

Then deep along the corridors of the great manor house, she hears mysterious night-time wailing and crying.

Who is wailing like that? It's Mary's poor crippled cousin, Colin, kept hidden away in far-away rooms of the manor. Colin is, if anything, even more nasty and more spoiled than Mary is, and he can match her in temper tantrums.

In between tantrums, Mary tells Colin about the secret garden. (After Colin's mother died, Colin's father ordered the garden locked, and he threw away the key. Mary was just lucky enough to find the key when a robin showed her where it was hidden.)

Colin had to arrive at the secret garden in a wheelchair.

But the secret garden turned out to have a very strange and powerful effect on the two cousins.

Picture your tea party in a secret garden like that, a garden full of roses but with high walls and a strange past—a special, secret place just right for a tea party.

A TEA PARTY PROJECT

The Menu
Cambric or herbal tea, with milk and lemon wedges

An assortment of tiny sandwiches

An assortment of fancy vegetables and fresh fruits

Tea party cookies

The Tea
For a truly old-fashioned tea party, try cambric tea. This is a sort of pretend tea that children used to make for their tea parties. It has no tea in it. And it's so easy to make that it almost doesn't need a recipe.

Or for a more grown-up sort of tea party, try hot herbal tea.

Suggestion: *For a hot-weather tea party, go outside and let the sun brew your own sun tea. For how to make sun tea, look at the OUTSIDE FOODS section.*

Old-Fashioned Cambric Tea
Here's what you need for old-fashioned cambric tea:

A teapot of hot water

A small pitcher of milk

A small bowl of sugar

Here's how to pour cambric tea:

1 Pour some milk into a tea cup.

2 Fill the cup with hot water.

3 Add a spoonful of sugar.

> : **THAT'S SIMPLE**
> : **OLD-FASHIONED CAMBRIC**
> : **TEA.**

Herbal Tea
Here's what you need for herbal tea:

A teapot of hot water (1 cup of hot water for each cup of tea you want)

Herbal tea (1 bag or 1 teaspoon of tea leaves for each cup of tea you want)

A small pitcher of milk

A small bowl of sugar

A plate of lemon wedges

Here's how to make herbal tea:

1 First, warm the teapot. Fill the teapot with very hot water, and let it sit for a few minutes. Then pour out the hot water, and you have a warmed teapot.

2 ***You decide the flavor of herbal tea you like best.***

3 For each cup of tea you want, put in one bag or measure one teaspoon of herbal tea leaves into the teapot.

4 For each cup of tea you want, boil one cup water. (You can boil water in the microwave on high power for about two minutes.)

5 Pour the boiling water over the tea leaves in the teapot.

> : *Caution: You need adult help*
> : *with boiling water.*

6 Let the teapot sit for about five minutes to steep the tea.

7 Pour the tea through a strainer into each cup.

8 Serve with milk, sugar, and lemon wedges.

TEA SANDWICHES

Suggestion: For ways to shape and design sandwiches, look at the sandwich design projects in FOODS TO PUNCH, TWIST, SHAPE, AND DESIGN.

You decide the tea party sandwiches you like best. Here are three traditional tea party sandwiches. (After all, part of the charm of tea parties is the tradition.)

Cucumber or Watercress Sandwiches
Here's what you need:

A cucumber or watercress

Butter

1 slice white bread

1 slice wholewheat bread

Here's how to make the sandwiches:

1 Cut the cucumber into very thin slices or chop the watercress.
2 For each sandwich, butter a slice of white bread.
3 Lay cucumber slices or watercress on the buttered white bread, and cover with a slice of wholewheat bread.

Cream Cheese and Olive Sandwiches
Here's what you need:

1 3-ounce package of cream cheese
2 tablespoons stuffed olives or salad olives

White bread

Wholewheat bread

Here's how to make cream cheese and olive sandwiches:

1 Soften the cream cheese by letting it stand at room temperature. Or place in a dish, cover, and microwave on high power for 30 seconds.
2 Finely chop the stuffed olives or salad olives, and mix with the cream cheese.
3 For each sandwich, spread the cream cheese mixture on a slice of white bread, and top with a slice of wholewheat bread.
4 Cut off the crusts, and slice into strips, triangles, or other good shapes.

NOW YOU HAVE ALL THE GRACE AND ELEGANCE OF YOUR OWN TEA PARTY.

. . . .
SCHOOL LUNCHES
. . . .

Is your lunch box so packed with delicious foods that you have to protect it from burglars?

In Beverly Cleary's book, *Dear Mr. Henshaw*, Leigh has to invent a burglar alarm for his lunch box.

Leigh's mother works for "Catering by Katy," and she brings home wonderful food delicacies for Leigh's lunch box. But Leigh hates it when the other kids steal his lunch, and he feels that he is turning into a "mean-eyed lunch-kicker."

Leigh has other problems, too. His parents are divorcing, and he's lonely—lonely enough to write dozens of letters to his favorite author, Mr. Henshaw.

Then Leigh invents his own lunch-box burglar alarm, an alarm that will go off with a terrible racket if anyone tries to open his lunch box.

The only difficulty, Leigh realizes too late, is that if he opens the lunch box in the school lunch room, he will set off the alarm himself.

Leigh can't imagine the consequences.

Would you like a lunch so good that you need a burglar alarm on it? Here's one to make yourself.

A School Lunch Project

The Menu
A Peanut Butter, Apple, and Raisin
Sandwich
A Ham and Pickle Sandwich
A Finger Vegetables and Packable
Fruits Assortment
Milk

Peanut Butter, Apple, and Raisin Sandwich
Here's what you need for about four sandwiches:

Half an apple
1 tablespoon raisins
½ cup peanut butter

Here's how to make the sandwiches:

1 Peel and core the apple. Then chop it into very small pieces. (You need only half for the sandwiches. You might as well snack on the other half.)
2 Mix the apple pieces with the raisins and peanut butter.
3 Spread the mixture on wholewheat bread.

Ham and Pickle Sandwich
Here's what you need for about four sandwiches:

¼ pound shaved lean ham
1 tablespoon chopped pickle or pickle relish
½ teaspoon mustard
1 tablespoon mayonnaise

Here's how to make the filling:

1 Mince the shaved ham into small pieces.
2 Mix in the chopped pickle, mustard, and mayonnaise.
3 Make the sandwich with wholewheat bread and lettuce or sprouts to add crunch.

Finger Vegetables and Packable Fruits

Veggie Suggestion: Try veggies that will stay crisp till noon—something like celery or carrot sticks.

Fruit Suggestion: Try fresh fruits that won't go soggy before lunch time—fruits like apple, grapes, nectarine, or plums.

Now You Have Your Own School Lunch.

It may not be safe without a burglar alarm.

··········
MAKING DO WITH WHAT YOU HAVE
·······························

What can you do with leftovers when you have nothing else but left-overs?

If you're creative (and lucky), you can figure out a delicious meal from scraps.

At least, that's what the all-of-a-kind family does.

The family of Sydney Taylor's *All-of-a-Kind Family* lives in New York City at the turn of the century. The family has a father and a mother—and five daughters.

(In time, the family becomes all-of-a-kind-plus-one when a baby brother is born to them.)

In one of the stories, the girls' aunt (their "Tanta") has just arrived to celebrate the Jewish holiday of Sukkot with the family. Their mother is due to arrive home any minute when the girls realize that they've neglected a fine holiday dinner. Their dinner is burned and ruined.

All they've got now is leftovers—and teamwork.

They create a "false soup."

The "false soup" doesn't have all the meat and bones and delicacies of regular soup, but the girls use what they do have. Everyone rushes around, working together on the soup.

In time, the soup is bubbling. The good smell of the soup drives away the unpleasant scorched smell of the burned dinner. The telltale pot is washed and shining brightly on a shelf again.

"We're lucky!" one of the littlest girls says. "We've got two Thanksgivings to celebrate—Succos and then our country's."

Now you use up your leftovers and serve a savory "false soup."

A MAKING-DO "FALSE SOUP" PROJECT

This is soup you can make in the blender.

You decide the combinations you want.

1 Begin with a creamy base for the soup. *Here are the possibilities*:

> *1½ cups chicken broth with ¾ cup milk*
> *OR*
>
> *1 cup vegetable liquid (water left over from cooking vegetables) with 1¼ cups milk*
> *OR*
>
> *1 cup water with 1¼ cups milk*

2 Next, you need a thickener for the soup. Look over your supplies, and then decide the thickener:

> *½ cup leftover cooked or mashed potatoes*
> *OR*
>
> *1 egg, slightly beaten*
> *OR*
>
> *¼ cup cornstarch*
> *OR*
>
> *¼ cup all purpose or unbleached flour*

3 Next, look over your leftover vegetables, and decide what to add:

> *1 cup cooked, cut-up vegetables*

4 Finally, get out onion and seasonings:

> *1 medium onion, chopped*
> *1 teaspoon salt*
> *1 teaspoon pepper*
> *1 teaspoon parsley*

Here's how to fix the soup:

1 In a blender or food processor, put the basic liquids (the broth, water, milk combination you decided), plus the thickener (the potato, egg, cornstarch, or flour), plus the vegetables, onion, salt, and pepper.

2 Cover, and blend until smooth.

3 Pour into a large saucepan, and heat over low heat until boiling. Then cover, and simmer for 20 to 30 minutes.

4 Sprinkle with parsley, and serve warm.

> **NOW YOU HAVE FOUR SERVINGS OF YOUR OWN CREAMY SOUP.**

. . . .

DIET FOODS

. . . .

Most everybody goes on a diet once in awhile, often not too seriously.

But some people really need a whole summer of low-calorie foods and lots of exercise. In Robert Kimmel Smith's *Jelly Belly*, Ned is ready for a summer like that—or at least that's what his parents think. Ned is so fat that the kids at school have been calling him "Jelly Belly."

Ned's parents are under the impression that a summer at diet camp is just what Ned needs to slim down and cheer up. At camp, Ned's bunkmate eats junk food in secret. And Ned decides that he himself has a lot to learn about food and about life.

Most kids who are worried about being fat find that, eventually, they can manage Life Without Junk Food. And they don't really have to go hungry.

In Robert Lipsyte's *One Fat Summer*, for instance, Bobby Marks conquers the problem of being fat when he takes a summer job mowing lawns. Before that he had hated summer because he couldn't hide his fat body inside heavy clothes.

Then, mainly because the weather is cool and he can wear a long-sleeved shirt outside his splitting pants, he decides to go to a Fourth of July carnival, and his whole life is changed.

For one example of low-calorie food that's packed with nutrition, try lettuce cups for lunch. (Lettuce cups have a lot more in them than lettuce.)

A Low-Calorie, High-Taste Lettuce Cup Project

Create a lettuce cup, and think what all you could put in it.

Here's what you need:

Leaves of lettuce

An apple

¼ cup orange juice

¼ cup raspberries, blueberries, or strawberries

¼ cup raisins or currants

Here's how to make a lettuce cup:

1 Select several crisp lettuce leaves from the inside of the head of lettuce. Wash and drain.

2 Wash, quarter, and core the apple. (Leave it unpeeled.) Chop the apple into small pieces. Soak the apple pieces in the orange juice. (The citric acid in the orange juice prevents oxygen reacting with the apple and turning it brown.)

3 Wash and drain the raspberries, blueberries, or strawberries. Cut up strawberries.

4 Curl the lettuce leaves into the shape of a cup. Drain the orange juice from the apple, and put in the apple pieces.

5 Top with berries and raisins or currants.

NOW YOU HAVE A LETTUCE CUP FULL OF NUTRITION AND TASTE.

. . . .
SPORTS POWER
. . . .

Did you ever think about what your favorite sports hero eats?

Most athletes take their food very seriously.

Athletes are even careful about the timing of their food. They eat complex carbohydrates before games (not candy bars or other sugars that might give them only a short-lived burst of energy).

And other times, athletes try to eat perfectly well-balanced diets. Of course, the commercials have the champions consuming everything from non-stop Wheaties and margarine to perpetual soft drinks and beer.

Find biographies of your own favorite athletes, and see where they really get their sports power.

A SPORTS POWER PITA POCKET PROJECT

A well-stuffed pita pocket can give you a good balance of protein, carbohydrate, and fiber—lots of what you need for sports power. And lunch-in-a-pocket is easy to carry to a sports event, whether you're playing or watching.

Here's what you need:

1 large wholewheat pita
Mayonnaise
3 very thin slices lean baked ham
2 thin slices provolone cheese
Shredded lettuce
2 thin slices Spanish onion
Tomato slices
Alfalfa sprouts

Here's how to fill the pita pocket:

1 Split open the pocket.
2 Spread the inside with mayonnaise, and fill with ham, cheese, shredded lettuce, Spanish onion slices, and tomato slices.
3 Top with alfalfa sprouts.
4 Wrap tightly. Refrigerate until you're ready to take it to the game.

NOW YOU HAVE ONE LARGE, STUFFED SPORTS-POWER PITA POCKET.

BRAIN FOOD

Eat fish and grow smart! Does that really happen?

Everyone seems to have a bright idea on what to eat to gain sports power, and everyone seems to have a great notion of what sort of food builds brain power.

Of course, there is no magic food to turn you into a super athlete or a world-power genius. Instead what people need is a variety of nutritious foods, all contributing to building healthy bodies and great minds.

But fish, all by itself, seems to have the big reputation as a brain food. And most seafood is nutritious. Seafood might help.

Actually, however, your brain cells were about 75% developed before you are born—and the other 25% of your brain cells developed before you were one year old.

So as you grow older, you may be getting smarter, but you aren't actually developing any more brain cells. The brain power is all there already.

Instead what your brain cells need now is oxygen. And that's where fish comes in. The hemoglobin in red blood cells carries oxygen around your body (and to your brain). Iron helps build hemoglobin. And fish is a source of easily absorbed iron.

Do you suppose that's why people thought fish was a brain food? Were people thinking scientifically? Or maybe someone long ago was just eating fish and bragging about his brain power?

Try delicious fish fillets, and see if you feel smart.

A MICROWAVE BAKED FISH PROJECT

Here's what you need:

*1 pound white fish fillets
(You decide your fish choice:
haddock, flounder, sole, cod)*

2 tablespoons butter or margarine

8 Saltine crackers

1 lemon

Fresh sprigs of parsley, if you wish

Here's how to bake fish fillets:

1 Spread the fillets in a single layer in a microwave-safe dish. Arrange so the thickest part is toward the outside of the dish.

2 Place the butter or margarine in a heatproof measuring cup. Microwave on high power for about 30 seconds, until the butter melts.

3 Crumble the crackers into the butter, and mix thoroughly.

4 Sprinkle the butter-cracker mixture over the fish.

5 Cut the lemon in half the long way, and cut into quarters. Squeeze the juice from one quarter of the lemon over the fish.

6 Cover the fish with clear plastic wrap, and place in the microwave oven.

7 Microwave on high power for ten to 12 minutes, or until the fish is opaque white and flakes easily. Let stand, still covered, for five minutes.

8 Use a spatula to place the fish fillets onto a warm platter. Slice the remaining lemon into six slices, and arrange them around the fish. Garnish with a sprig of fresh parsley on each fillet.

**NOW YOU HAVE FOUR
SERVINGS OF FISH FILLETS.**

Serve with baked potatoes, peas, and salad.

FOOD FOR ASTRONAUTS

At zero gravity in a spaceship, astronauts have problems with food that we've never had to think about on earth.

At zero gravity, for instance, dishes, trays, and the astronauts themselves are always in danger of just floating away.

Successful foods for spaceships come out a little odd.

The foods are often sealed into individual packets, called "retort pouches." The "cook" astronaut who needs to add water uses a hollow needle to punch a hole in the retort pouch. The hollow needle connects directly to a supply of water, and lets the exact amount of water into the food without any exposure to the air.

Otherwise, drops of water—or bits of food—would be floating around the spacecraft.

The only way to heat food is by forcing air around it from a special oven.

Other food pouches the astronauts can cut open with scissors.

To eat, the astronauts need to tie the food down. They use Velcro to fasten down their trays—and then they have to tie themselves into their chairs, too.

Otherwise, the astronauts could float away, with their dinners flying every which way.

Then they have to put the food in their mouths all in one bite, without one crumb left over.

Otherwise, crumbs would float around the spacecraft. A runaway crumb could get into delicate machinery and wreck something fragile.

And the astronauts must clean everything (their mouths, dishes, trays) perfectly.

Try some spaceship cookies—just the right size to put into your mouth, all in one bite, with not one crumb left over.

A BITE-SIZED SHORTBREAD COOKIES PROJECT

Because they are bite-sized, these shortbread cookies are suitable to take on a spaceship.

Here's what you need:

- ½ cup (1 stick) butter or margarine
- ¼ cup sugar
- 1¼ cups all purpose or unbleached flour

Here's how to mix the dough:

1 Cream the butter or margarine and sugar until thoroughly combined. You can use an electric mixer for this step.

2 With a wooden spoon, stir in the flour until it is well combined.

3 Form the dough into a ball. Wrap in plastic. If you wish, you can chill the dough in the refrigerator overnight, but you don't need to.

Here's how to roll out the cookies:

1 Preheat the oven to 350°F (180°C).

2 Sprinkle a pastry cloth with flour, and roll out the dough until it is about ⅓ inch thick.

3 Use a sharp knife to cut the dough into 1- to 1½-inch squares. Or use the center of a doughnut cutter to cut the dough into small round bites.

4 Bake on an ungreased baking sheet for 20 minutes, or until lightly browned.

5 Cool on wire racks.

: **NOW YOU HAVE ABOUT 32**
: **BITE-SIZED SHORTBREAD**
: **COOKIES, SUITABLE FOR**
: **TAKING ON A MISSION INTO**
: **SPACE.**

. . . .

SHORTBREAD

. . . .

Because shortbread originated in Scotland, it is often called Scotch shortbread.

Scottish bakers pat the dough into a circular shape, score it in wedge-shaped pieces as if it were a pie—and then bake it on a pie plate.

And it's called shortbread since an antique meaning for the word "short" is just plain flat.

The Scottish people serve shortbread on Christmas and on other important occasions, and sometimes they score the wedges with holiday designs.

You might enjoy the inventive names of other Scottish foods.

Bubble and squeak is meat and cabbage, fried together, sometimes with a potato thrown in. Bubble and squeak is named more for the humor of the name than for the ingredients of the dinner.

Haggis is a sort of round, gray Scottish sausage. The gray ball is the stomach of a sheep, and in it are sewn the sheep's heart, lungs, and liver, along with oatmeal and onions.

On patriotic holidays in Scotland, the arrival of the haggis is announced with the solemn music of the bagpipes.

If you like hot dogs, you could probably eat haggis. But if you eat haggis, you must eat it with reverence, enthusiasm, and a sense of importance.

PIG-OUT FOODS

If you want a polite term for pig-out foods, you could call them comfort foods.

They are the foods you eat when you're under stress. They are the foods that make you feel better.

They're the foods you can't stop eating.

In Paula Danziger's *The Pistachio Prescription*, Cassie is feeling like "the first teenage bomb in captivity."

At school Cassie is running for "freshperson class president" and conducting "Operation Overthrow." At home her parents are battling, and she feels as if she is living through World War III.

In between she eats red pistachio nuts.

"Pistachio nuts, the red ones, cure any problem," Cassie says. "When I'm upset or nervous I always eat them. My best friend, Vicki, says that's the silliest thing she's ever heard. She says it's jelly beans that work . . ."

What pig-out food works for you? We suggest just a few of your own home-made cheese puffs.

A PIG-OUT CHEESE PUFFS PROJECT

Here's what you need:

- ¼ pound Cheddar cheese
- ¼ cup all purpose or unbleached flour
- ¼ teaspoon salt
- ¼ teaspoon pepper
- ¼ teaspoon paprika

Here's how to make cheese puffs:

1 Preheat the oven to 375°F (190°C).

2 Place the Cheddar cheese in a large, heatproof glass bowl. Soften the cheese in the microwave oven at low power for two minutes.

3 Stir in the flour, salt, pepper, and paprika.

4 Form the cheese mixture into ¾-inch balls. Be especially sure to wash your hands before you begin shaping the cheese balls.

5 Line up the cheese balls on a greased baking sheet. Bake for 12 to 15 minutes, until they puff up to a golden brown.

6 Eat warm or cool, as you wish.

> **NOW YOU HAVE ABOUT EIGHT TO TEN CHEESE PUFFS, WITH PIG-OUT POTENTIAL.**

. . . .

GROSS-OUT FOODS

. . . .

Some of today's favorite foods were once considered nasty and gross—or even poisonous.

Once Americans thought tomatoes were poison.

A courageous farmer proved otherwise. On September 26, 1820, Robert G. Johnson of Salem, Oregon, stood in front of a crowd and proceeded to eat a whole basketful of tomatoes. His doctor stood by—saying that he would attempt to save Mr. Johnson, but that he feared the effort would prove hopeless.

Of course, Robert Johnson lived and proved that tomatoes are not poisonous.

In Thomas Rockwell's book *How to Eat Fried Worms*, Billy undertakes a bet that he can manage to eat 15 worms. Billy can eat the worms any way he wants, along with any "flavoring" from peanut butter to horseradish.

Billy wins his bet.

Would you like to try some fried worms? Fix up the next recipe—if you dare.

A FRIED WORMS GROSS-OUT PROJECT

Don't worry. You'll like fried worms.

Be especially sure to wash your hands before you begin this project. You wouldn't want to get the worms dirty.

Here's what you need:

2 cups all purpose or unbleached flour

½ teaspoon salt

2 eggs

2 tablespoons warm water

Here's how to make fried-worm dough:

1 Mix the flour and salt, and pour out onto a board or pastry cloth.

2 Make a well in the center.

3 Beat the eggs in a small bowl, and stir in the water.

4 Pour the egg mixture into the center well of the flour.

5 Use your hands to mix flour into the egg mixture. Work the dough, pushing it with the palms of your (clean) hands and then turning over a new surface to push again. Knead until smooth.

Hint: Add a little more water if necessary. The dough ought to be stiff but workable.

6 Divide the dough in half. Cover with a clean dish towel, and let the dough rest for about 30 minutes.

FRIED WORMS
continued

Here's how to make the "worms":

1 Go back to the board or pastry cloth. Roll out each half of the dough as thinly as possible.

2 Let the dough dry for a few minutes.

3 Then roll up the dough loosely, and cut the dough roll into long strips. Keep the strips as even as you can.

4 Spread out the strips and let them dry. When they are dry, you can cook them immediately. (Or, if you don't want "fried worms" immediately, you can store them in a tightly covered container in a cool, dry place. Use within a week.)

Here's how to cook the "worms":

: *Caution: You need adult help*
: *with boiling water.*

1 Bring water to boil in a large pan. Add one teaspoon salt to the water.

2 Drop the "worms" into the water and boil for five to ten minutes (depending on the thickness).

3 Drain the "worms" into a colander over the sink, and rinse with cold water.

4 Let cool for a few minutes.

Here's how to fry the "worms":

: *Caution: You need adult help*
: *with frying.*

1 In a heavy skillet, heat two tablespoons butter, margarine, or cooking oil.

2 Put the "worms" into the skillet over medium-high heat. Stir to keep them from sticking or burning. In just a few minutes, they will be brown and hot, ready to eat.

3 Serve immediately with meat, fish, or a little tomato sauce.

: **NOW YOU HAVE SIX**
: **SERVINGS OF FRIED**
: **WORMS.**

Aren't you glad?

GREAT-GRANDMOTHER'S FAVORITE RECIPES

Maybe your great-grandmother came to America from Ireland or Africa, Mexico or China.

Or perhaps she was a Native American whose civilization had already flourished here for thousands of years.

Your ever-so-great-grandparents might have been pioneers out West. They might have been immigrants who came across an ocean to get to America.

Your ancestors probably couldn't bring much with them.

But they could bring their memories of traditions, of holiday customs, and of special foods.

Here are a few great-grandmothers' recipes to try—all updated.

But these are from other people's great-grandmothers. Who were your ancestors, and what memories did your great-grandfamily leave for you?

AN EMPANADAS PROJECT

If your great-grandmother came from Spain, Mexico, or Texas (or other parts of the southern United States), she might have lunched on meat pie empanadas. This is an updated empanada—a turnover, with a choice of fillings.

Here's what you need for the pastry:

- *3 cups all purpose or unbleached flour*
- *1 teaspoon salt*
- *A pinch of ground anise seed*
- *½ cup olive oil*
- *½ cup cold water*

You decide what kind of filling you want: Ham or tuna.

Here's what you need for ham filling:

- *1 clove minced garlic (or ⅛ teaspoon garlic powder)*
- *1 large onion*
- *2 small tomatoes*
- *½ pound cooked or baked ham*
- *2 hard-cooked eggs*
- *2 tablespoons olive oil*
- *Sprinkling of pepper and salt, if you wish*

Here's what you need for tuna filling:

- *1 large onion*
- *2 medium tomatoes*
- *7-ounce can of water-packed tuna*
- *2 hard-cooked eggs*
- *⅓ cup olive oil*
- *Sprinkling of salt, if you wish*

Here's how to make the pastry:

1 Measure the flour into a large bowl. Stir in salt and anise seed.

2 Make a hole in the center of the flour, and pour in the olive oil and water. Mix the dough thoroughly with your fingers or with a fork.

3 Roll the dough into a ball, and let it rest while you prepare the filling.

Here's how to get the ingredients ready for ham filling:

1 Chop the onion and the tomatoes.

2 Dice the ham.

3 Peel and mash the hard-cooked eggs.

Here's how to get the ingredients ready for tuna filling:

1 Chop the onion and the tomatoes.

2 Drain the tuna, and break it into bits.

3 Peel and mash the hard-cooked eggs.

....

EMPANADAS
continued

Here's how to cook the ham or tuna filling:

1 Heat the olive oil in a skillet over medium heat.

2 Stir and fry the onions slowly until they are soft and transparent.

> : *Caution: You need adult help*
> : *with frying the onions.*

3 Add the chopped tomatoes (and minced garlic).

4 Turn down the heat. Stir frequently and simmer for about five minutes, or until the liquid evaporates.

5 Add the ham or tuna pieces and the mashed hard-cooked eggs. Stir over low heat for two to three minutes more. Remove from heat.

6 If you wish, sprinkle on pepper and salt.

Here's how to finish the turnovers:

1 Preheat the oven to 425°F (220°C).

2 Sprinkle flour on a pastry cloth or board. Roll out the dough to ¼ inch thick. Then cut circles or squares about 6 inches across. Use the rim of a can to help cut them right, or use a paper model—or just mark with a knife point, and cut them when they seem right.

3 Spoon about two tablespoons filling onto half of each circle or square. Leave the edge of the pastry clear.

4 Here's the fun part; turning over the turnovers. Fold the other half of each circle or square over the filling. Pinch the edges together, and press with a fork all around each edge.

5 Brush each turnover lightly with a beaten egg.

6 Prick the top of each with a fork.

7 Bake on a greased baking sheet for 25 minutes—until the turnovers are brown and crisp.

> : **NOW YOU HAVE ABOUT TEN**
> : **EMPANADAS THAT YOUR**
> : **GRANDMOTHER WOULD**
> : **LOVE TO TASTE.**

A CORN ON THE COB PROJECT

In Central America, Columbus ate corn with one of his first New World meals. In North America, native Americans served corn to the earliest European settlers—and taught them how to grow their own corn.

And to this day, everyone still likes corn on the cob.

Use a microwave oven to make modern corn on the cob.

Here's one way to get the corn ready:

1 Remove the outside husks from fresh corn on the cob. Leave the inner husks attached, but spread them apart and remove the corn silk. (Be patient.)

Hint: This can be a messy job. Take it outside, or husk the corn over an open bag to catch the huskings.

2 If you wish, butter the corn at this point.

3 Replace the inner husks as the "wrapping." If they do not stay together, tie them together at the tip with string.

Here's another way to get the corn ready:

1 Husk the corn, and remove the corn silk.

2 Wrap each ear of corn in waxed paper. If you wish, butter the corn at this point.

Here's how to microwave corn on the cob:

1 Place the ears of corn on a microwave-safe plate.

2 Roast in the microwave oven on high power:
four to six minutes for two ears of corn
six to eight minutes for four ears of corn
ten to 12 minutes for six ears of corn

3 Let stand for two or three minutes after roasting.

NOW YOU HAVE YOUR OWN ROASTED CORN ON THE COB.

A PICKLES PROJECT

Down on the farm, people used to make their own pickles. You can, too, just as easily.

Here's what you need:

1 medium onion
1 large cucumber
½ cup vinegar
5 tablespoons water
5 tablespoons sugar
½ teaspoon salt
2 or 3 shakes of pepper
1 tablespoon chopped parsley, if you wish

Here's how to make pickles:

1 Cut the onion into thin slices.

2 Wash the cucumber.

3 Using a fork or a vegetable peeler, scrape the length of the unpeeled cucumber up and down. Make stripes all the way around.

4 Then cut the cucumber into thin slices.

5 In a one-quart glass jar or bowl, toss the onion and cucumber slices together.

6 In a separate bowl, mix the vinegar, water, sugar, salt, and pepper.

7 Pour over the onion-cucumber mixture.

8 Cover and refrigerate for at least 24 hours before eating.

9 After that, keep the pickles in the refrigerator.

Hint: When the pickles are finished, save the brine to make more pickles. (The brine is the liquid the pickles have been sitting in.)

HELP YOURSELF TO YOUR OWN FRESH HOMEMADE PICKLES.

AN OLD-FASHIONED WAFFLES PROJECT

Your great-grandparents probably owned a waffle iron. If you have one, you can make waffles just like theirs.

Here's what you need:

- 2 eggs
- 2 cups milk
- 1 cup (2 sticks) butter
- 2½ cups all purpose or unbleached flour
- 2 tablespoons sugar
- 1 tablespoon baking powder
- 1 teaspoon salt

Here's how to make waffles:

1 Start heating the waffle iron.

2 Separate the egg yolks from the whites, egg whites into a small mixer bowl and egg yolks into a large mixer bowl.

3 Use the electric mixer to whip the egg whites at high speed until they stand in stiff peaks.

4 Add one cup of the milk to the egg yolks in the large bowl. Use the electric mixer to beat. Add the other cup of milk, and beat a little more.

5 Melt the butter on high power in the microwave oven for one minute. Mix the melted butter into the egg-milk mixture.

6 In a separate bowl, mix the flour, sugar, baking powder, and salt. Add to the egg-milk mixture and beat until smooth.

7 Carefully fold the egg whites into the batter.

8 Now the batter is ready for the waffle iron. Pour ¼ to ⅓ cup batter onto each side of the waffle iron, and close the lid. Heat until the waffle iron stops steaming.

9 Serve immediately with maple syrup or with cinnamon and sugar.

NOW YOU HAVE ABOUT 24 OLD-FASHIONED FOUR-INCH WAFFLES.

A BUTTERMILK BISCUITS PROJECT

Picture gathering around the chuckwagon after riding herd all day in the Old West. You're ready for chow—and you're hoping for buttermilk biscuits.

Here's what you need:

2 cups all purpose or unbleached flour

½ teaspoon baking soda

½ teaspoon salt

3 tablespoons butter

1 cup buttermilk or thick sour milk

Here's how to bake easy buttermilk biscuits:

1 Preheat the oven to 425°F (220°C).

2 In a large bowl, combine the flour, baking soda, and salt.

3 Blend in the butter with a pastry blender or two knives. This is called "cutting in" the butter. Work with the pastry blender or two knives until the mixture looks like coarse crumbs.

4 Stir in the buttermilk quickly.

5 Sprinkle a pastry cloth or board with flour. Turn the dough out onto the board, and knead once or twice. Pat out to ½-inch thickness.

6 Cut out biscuits with a biscuit cutter or round cookie cutter. Arrange on an ungreased baking sheet an inch apart.

7 Bake for 12 to 15 minutes, until the biscuits are light brown and puffy.

8 Serve warm.

> **NOW YOU HAVE EIGHT TO TEN BUTTERMILK BISCUITS.**

Traveling Down the Road with Johnnycake

Johnnycake may have started out as "journey cake."

It's true that johnnycake is easy to bake, and it's just the sort of food that would have kept well over a long journey (even stuffed into saddlebags).

But there may be another origin to the name. Johnnycake may have started as Shawneecake, because the Shawnees were very good at making it. (Does the word "johnnycake" sound a lot like "Shawnee cake"?)

But making cornbread had not started out easy for the Shawnees.

Long ago, the Shawnee women had to grind corn by standing over a hollow tree trunk and pounding for hours until hard kernels of corn finally turned into cornmeal.

The result was a sort of porridge (called "samp"), which the Shawnees concocted of soggy cornmeal and then cooked over an open fire.

The early European settlers improved the taste of cornmeal by adding milk, butter, and sugar. Then they tried cooking cornbread on a griddle like pancakes, and both the Shawnees and the Europeans were very pleased with the results.

By the 1630s the colonists had built gristmills, so that grinding corn was no longer the dreadful chore it had been for the Shawnees.

But you'll find no one named Johnny who can claim credit for johnnycake.

(By the way, in Rhode Island, you'll find johnnycake is spelled jonnycake. And Rhode Island bakers are specially proud of their delicious jonnycakes baked with fine white cornmeal.)

A JOHNNYCAKE PROJECT

Here's real old-fashioned johnnycake—but not so old-fashioned that you have to pound corn over a hollow tree trunk. Instead, you can have the batter mixed up in minutes.

Here's what you need:

1 cup cornmeal
½ teaspoon baking soda
1 teaspoon cream of tartar
¼ teaspoon salt
1 egg
1 cup milk
¼ cup honey
1 tablespoon molasses
1 tablespoon butter

Here's how to make johnnycake:

1 Preheat the oven to 425°F (220°C).

2 In a large bowl, mix together the cornmeal, baking soda, cream of tartar, and salt.

3 In a separate large bowl, beat the egg with a fork. Then stir in the milk, honey, and molasses.

4 Melt the butter in the microwave oven on high power for 30 seconds. Stir the melted butter in with the egg-molasses mixture.

5 Pour the egg-molasses mixture into the cornmeal mixture. Stir briefly, just until they are well combined.

6 Pour the batter into a greased 8-inch square cake pan.

7 Bake for 30 minutes.

8 Serve hot.

NOW YOU HAVE ABOUT 16 SQUARES OF JOHNNYCAKE, GOOD AT HOME OR ON A LONG JOURNEY.

ENGLISH PUDDING AND INDIAN PUDDING

The early settlers in New England used to dream of the rich holiday puddings they had enjoyed back home in Old England.

No such puddings seemed possible in the New World. In the first years, the settlers had no flour and they had very few dairy cattle, so they were short of milk and butter.

But the early English settlers did have the cornmeal that the native Americans taught them to make, and they had tasted the flat cornmeal-porridge, "samp."

So they set about creating pudding out of samp. (They were already developing samp into the first johnnycakes.)

As more dairy cattle arrived in New England, the colonists had more of the traditional pudding ingredients they wanted. They tried enriching samp with milk, butter, eggs, spices—and molasses.

The English colonists gave credit to the original native American invention by naming the results "Indian pudding."

Soon molasses seemed absolutely necessary to create a good American holiday pudding. The colonists in New England began to look eagerly for ships to arrive carrying molasses from the West Indies. Report is that one of the first Thanksgiving feasts in the New World had to be delayed.

The colonists were still waiting for the molasses to arrive.

Then they could celebrate.

AN INDIAN PUDDING PROJECT

Perhaps your ancestors were delighted with their invention of a rich and sweet cornmeal pudding.

Now you can make Indian pudding in a microwave oven.

Here's what you need:

2 cups hot milk

¼ cup cornmeal

½ teaspoon salt

½ teaspoon ginger

½ teaspoon cinnamon

⅛ teaspoon baking soda

½ cup molasses

1 cup cold milk

⅓ cup raisins (if you wish)

Here's what you do:

1 Measure milk into a one-quart heatproof casserole dish. Heat, uncovered, in the microwave oven on high power for three to four minutes, or until steaming.

2 Add the cornmeal slowly, while stirring.

3 Cover and heat the mixture on high power for 1½ minutes. Stir and heat again for another 1½ to two minutes, or until the mixture is thickened.

4 Stir in salt, ginger, cinnamon, molasses, and eggs. Add raisins, if you wish.

5 Cover and cook on medium-high power for 20 to 25 minutes, until a knife comes out clean when inserted one inch from edge of bowl.

6 Serve warm, with vanilla ice cream or whipped cream on top.

NOW YOU HAVE ABOUT SIX SERVINGS OF YOUR OWN NEW WORLD PUDDING WITH OLD WORLD ADDITIONS.

. . . .

A STORY OF GRAHAM CRACKERS

. . . .

Back in the early 1800s, a Presbyterian minister from Connecticut, the Reverend Sylvester Graham, began traveling all around the United States to preach the virtues of good diet and healthful living.

Rev. Graham wanted Americans to stay healthy with daily exercise, good food, and cheerful dispositions.

Do you suppose your ancestors went to hear any of Rev. Graham's lectures?

Rev. Graham was also in favor of hard beds, cleanliness (cold showers at least three times a week), sensible clothes, and open bedroom windows for fresh air (even in the winter). He was against alcohol, meat, and spicy foods.

Particularly, Rev. Graham objected to white flour.

Back then, white flour was milled (and often still is) so as to destroy the wheat germ and bran—and other nutritious elements. Rev. Graham wanted the wheat germ and bran back in the flour so that Americans would have more fiber in their diet.

So he invented a new type of wholewheat flour, called graham flour. You can still find it for sale.

And, of course, the crackers named after Rev. Graham are graham crackers. You can still find graham crackers for sale, too—or you can make your own.

A GRAHAM CRACKERS PROJECT

Here's what you need:

1 cup graham or wholewheat flour
1 cup all purpose or unbleached flour
1 teaspoon baking powder
1 teaspoon salt
¼ cup (1 stick) butter
¼ cup honey
¼ cup milk

Here's how to make graham crackers:

1 Preheat the oven to 400°F (200°C).

2 In a large bowl, combine the flours with the baking powder and salt.

3 Using a pastry blender or two knives, cut in the butter until the mixture looks like coarse crumbs.

4 Stir in the honey.

5 Add the milk, a little at a time, until you have a stiff dough. (You may need a little more or a little less than ¼ cup.)

6 Sprinkle flour on a pastry cloth or board. Roll out the dough very thin, no more than ¼-inch thick.

7 Cut into three-inch squares. Prick the surface of each square with a fork.

8 Brush each square lightly with milk.

9 Bake on an ungreased baking sheet for about 18 minutes, or until golden brown.

10 Cool thoroughly on wire racks, and store in a tightly covered container.

> **NOW YOU HAVE ABOUT A DOZEN HOMEMADE GRAHAM CRACKERS.**

··········
A STRAWBERRY SHORTCAKE PROJECT
·································

Imagine how good the first strawberries must have tasted to your great-grandparents after a long winter without fresh fruits. The first fresh strawberries still do taste better than anything else in the world.

Here's what you need:

1 quart fresh strawberries (or frozen whole strawberries, partially thawed)

¼ cup sugar

2 cups all purpose or unbleached flour

½ teaspoon salt

4 teaspoons baking powder

2 tablespoons more sugar

½ cup (1 stick) butter or margarine, softened

⅔ cup milk or light cream

1 cup (½ pint) whipping cream

Here's how to prepare the strawberries.

Wash the strawberries and remove the hulls. Save six of the best whole strawberries to top off your strawberry shortcake. Slice the rest. Sprinkle them with ¼ cup sugar, and refrigerate while you make the shortcake.

Here's how to mix shortcake dough:

1 Preheat the oven to 450°F (230°C).

2 In a large bowl, combine the flour, salt, baking powder, and two tablespoons sugar. Stir thoroughly.

3 Cut the butter or margarine into about six pieces, and add to the flour mixture.

4 With a pastry blender or fork, work the butter into the flour until the mixture looks like coarse crumbs.

5 Add ⅔ cup milk or light cream, and stir in quickly.

· · · · · · · · · ·

STRAWBERRY SHORTCAKE
continued

Here's how to finish:

1 Knead the dough lightly three or four times. Turn the dough out onto a floured pastry cloth or board. Pat or roll out the dough to ½-inch thickness.

2 Use a biscuit cutter to cut six biscuits. Line up the biscuits on a lightly greased baking sheet.

3 Bake for about ten minutes, until golden brown.

4 Cool briefly on a wire rack.

5 Use an electric mixer to whip the whipping cream at high speed.

6 Split the six shortcakes. Butter each bottom layer. Fill with strawberries, and top with whipped cream. Add the tops, and cover with more strawberries and whipped cream.

> NOW YOU HAVE SIX
> SERVINGS OF YOUR OWN
> LUSCIOUS HOMEMADE
> STRAWBERRY SHORTCAKE.

· · · · · · · · · ·

DO THE HOKEY-POKEY, AND TURN YOURSELF ABOUT

· ·

If they were city children, your great-grandparents might have eagerly waited for the arrival of the hokey-pokey man.

The hokey-pokey man sold hokey-pokey—ice cream treats for children.

And if your great-grandparents lived in New York City, they might have heard a familiar cry from the street vendors who sold ice cream:

"I Scream / Ice Cream!"

A MULLED CIDER PROJECT

"Mulled" is an old-fashioned word that means flavored with spices. This hot mulled cider is perfect for a cold winter day.

Here's what you need:

 1 quart apple cider
 1 cinnamon stick
 5 whole cloves
 ¼ cup brown sugar, well packed

Here's how to fix mulled cider:

1 Pour the apple cider into a large pot, and stir in cinnamon stick, cloves, and brown sugar.

2 Bring to a boil over medium-high heat.

3 Lower the heat. Cover and let simmer for 15 to 20 minutes.

4 Serve warm.

> **NOW YOU HAVE ONE QUART OF OLD-FASHIONED MULLED CIDER.**

FAST FOOD THE PIONEER WAY

Your pioneer ancestors might have fixed up a large pot of soup or stew, and then taken it outside to freeze right in the pot—with a large spoon sticking out the top of the pot.

When the soup was frozen solid, they removed the pot and used the spoon as a hook by which to hang up the frozen soup.

They could cut off a frozen chunk whenever they wanted a heat-and-eat fast dinner.

FUN FOOD WITH SECRET MESSAGES

These projects give you a chance to send hidden messages.

You can write "I Love You" with applesauce. You can hide messages inside party cupcakes. You can spell words with alphabet soup, or turn a cake upside down and uncover a hidden design.

You might even receive a message or two as a reward for all your efforts.

. . . .

AN APPLESAUCE PROJECT THAT SAYS "I LOVE YOU"

. . . .

First make your own pure delicious applesauce. Then write an applesauce message.

Applesauce
(With or Without a Microwave)

Here's what you need:

- 2 pounds apples (about 6 small apples)
- ¼ cup water or orange juice
- 1 tablespoon lemon juice

Here's how to cut the apples:

Cut each apple into four pieces, and cut out the core. You don't need to peel the apples, but make sure you get rid of the seeds, stem, and other parts of the apple core that are not good to eat.

Here's how to microwave the apples:

1 Put the apple pieces into a large microwave-safe dish.

2 Pour in the water or orange juice and the lemon juice.

3 Cover the dish, and heat in the microwave oven at high power for five minutes.

4 Stir the apple pieces. Then heat at high power for another five minutes.

5 The apples ought to be soft and tender, with the peels almost falling off.

Here's how to cook the apples without a microwave:

1 Put the apple pieces into a large pan. Add the ¼ cup water or orange juice and the lemon juice.

2 Cook the apples over low heat for about 40 minutes, until they are soft and tender.

APPLESAUCE
continued

Here's how to turn the apples into applesauce:

1 Put a strainer into the sink. Pour the apples into it so that you can drain out the water. Use oven mitts and keep your face out of the way. Steam is invisible, but hot.

2 Spoon the mushy apples into a food mill. Hold the food mill over a large bowl, and crank out applesauce. The peels will fall right off.

3 If you don't have a food mill, spoon the mushy apples into a blender or food processor. Put on the lid, and process just a minute or two until the apples turn into applesauce. This sort of applesauce will be chunky because it still has bits of peel in it.

Here's how to flavor the applesauce:

1 *You decide how to flavor the applesauce.* Applesauce is very good plain, but you might want to stir in:

    1 teaspoon nutmeg
      OR
    1 teaspoon cinnamon
      OR
    ½ teaspoon ginger

2 Serve warm or cold. Keep in the refrigerator.

> **NOW YOU HAVE ABOUT TWO CUPS OF YOUR OWN PURE APPLESAUCE.**

Here's how to write an applesauce message:

1 Spoon applesauce into a dish, and write a message with bits of fruit. *You decide what to use for your message:*

    Strawberry pieces
      OR
    Blueberries
      OR
    Raisins
      OR
    "Red hot" cinnamon candies

2 Try outlining a heart or writing "I ♡ U."

COOKING WIZARDRY FOR KIDS

APPLE TIDBITS

. . . .

In what family of plants do apples belong?
   Roses. Really.

How is an apple a good toothbrush?
   When you eat an apple, the fibers in the apple clear out any bits of food stuck around your teeth. After you eat something sticky or gooey, eat an apple.

Don't plant seeds from your best apple.
   Strangely enough, seeds are usually not the best way to start apple trees. They'd probably grow into inferior trees with bad-tasting apples.
   Apple farmers create new apple trees by grafting buds from one good tree onto the branches of another good tree.

Did Johnny Appleseed really exist?
   Yes. His name was John Chapman, and he lived from 1774 to 1845. He was a kind man who said that he never harmed a living creature. He traveled across America with his Bible, a bag of apple seeds, and wonderful plans.
   Some of his plans didn't work. The trees he planted were often poor straggly things. He also carried seeds for herbs that he thought people could use for medicine. But those seeds turned out to grow weeds.
   Johnny Appleseed is famous, though, because he inspired the early settlers to plant apple orchards. Then they could have apples all winter, and on the harsh frontier, that could make the difference between life and death.
   And maybe people don't like poor straggly apple trees. But the animals loved them, and the winter apples make the difference between life and death for them, too.

Did you know that an apple is 85% water?
   That's not so strange. People are about 65% water.

How can you find a star inside an apple?
   Slice through the apple crosswise, and look at the starry core.

When you say something is "as American as apple pie," do you mean it?
   No. Europeans ate apple pie before they had ever heard of America. What we really ought to say is "as American as cranberries."

Does an apple a day really keep the doctor away?
   Yes. Eating apples, along with other fruits and vegetables, helps to keep you healthy, and then you won't have to see your doctor so much.
   But, of course, doctors eat apples, too. So you just might find a doctor at the orchard, or maybe in the kitchen making a fine apple pie.

AN APPLE STORY

Almost two hundred years ago, in 1796, a Canadian farmer found a mysterious grove of apple trees in the forest near his farm. The apples were the most delicious he had ever tasted.

They seemed almost like magic to him.

With much work, the farmer transplanted 20 of the trees so that they could grow near his house. He wanted his family to be able to care for the trees and to enjoy the brilliant red apples.

And so the family did for some 30 years.

The farmer was so proud of his wonderful apple trees that he helped his neighbors to grow other trees from them.

Soon his apples were the favorite apple all over Canada, then all across the United States, and then around the rest of the world.

The farmer named the apples after himself and after their color. The farmer's name was John McIntosh, and so the apple became McIntosh Reds.

Then, one by one, the trees began to die. By 1830, all of the trees were gone except for one last tree.

More trouble followed. In 1893, a fire struck and burned almost all of the last great tree.

Only one side was still alive, but that part of the tree kept on bearing apples for years. Altogether, the tree lived 112 years.

Now we still eat McIntosh apples.

John McIntosh would probably not be surprised. But he might be surprised to learn that people like his apples so well that they named a computer after them.

After all, you can't eat a computer.

....
AN APPLE TASTE TEST
....

What kind of apples do you like best?

You'd have a hard time finding out.

Every apple seed produces a whole new kind of apple tree. Right now, you could find about 3,000 kinds of apples for sale somewhere or another. Some have lovely strange names, like Wolfe Rivers, Rhode Island Greenings, Winesaps, or Northern Spys. In England, the names of apples ring with even stranger tones: Blanderells, Costards, Pearmains, or Pomewaters.

Try a taste test in the fall when you can have your choice of fresh apples.

....
TELL YOUR FORTUNE WITH APPLE GAMES
....

Here are some old-fashioned ways to tell your fortune with apples.

This one is from Kentucky. Save the seeds from an apple, and count them, one by one, with the rhyme:

> He loves me / He don't
> He'll marry me / He won't
> He would if he could / But he can't.

See where you end up.

This one is from England. Walk in a circle holding an apple seed between your thumb and forefinger. Say:

> Pippin, pippin, paradise /
> Tell me where my true love lies.

The seed is supposed to fly off toward the house of your future wife or husband. (A pippin is a small apple or an apple seed.)

This one is from New England. Peel an apple. See how many times the peel breaks, and that is how many children you will have.

This one is from Russia. Dream of an apple, and that means you will have a long life. You will succeed in your career, and you will find a good wife or husband.

Happy apple dreams.

AN ALPHABET SOUP PROJECT

You'll find secret messages in your alphabet soup, but the messages may be a little scrambled.

Alphabet soup is a good way to use leftover chicken and leftover vegetables.

Here's what you need:

2 quarts water
8 chicken bouillon cubes
¼ cup diced onion
¼ cup alphabet noodles
1 cup cooked diced chicken
½ cup cooked carrots
½ cup cooked green beans
¼ cup cooked corn kernels

Here's how to make alphabet soup:

1 Bring the two quarts of water to a boil.

2 Carefully add the bouillon cubes, onion, and alphabet noodles.

: *Caution: You need adult help*
: *with boiling water.*

3 Turn the heat down, and simmer the soup for ten minutes.

4 Add the chicken, carrots, green beans, and corn.

Hint: Use either leftover or canned carrots, green beans, and corn. Or instead of green beans, use peas or lima beans.

5 Heat the soup for about five more minutes.

: **NOW YOU HAVE ABOUT 11**
: **CUPS OF ALPHABET SOUP.**

See what words you can spell as you eat.

A CUPCAKES PROJECT FULL OF GOOD-LUCK MESSAGES

Bake honey-sweet party cupcakes, and hide special good-luck messages inside.

Honey Cupcakes
Here's what you need:

- 1 cup (2 sticks) butter or margarine
- 1½ cups honey
- 4 eggs
- 2 cups sifted all purpose or unbleached flour
- 2 teaspoons baking soda
- 1 teaspoon cinnamon
- 1 teaspoon ginger
- ¼ teaspoon salt
- 1⅓ cups sour cream

Here's how to make the cupcake batter:

1 Preheat the oven to 350°F (180°C).

2 Mix together the butter and honey in the large bowl of an electric mixer. Beat until smooth.

3 Break the eggs into a separate bowl, and beat them lightly with a fork. Then beat them into your batter.

4 Sift the flour with the baking soda, cinnamon, ginger, and salt.

5 Add the flour mixture and the sour cream to the batter, alternately. Add each a bit at a time, and beat well.

Here's how to bake the cupcakes:

1 Spoon the batter into paper baking cups until each cup is almost—but not quite—full.

2 Bake in a cupcake pan for 25 minutes. Put just one pan in the oven at a time.

3 Let cool before frosting.

> NOW YOU HAVE 24 HONEY CUPCAKES.

GOOD-LUCK CUPCAKES

Cream Cheese Frosting
Here's what you need:

1 8-ounce package cream cheese
2 tablespoons honey
1 teaspoon vanilla extract

Here's how to make the frosting:

1 In the small bowl of an electric mixer, beat together the cream cheese, honey, and vanilla extract. Beat at high speed until smooth.

2 **You decide if you want colored frosting.** If you do, stir in four or five drops of food coloring. Add, one drop at a time, until you get the right shade.

How to Hide the Good-Luck Messages

1 Write your secret message on a small piece of an index card, cardboard or stiff paper. Your message ought to be no bigger than $1 \times 1\frac{1}{2}$ inches. (You need for the messages to be small enough to hide inside cupcakes.)

2 Wrap the message tightly in aluminum foil.

3 Punch a small hole in the top of the foil, and tie on a ribbon or bow.

4 Cut a slit in the top of the cupcake, and carefully push in your message. The ribbon or bow stays on top of the cupcake as part of the decoration.

How to Receive the Good-Luck Messages

Just pull on the bow, and out comes the special wrapped message.

. . . .

HONEY SWEETENERS

. . . .

Just how sweet is honey?

Honey is the sweetest food there is, sweeter even than sugar.

Can honey make you fat?

Honey can make you fat if you eat lots of it. But honey tastes so sweet that, often, a very small amount will do.

How can you use honey instead of sugar?

Honey makes a good substitute for sugar. If a recipe calls for one cup sugar, for instance, you can use ½ cup honey. That's good because you get a delicious sweet taste with fewer calories.

How old is the human sweet tooth?

We figure at least ten thousand years. We think so because cave explorers have found paintings on caves in Spain that show people getting honey from beehives. The prehistoric artists who painted those pictures probably lived that long ago.

How do flowers and bees work together to make honey?

Bees and flowers are necessary to one another.

The bees carry pollen for many types of flowers.

Without that help, those flowers could not produce seed, and they would not be able to reproduce.

And while the bees transport pollen for the flowers, the flowers produce nectar for the bees—nectar from which the bees can make their honey.

(Bees are not the only helpers. Many other insects and birds work at collecting nectar and pollen from their favorite flowers. Some flowers, such as dandelions, scatter their pollen in the wind. Even animals might unknowingly help flowers by transporting pollen caught in their fur.)

What do bees get from the flowers?

Flowers put out a sugary sap called nectar. The bee thrusts her head into the blossom to suck out the nectar. Or she may actually crawl inside a large flower. She stores the nectar inside her body in a special honey sac.

At the same time, the bee picks up pollen from the flower.

(We call the worker bees "she" because the worker bees are all females of a sort, although only the queen bee can lay eggs.)

The nectar and some of the pollen from the flower go to make honey, and that's good for the bees. Some of the pollen goes to fertilize the flowers, and that's good for the flowers.

· · · · · · · · · · ·

HONEY SWEETENERS
continued

How do bees know where to find the right flowers?

The flowers send messages. The bright colors and beautiful fragrances of flowers are part of the messages.

A type of worker bees, called "foraging bees," go out to explore until they see or smell the flowers.

Then when a foraging bee finds the flowers, she returns to the hive and tells the other bees. She dances in a particular code that tells the other bees how far to fly and in what direction.

How do bees make the nectar and pollen into honey?

Back in the hive, "house" bees take over the work.

The house bees treat the nectar with chemicals from their bodies and work to transfer it into honey and to store it all properly into honeycombs.

Young worker bees feed mostly on pollen because it is high in protein and can help them grow rapidly. Older bees eat only honey.

The queen bee eats a special concentrated "royal jelly." She needs extra strength to lay hundreds of eggs.

What kind of work goes into making honey?

The hard-working foraging bee can make 25 round trips a day, out to the flowers and back to the hive.

She carries a load of nectar and pollen that is half her own weight.

But she is so very tiny that she cannot carry much. Her load probably weighs only .002 ounce. In her whole lifetime of work, she will carry only a fraction of an ounce.

To bring us just one jar of honey, bees have to fly millions and millions of miles.

What would happen if a baby ate royal jelly, the special honey concentrated for a queen bee?

Find out by reading Roald Dahl's story, *Royal Jelly*.

A HONEY TASTE TEST

Bees make honey all alike.

But flowers make nectars all different.

When you buy honey, look at the label to see what sort of flower the bees used to make that honey.

You might find:

Clover

Heather

Lavender

Orange Blossom

Can you taste the difference in the flowers?

Are the colors different? Is one honey more or less sticky?

Do you suppose the bees can tell the difference?

AN APPLE ELIZABETH PROJECT

For mysterious reasons, this dessert used to be called Apple Brown Betty.

Here's what you need:

- ½ cup brown sugar, well packed
- 1 teaspoon cinnamon
- 2 or 3 slices of bread
- 4 or 5 apples
- 1 teaspoon lemon juice
- 2 tablespoons butter or margarine
- ½ cup hot water

Here's how to start Apple Elizabeth:

1 Preheat the oven to 375°F (190°C).

2 Butter the bottom of a nine-inch square pan. Or use a 1½-quart casserole dish.

3 Mix the brown sugar and cinnamon.

4 Peel the apples, and slice them very thin. Measure two cups apple slices.

Here's how to make bread crumbs:

Cut off the crusts, and tear the bread into pieces. Whirl the bread pieces around in a blender or food processor for a few seconds until they turn into crumbs. Measure one cup bread crumbs.

Make layers:

1 First spread a layer of ⅓ cup of bread crumbs in the buttered baking dish. Then spread a layer of about half the apple slices. Sprinkle with about half the brown sugar-cinnamon mixture. Sprinkle with ½ teaspoon of lemon juice. Dot with just a little butter.

2 Then start again with another layer of ⅓ cup of bread crumbs. Spread on the rest of the apple slices. Top with the rest of the bread crumbs and the brown sugar-cinnamon mixture. Sprinkle with the rest of the lemon juice. Dot with butter.

3 Pour the hot water over the layers.

4 Bake for 40 to 45 minutes.

5 Apple Elizabeth is good plain. Or top with ice cream or whipped cream.

· · · · · · · · · ·

FOOD NAMES

· ·

Many chefs name their cooking inventions after people. Sometimes they want to honor an important person like a queen or a general. Or maybe they are thinking of an unusual way to say hello to a friend.

Or often the name never applied to any particular person. The name got attached to the food by some more roundabout means.

Think of foods that have human-sounding names:

Bismarcks and Napoleons—(These delicate pastries are named after military leaders and rulers who were anything but delicate.)

Chicken à la King

Cracker Jacks—(This sugar-coated popcorn has been popular for more than a hundred years.)

Crepes Suzette

Eggs Benedict

Graham Crackers—(Over 150 years ago, Rev. Sylvester Graham invented graham crackers to improve nutrition in America.)

Johnnycake—(Look for the recipes for both these old-fashioned foods in the GREAT-GRANDMOTHER'S FAVORITE RECIPES section.)

Melba Toast, Peach Melba—(A famous opera singer, Nellie Melba, inspired both the peachy dessert and the thin, crunchy toast.)

Shirley Temples—(Shirley Temple is a grown-up woman now, but as a child star everybody loved her—so much that they still call children's cocktails Shirley Temples.)

Sloppy Joes

Who will you call your next cooking project?

A SANDWICH STORY

A good deal more than two hundred years ago, John Montagu, the fourth Earl of Sandwich, named an important type of food for himself.

Once the Earl of Sandwich was very busy playing cards.

Actually, he was often very busy playing cards. He didn't have time for regular dinners.

He ordered his meat brought to him between two slices of bread.

Then he could eat with one hand, without putting down his cards.

And so the Earl of Sandwich accidentally invented the sandwich.

Lucky for our tastebuds, sandwiches have nothing to do with sand.

And just think. John Montagu, the fourth Earl of Sandwich, could have called his new food invention "John" or "Montagu"—or even "Earl."

A Pineapple Upside Down Cake Project

Bake a basic yellow cake. The cake looks a little plain and ordinary—but turn it upside down, and suddenly it's something special.

Here's what you need:

Basic yellow cake batter

Suggestion: *For directions on how to make yellow cake, look back at the make-your-own cake mix project in the FOOD FACTORY section.*

½ cup (1 stick) butter or margarine

1 cup brown sugar, well packed

A 1 pound, 4-ounce can pineapple slices

A 4-ounce jar maraschino cherries

Walnut halves (if you wish)

Here's how to make an upside down cake:

1 Preheat oven to 350°F (180°C).

2 Make basic yellow cake batter.

3 Place the butter or margarine in a 9 × 13-inch baking pan. Set in the oven for a few minutes until the butter melts.

4 Stir the brown sugar into the butter, and spread evenly over the bottom of the pan.

5 Arrange pineapple slices over the bottom of the pan, with a cherry in the center of each. If you wish, complete your design with walnut halves (broken ends upward).

6 Carefully pour the cake batter into the pan (on top of the pineapple design).

7 Bake for 35 to 40 minutes. The cake should be lightly browned and spring back when touched.

8 Let the cake cool in the pan for ten minutes. Run a knife or spatula around the edge of the cake. Place a large, flat platter on top of the pan and flip both of them over in one motion. Remove the pan easily.

NOW YOU HAVE AN UPSIDE DOWN CAKE THAT'S RIGHTSIDE UP—WITH YOUR HIDDEN DESIGN ON TOP.

A NOT-REALLY ICE CREAM PROJECT

Trick your friends in the most surprising way. This strawberry ice cream is not really strawberry ice cream. It's strawberry ice tofu cream.

You'll need an ice cream maker.

Here's what you need:

⅓ pound soft tofu

¼ cup fruit juice or fruit-flavored syrup

½ cup strawberry pieces

2 tablespoons honey

1 teaspoon vanilla extract

Here's how to make not-really ice cream:

1 Blend the tofu, fruit juice or syrup, strawberries, honey, and vanilla extract until very smooth. Use a blender or a food processor.

2 Pour your blended mixture into the frozen ice cream maker container, and crank according to the instructions that come with the machine. You will have ready-to-eat not-really ice cream in just about 20 minutes.

3 You can always double or triple the ingredients if you want to make not-really ice cream in a larger ice cream maker.

NOW YOU HAVE ABOUT TWO CUPS OF YOUR OWN SURPRISE ICE TOFU CREAM.

OUTSIDE FOODS

These are foods you can make outside—and eat outside.

You can even let the sun help you cook. Hot sunshine does the brewing for sun tea. Scout or not, you may always want "s'mores." And it's always fun to roast marshmallows, corn, or potatoes over a fire. You can even cook something unusual outside—like a banana.

Just be sure to have adult help around a barbecue grill or a camp fire. And be extra, extra careful, even after you think the fire is out.

....

A TRAIL MIX PROJECT

....

Pack up this trail mix and you always have something to munch on as you hike.

Here's what you need:

1 cup unsalted peanuts

1 cup sunflower seeds

1 cup coconut chips

1 cup chocolate chips

1 cup raisins

Here's how to mix trail mix:

1 Just mix together the peanuts, sunflower seeds, coconut chips, chocolate chips, and raisins. For easy carrying, pack in small plastic bags.

2 *You decide what else to add.* Here are other options to vary the trail mix:

1 cup dried fruit

1 cup pecans, walnuts, or almonds

> **NOW YOU HAVE 15 SERVINGS OF TRAIL MIX (⅓ CUP EACH).**

....

A SUN TEA PROJECT

....

You can brew tea in the hot sun. When summer arrives in some neighborhoods, you can see a jar of sun tea on every doorstep.

Here's what you need:

1 gallon water

8 tea bags of herbal tea

Here's how to make sun tea:

1 *You decide what sort of herbal tea to fix.* You might like camomile or cranberry, apple or almond, rose hip or mint—or a mixture of more than one kind.

2 Pour the water into a one-gallon jug or glass pitcher, and put in the tea bags.

3 Cover the top with plastic wrap.

4 Set out in the hot sunshine for three to four hours.

5 Serve with ice. If you want, stir in honey or sugar, or top with lemon wedges.

> **NOW YOU HAVE ONE GALLON OF YOUR OWN SUN TEA.**

A S'MORES PROJECT

S'Mores are a traditional favorite cook-out food with Boy Scouts and Girl Scouts. Fix these outside over your campfire or barbeque fire—or fix inside in the microwave oven.

Here's what you need:

Graham crackers

Large marshmallows

Small plain chocolate bars

Here's how to roast s'mores over a fire:

1 Prepare a long stick for each person who wants to make s'mores. Clean the bark off one end. Shave the end to a point.

> *Caution: You may need adult help with preparing the sticks.*

2 Put half a chocolate bar on a graham cracker square.

3 Spear a marshmallow on the end of the stick, and hold the marshmallow over the hot coals of the fire (not directly in the fire). Turn the marshmallow slowly until it starts to sizzle and turn brown all around.

4 Put the marshmallow (still on the stick) onto the chocolate-and-graham cracker square. DO NOT TOUCH THE MARSHMALLOW. IT IS HOT. Cover with another graham cracker square. Holding the graham cracker squares firmly around the marshmallow and chocolate bar, slowly pull the stick out, leaving the marshmallow inside.

> *Caution: You need adult help around the campfire or barbeque fire.*

> *Another Warning: Be sure you understand how to take the hot marshmallow off the stick before you are actually in the process.*

Here's how to fix s'mores in the microwave oven:

1 Make a sandwich of the graham crackers, ½ chocolate bar, and the marshmallow.

2 Set them on a paper towel in the microwave oven.

3 Microwave on medium-high power for 30 to 40 seconds until the marshmallow and chocolate have melted.

> **NOW YOU HAVE YOUR OWN S'MORES, INSIDE OR OUTSIDE.**

··········
PICNIC NAPKIN RINGS
·······························

Make napkin rings to hold napkins, knives, forks, and spoons at a picnic.

Cut the rings out of a cardboard paper-towel roll (about eight 1-inch rings from one roll). Use markers, crayons, or tempera paints to decorate the rings.

These napkin rings aren't just pretty. They're practical, too, especially when the wind is blowing over your picnic.

··········
A POTATO-GRILLED-IN-FOIL PROJECT
·······························

Fix delicious potatoes to roast on a barbecue grill or over a campfire.

Here's what you need:

1 baking potato per person
1 tablespoon butter for each potato

Here's how to get the potatoes ready:

1 With a peeler, thinly peel each potato. Cut each potato in half, and slice each half into very thin ⅛-inch slices.

2 Place each sliced half on a double thickness of foil. Put 1 tablespoon butter on top of each, and sprinkle with salt and pepper, if you wish. Then very lightly sprinkle your choice of chives, dill weed, Parmesan cheese, garlic powder, or onion powder.

3 Wrap the foil around each potato to form a package.

Here's how to grill and serve the potatoes:

1 Put the packages on the hot coals of the grill (or on the hot ashes of the campfire) to roast for 20 to 30 minutes.

2 Serve in the foil. Use scissors to cut open the packet.

NOW YOU HAVE YOUR OWN GRILLED-IN-FOIL POTATO.

A Yummy-Banana-Cookout Project

Did you ever think of eating a hot grilled banana? Fix these on a barbecue grill or over a campfire.

Here's what you need:

1 banana per person

1 to 2 teaspoons brown sugar for each banana

Here's what you do:

1 Cut the stem off each banana.

2 Cut the banana lengthwise on the inward curving side, without cutting through the skin on the outward curving side.

> **Caution: You need adult help with cutting the bananas.**

3 Carefully and gently spread each banana open, and sprinkle with brown sugar.

4 Close each banana, and wrap in foil.

5 Place on the hot coals of the grill (or on the hot ashes of the campfire) to roast for about 15 minutes.

6 Allow to cool slightly before eating.

FEED THE ANIMALS

Delight your pet with a food treat. Visit a horse with snacks in hand. Help out the wild birds.

For all your favorite animals, have some guidelines in mind:

The best treat you can give any animal is clean, fresh water.

Don't overfeed your pets with too many treats.

Don't feed your pets from your own food. Don't leave food out where your pet might grab it.

Don't feed bones to your dog or cat. The bone might choke your pet, or damage its intestines. Don't take the chance.

Use food as a reward only for good behavior. Never use food to "make up" after your pet has done something bad, or to try to get the pet into a better mood. Your pet might just think you're giving out awards for bad behavior.

Watch your pets to be sure that they don't eat something really bad for them. Many pets have no judgment about what to eat, and, by accident, can eat even things like dirt or stones.

Don't leave uneaten pet food around to spoil. If your pet doesn't care for the dinner you served, remove it.

Check pet food (especially bird seed, pellets, hay, and dry dog or cat food) to make sure the food is clean and free of mold, dust, and insects. Serve your pet food in clean dishes.

Clean up bird seed leavings before they spoil or get contaminated. Clean up after a pet bird in a cage, and also clean up under an outside bird feeder.

Don't feed wild animals unless you want to attract them.

A CAT BIRTHDAY "CAKE" PROJECT

Here's what you need:

¼ pound ground beef
¼ cup leftover cooked noodles
¼ cup leftover cooked green beans
½ teaspoon minced garlic
Chunks of mild cheese

Here's what you do:

1 If you are starting out with raw ground beef, place it in the microwave oven on a plate covered with a white paper towel. Cover with another paper towel or with waxed paper. Microwave on high power for 2 to 2½ minutes, until the beef is cooked throughout.

2 OR you can use leftover cooked ground beef.

3 Crumble the ground beef into your cat's dish as the first "layer" for the birthday treat.

4 Put on a layer of leftover noodles.

5 Put on a layer of leftover green beans.

6 Sprinkle on minced garlic.

7 Top with ½-inch chunks of mild cheese.

> **NOW YOU HAVE A KITTY BIRTHDAY "CAKE," SUITABLE FOR DELIGHTING YOUR CAT.**

Serve along with a bowl of fresh, clean water.

A Bone-Shaped Dog Biscuit Project

Here's what you need:

1 egg

½ cup milk

¼ cup vegetable oil

¼ cup honey

1½ cup all purpose or unbleached flour

¾ cup bran cereal

¼ cup rolled oats

Here's how to make dog biscuits:

1 Preheat the oven to 350°F (180°C).

2 Lightly beat the egg.

3 In a large bowl, stir together the egg, milk, vegetable oil, and honey. Use a large spoon. This is not a job for an electric mixer.

4 Combine the flour, bran cereal, and rolled oats. Add them to the egg-milk mixture, and stir until you've created a stiff dough.

5 Sprinkle flour on a pastry cloth or board, and roll out the dough to about ¼-inch thick.

6 Use a knife or toothpick to mark bone shapes, each about two inches long, in the dough. (You may want to make a paper model first.) Then cut out bone-shaped biscuits.

7 Roll up the scraps of dough, and cut out more biscuits.

8 Line up the biscuits on a lightly greased baking sheet. Bake for about 15 minutes.

Now You Have About Two Dozen Bone-Shaped Biscuits For Your Dog.

Don't forget a bowl of fresh, clean water.

A Treat for Gerbils and Hamsters Project

Here's what you need:

1 tablespoon unsalted peanuts

1 tablespoon raisins

1 tablespoon sunflower seeds

1 teaspoon wheat germ

Leftover potato peelings, if you have some

Chopped apple bits

A lettuce leaf

Here's all you do:

Combine the peanuts, raisins, sunflower seeds, wheat germ, potato peelings, and chopped apple bits. Serve on a lettuce leaf.

Caution: Don't leave uneaten food in the cage for more than a couple of hours.

NOW YOU HAVE A HEALTHFUL TREAT FOR GERBILS AND HAMSTERS.

Serve with a fresh supply of water.

A Rabbit Treat Project

Here's all you need:

Serve your rabbit a treat of a carrot, a sweet potato, a turnip, or lettuce leaves.

Caution: It's important not to overfeed pet rabbits. Serve only small, nutritious treats.

NOW YOU HAVE A BUNNY TREAT.

Serve along with fresh, clean water.

A TREAT FOR PARAKEETS PROJECT

Other cage birds will love this treat, too.

Here's what you need:

1 small carrot
2 or 4 seedless grapes
1 eggshell
Leaves from 1 stalk of celery

Here's what you do:

1 Scrape the carrot, and dice it into very small pieces.

2 Cut the grapes into small pieces.

3 Pound the eggshell with a spoon or wooden mallet until it is completely ground. (Birds have no teeth, so they need "grit," such as ground eggshell, to help them digest their food.)

4 Tear or cut the celery leaves into small bits.

5 Mix carrot bits, grape bits, ground eggshell, and pieces of celery leaves.

> *Caution: Don't leave this treat in the bird cage for more than two hours. If your bird doesn't eat it soon, remove it.*

NOW YOU HAVE A BIRD TREAT.

Serve with a dish of fresh water. Your pet bird would love for you to clean up seed hulls and leavings.

A WILD BIRD FEEDING PROJECT

Here's what you need:

¹/₂ cup cornmeal

¹/₂ cup shortening

¹/₄ cup sunflower seeds

¹/₄ cup raisins

Here's what you do:

1 Mix together the cornmeal, shortening, sunflower seeds, and raisins. Form into a ball.

2 Chill until firm, 30 minutes or longer.

3 Place in a suet-type wire bird feeder, or hang a foil cup in a tree.

: **NOW YOU HAVE 1½ CUPS**
: **WILD BIRD FOOD.**

A HORSE SNACKS PROJECT

When you visit a horse, don't offer a snack without the owner's permission. Some horses have problems with overeating, and horses can be fussy and unpredictable about their food.

Here's all you need for the best horse snacks:

Carrots

Apples

Here's all you do:

1 Cut the carrots into large pieces, and cut the apples in half.

2 When you offer carrots and apples to a horse, hold the food with the palm of your hand upward and your fingers curved downward. You don't want the horse taking a nip out of your hand by mistake.

: **NOW YOU HAVE THE BEST**
: **SNACK FOR A HORSE.**

Serve with a bucket of clean water.

GLOSSARY OF TECHNIQUES

Bake   To cook with hot, dry air in an oven.

Barbecue   To cook on a grill with direct intense heat from a flame, hot coals, or gas. Or the grill itself, often meant to be used outside. May be used to mean the same as *grill*.

Baste   To moisten food while cooking. Basting adds flavor and keeps food from drying out.

Beat   To mix hard over and over, round and round with a spoon, a fork, a whisk, an electric mixer, or an egg beater.

Blend   To mix ingredients until smooth, often with an electric blender or food processor.

Boil   To heat liquid until bubbles break on the surface.

Beat   **Blend**   **Boil**

Broil   To cook with direct intense heat from a flame, hot coals, or the broiling unit of an oven.

Brown   To cook quickly at a high temperature until light brown.

Chill   To refrigerate until cold.

Chop   To cut into pieces with a knife, a chopper, a food processor, or a blender.

Cool   To let hot food sit at room temperature until no longer hot.

Cream   To beat until soft and creamy, as when mixing butter and sugar.

Cube   To cut into ¼- to ½-inch squares.

• • • • • • • •

Cut in   To mix fat, such as shortening or butter, into a flour mixture by using a pastry blender, a fork, or two knives, one in each hand, chopping against each other.

Dice   To cut into very small squares, about ¼ inch across.

Dot   To drop bits of something, usually butter or margarine, here and there on food.

Drain   To strain or pour off liquid.

Flour   To dust lightly with flour. When you flour a greased pan, coat the bottom and sides lightly and shake off any excess flour that fails to stick.

Fold   To mix very gently, by bringing spoon or spatula down, up, and over to bring whatever is at the bottom of the bowl to the top. Folding allows you to mix in a new ingredient without losing volume or air in foods such as beaten eggs or whipped cream.

Garnish   To decorate food with colorful additions such as lemon or orange slices, parsley or mint, radish roses or tomato slices.

Grate   To tear food into small bits by rubbing against a grater or by chopping in a blender.

Grease   To rub a dish or pan with butter, margarine, oil, or shortening so that food does not stick.

Grill   To broil with direct intense heat from the broiler unit of an oven or over a flame, hot coals, or gas. Or a cooking device that delivers intense heat, often meant to be used outside. May be used to mean the same as *barbecue*.

Knead   To work dough with the hands by folding and pressing. Press down with the heels of your floured hands; then fold the dough over and press down again and again, until the mixture becomes smooth and elastic. Or to work with the dough hook of an electric mixer.

Knead

• • • • • • • •

Marinate To cover food with a liquid intended to add flavor and to break down fibers, making the food more tender.

Melt To heat until a solid, such as butter or chocolate, becomes liquid.

Mince To chop or cut into very tiny pieces.

Pan-fry To cook in hot fat in a frypan or skillet.

Pare To remove peels from vegetables or fruits with a parer or knife.

Peel To pare. Or to remove skins from citrus fruits and bananas by pulling them off.

Pinch A small amount of salt or seasoning that you can hold between your thumb and forefinger.

Preheat To heat an oven to a certain temperature before using. Most ovens take about 10 minutes to preheat to a moderate temperature.

Puree To mash, strain, or grind food to a smooth pulp.

Roast To cook with hot, dry air in an oven, usually referring to meats rather than baked goods.

Roll out To flatten and spread dough with a rolling pin.

Sauté   Season

Sauté To cook briefly in a small amount of fat in a frypan or skillet.

Scald To heat milk to just below the boiling point, until tiny bubbles from around the edge of the milk and steam begins to rise.

Season To flavor food by adding salt, pepper, spices, or herbs.

· · · · · · · ·

Shred   To cut into very thin, long, narrow strips.

Sift   To put flour or other powdery ingredient through a fine sieve or sifter in order to make the ingredient lighter and to remove any lumps or coarse particles. One cup of sifted flour contains less flour than one cup of unsifted flour. Be sure to notice what's called for in the recipe.

Simmer   To cook in a liquid that is almost boiling but not bubbling. Usually the surface moves slightly.

Stir   To mix round and round with a spoon or fork.

Toss   To mix together lightly.

Whip

Whip   To beat with a whisk, electric mixer, or egg beater to add air. Eggs and heavy cream become thick and fluffy as you beat in air.

Whisk   To beat lightly and quickly. Or the utensil, consisting of several loops of wire attached to a handle, used for whipping.

CONVERSION TABLES

SOLID MEASURES

For cooks measuring items by weight, here are approximate equivalents, in both Imperial and metric. So as to avoid awkward measurements, some conversions are not exact.

	U.S. CUSTOMARY	METRIC	IMPERIAL
Butter	1 cup	225 g	8 oz
	1/2 cup	115 g	4 oz
	1/4 cup	60 g	2 oz
	1 Tbsp	15 g	1/2 oz
Cheese (grated)	1 cup	115 g	4 oz
Fruit (chopped fresh)	1 cup	225 g	8 oz
Herbs (chopped fresh)	1/4 cup	7 g	1/4 oz
Meats/Chicken (chopped, cooked)	1 cup	175 g	6 oz
Mushrooms (chopped, fresh)	1 cup	70 g	2 1/2 oz
Nuts (chopped)	1 cup	115 g	4 oz
Raisins (and other dried chopped fruits)	1 cup	175 g	6 oz
Rice (uncooked)	1 cup	225 g	8 oz
(cooked)	3 cups	225 g	8 oz
Vegetables (chopped, raw)	1 cup	115 g	4 oz

LIQUID MEASURES

The Imperial pint is larger than the U.S. pint; therefore, note the following when measuring liquid ingredients.

U.S.	IMPERIAL
1 cup = 8 fluid ounces	1 cup = 10 fluid ounces
1/2 cup = 4 fluid ounces	1/2 cup = 5 fluid ounces
1 tablespoon = 3/4 fluid ounce	1 tablespoon = 1 fluid ounce

U.S. MEASURE	METRIC APPROXIMATE	IMPERIAL APPROXIMATE
1 quart (4 cups)	950 mL	1 1/2 pints + 4 Tbsp
1 pint (2 cups)	450 mL	3/4 pint
1 cup	236 mL	1/4 pint + 6 Tbsp
1 Tbsp	15 mL	1 + Tbsp
1 tsp	5 mL	1 tsp

CONVERSION TABLES
continued

DRY MEASURES

Outside the United States, the following items are measured by weight. Use the following table, but bear in mind that measurements will vary, depending on the variety of flour and moisture. Cup measurements are loosely packed; flour is measured directly from package (presifted).

	U.S. CUSTOMARY	METRIC	IMPERIAL
Flour (all-purpose)	1 cup	150 g	5 oz
Cornmeal	1 cup	175 g	6 oz
Sugar (granulated)	1 cup	190 g	6 1/2 oz
(confectioners)	1 cup	80 g	2 2/3 oz
(brown)	1 cup	160 g	5 1/3 oz

OVEN TEMPERATURES

Fahrenheit	225	300	350	400	450
Celsius	110	150	180	200	230
Gas Mark	1/4	2	4	6	8

INDEX